ENCLOSURE RECORDS
for Historians

Artist's impression of an enclosure commission meeting. Most such meetings were held in inns and lasted for many days – in some cases, as long as a week or more during which time, large quantities of food, ale, wine and spirits were consumed. Seated in the centre of the table are three commissioners, talking to the surveyor who is armed with draft plans of the new enclosures. Seated on the far right is the commissioners' clerk who is taking the minutes of the meeting and counting out some of the proprietors' enclosure rate payments. He could look forward to receiving a substantial fee for his services. Drawn by C.J. Fiddes.

ENCLOSURE RECORDS
for Historians

Steven Hollowell

 Phillimore

2000

Published by
PHILLIMORE & CO. LTD.
Shopwyke Manor Barn, Chichester, West Sussex

ISBN 1 86077 128 9

Printed and bound in Great Britain by
BUTLER & TANNER LTD.
London and Frome

Contents

List of Figures

List of Tables

Acknowledgements

In writing this book, I am grateful for the help received from a number of people. In particular, though, I should like to mention the archivists and staff of the record offices and archive repositories listed below. During the past year, I have had the pleasure of visiting nine of the county record offices from Kendal and Durham in the north to Exeter and Lewes in the south. Almost without exception, I have been met by helpful and enthusiastic staff. Of the remaining record offices that I have not visited personally, I am equally grateful for their help and assistance which has been conducted by correspondence—even where I have not been able to use material in this publication or where there was a nil return.

A number of documents reproduced in the book come from private collections. I should like to extend my thanks to their owners for their help and consent in allowing the use of them. They include Lord Hothfield; Lord Strathmore; the Earl of Devon; the Sussex Archaeology Society; the Dean and Chapter of Peterborough Cathedral; Christopher Davidge and Captain R. de C. Grant-Rennick and his heirs.

I also extend my thanks to Amanda Smith for reading the proofs and to Leicester University Library and Cambridge University Library who both afforded me the use of their collections free of any charge.

County Record Offices
Berkshire
Cambridgeshire
Carmarthenshire
Cheshire
Cornwall
Cumbria (Kendal)
Denbighshire
Derbyshire
Devon (Barnstaple)
Devon (Exeter)
Dorset
Durham
East Riding of Yorkshire
East Sussex
Flintshire
Glamorgan
Northamptonshire
Pembrokeshire

Preface

From lounge bars to university lecture halls, few topics of debate have generated so much heat and controversy as that of enclosure. From the barrack room lawyer with a vague but firmly held belief of social injustice to the social and economic historians armed with data and statistics, enclosure remains one of the great unresolved events in our history. However, despite the lack of agreement on many of the effects of the enclosure of open fields, wastes, moorland and commons, the investigation of it is well within the means of the keen amateur historian for whom this book has been written. Equally, though, it is hoped that the second- or third-year history undergraduate; the solicitor dealing with a modern boundary dispute; the rambler faced with a rights of way problem, as well as many other people with an interest in the countryside, will find this an interesting and useful source.

As well as providing an introduction to the contemporary documents generated by enclosure, the historical background and some of the debates that surround it are also examined. The different methods used over time to introduce enclosure are similarly described along with the issues that surrounded them.

A number of research topics are suggested for local historians with an interest in this area. In particular, several important aspects of enclosure are explained and ways suggested in which the reader might investigate them. One of these is the relationship between enclosure and agricultural improvement. As we shall see later, agricultural improvement was one of the postulated aims of the enclosure movement. How, then, do we find out more about this and perhaps test the results of enclosure on a group of villages? Also, what happened to the small farmers after enclosure; did they really suffer, as many historians have claimed? Both questions can be addressed once the researcher has unearthed all the documentary evidence and made sense of it.

Enclosure is a fascinating topic and also one which is equally within the grasp of the experienced local historian or a comparative newcomer. Documents are almost exclusively written in English and so very little Latin is required. Because, originally, several copies of the principal documents were produced, there is a comparatively good survival rate with at least one of them being extant. The handwriting for the early documents is difficult and some experience of palaeography is desirable but not necessary; some useful tips are given later.

Examples of many of the documents are shown. Because many were very long and written on large membranes, they cannot be accurately reproduced in a book. Copies of smaller documents are shown, sometimes with transcriptions, where necessary, in order to convey their meaning to the reader. In some cases, extracts from longer documents are dealt with in the same way. Where the aim is merely to show the reader the general appearance of a large document rather than to discuss its content, a photograph is provided but no attempt may be made to transcribe it.

A few brief words need to be said before the reader embarks on a research project. The first concerns the whereabouts of the records themselves. In most cases the locally generated records can be found at the county record office. There are exceptions to this rule and occasionally an out-of-county visit may have to be made, in which case it is advisable to consult *Record Repositories in Great Britain*, published by the Public Record Office,[1] which is a list of public and private archive repositories including record offices, libraries and university manuscript departments.

It is important to check on record offices before making a long journey—usually a telephone call is enough to find out what, if any, local rules for their use exist. For example, is it necessary to book a seat in advance or is a readers' card required? If you know which documents you require, it may be possible to book them by telephone so that they are already waiting for you when you arrive. *Record Repositories in Great Britain* lists each record office, its address, telephone and fax numbers, the archivist's name and all other relevant information.

Most record offices (but not all) are divided into two areas. The first is the index room where all the descriptions and index numbers of the records are kept. Expect to spend at least a day in this room before moving on to look at the documents. This room may also have micro-film or micro-fiche readers. Many researchers never get beyond this room. The other area is the search room where the original documents are produced for researchers. You may be expected to place some documents on a wooden lectern, a tall stand in the case of parchment rolls or, for bound books, a pillow. Some record offices provide a transparent sheet of acetate to lay on the document so that the chemicals in your skin do not cause damage.

For those people not familiar with record offices, there are a few basic rules to be observed. Work is usually carried out in low levels of noise, not unlike a public library. Most importantly, researchers are not allowed to use ink pens of any description, to avoid accidents with old and often unique documents. So, go armed with a large note-pad and several sharp HB pencils.

Nowadays, many researchers use lap-top computers in record offices. Always ask permission first, especially if you intend to use their electricity. If the computer has a number of keyboard settings, you should choose the one that produces the least noise. Do not attempt to remove a document from the search room to another part of the record office without permission.

If you wish to take a copy of a manuscript, most record offices will arrange this for you up to A3 or B4 size. They may not be able to do it while you wait but will be pleased to send it on. Some documents cannot be copied in this way. Tightly bound books, large or fragile documents and, sometimes, documents with wax seals are usually unavailable for photocopying. It may also be that the record office does not own the copyright to some of its archives, in which case they will be unable to supply photocopies. In all cases, the decision of the duty archivist is final.

Sometimes, as an alternative to photocopying, it is possible to photograph the manuscript. A professional service is offered by some record offices but in others you may be expected to do it yourself. If you do attempt to photograph the document yourself, you must still first obtain the agreement of the duty archivist. The best results are obtained from a slow, black and white film. A 50 ASA speed will produce good results, a 25 ASA speed even better. It is unlikely, though, that there will be enough light in the search room for either, so be prepared with extra lights or a flash. As in all cases, if in doubt, consult the archivist. A 35mm camera will produce quite good results but a 120 camera (less common today than a few years ago) provides photographs with even finer detail. When the film has been developed, ask to have it printed on a high contrast paper which will tend to ignore grey smudges but concentrate on the darker characters. Although the amateur can produce some attractive copies of old documents in this way, it is still much easier to read the originals.

By following the debates and the advice given in the following chapters, competent local historians should find it quite easy to investigate their own enclosure or group of enclosures in a way that will allow them to be aware of the issues and to see their own study in the light of the national framework. So much of the landscape of England and Wales has been fashioned over the centuries by enclosure. Many of the hedges, country lanes and public footpaths owe their existence to the enclosures of old. The research into them can be both fascinating and rewarding.

Finally, enclosure in one form or another, and at different times in history, has visited and left its mark on most parts of the British Isles. An attempt has been made here to include examples and test cases from as wide a variety of English and Welsh regions as possible. The reader may notice, however, that several enclosures from the author's own county of Northamptonshire are included in the text. The reason for this, as will be discovered later, is that Northamptonshire was, to use W.E. Tate's much-quoted phrase, *the* county of enclosure. To have omitted the extensive evidence from counties such as Northamptonshire and its neighbours would have therefore painted an imbalanced picture. Only a lack of space in this volume compels the exclusion of case histories from all parts of the United Kingdom. Nevertheless, it is hoped that this book will help the reader to understand more about enclosure and the issues to which it has given birth. Perhaps also, it will encourage them to begin research projects of their own.

Introduction

Ultimately, there became three methods of enclosing land for agricultural use: informal enclosure; enclosure by formal agreement (but often confirmed by a legal court of law); and enclosure by Private or General Act of Parliament. None of the three belonged to a strict period in time, although informal enclosure was the first method to appear and parliamentary was the last. By the end of the 18th century, though, all three methods were in use. Parliamentary enclosure, which will be dealt with in detail in the following chapters, was the form most commonly studied until recently. There is, however, a growing realisation that, firstly, the 17th century was of at least equal importance to the introduction of enclosure[1] and that, further, non-parliamentary enclosure was nationally the dominant form and remained highly significant in the 18th and 19th centuries.[2]

Enclosure, as it implies, is usually concerned with the erecting of physical boundaries such as fences, hedges and ditches around and across agricultural holdings. It does, however, mean much more than this. Enclosure is a legal term which refers to the process whereby it becomes possible to farm land in severalty—independently of other farmers. The land being enclosed could be either open arable or pasture, or wastes such as heaths, commons, moorland or fens. In times of a dearth of good land, it could even include mountains. In order to be able to farm independently, any common rights held by others over the land to be enclosed had to be extinguished—usually with the payment of any compensation that the commoners might be due. The most important implications of enclosure arose following the loss of common grazing at certain times of the year. Enclosure of one sort or another seems to have occurred for many centuries without any recorded troubles. As Dr. J. Thirsk has pointed out, during the early Middle Ages enclosure from the wastes was as common a part of the annual agricultural cycle as ploughing.[3] Although doubts and concerns have been raised about the methods employed during the lawless years of the Wars of the Roses, this period has received very little attention from local historians. Very closely associated with the often complex notion of enclosure is 'engrossing'. This was the consolidation of two or more farms into one holding. The spare farmhouses were either downgraded to cottages, converted to barns or allowed to decay. The latter two led to a decrease in the total of houses in the village or manor. The differing effects of enclosure and engrossing were often inter-related and confused conclusions about them were drawn by many contemporary commentators.

Still very much under-researched is another aspect of enclosure, that which was used to create hunting parks for the landed gentry. Their effect on local economies and populations is still largely unknown. In Wiltshire, Kenneth Watts has identified a possible 90 or more such parks.[4] Of these, up to 27 appear to date from 1485 with many being constructed in the post-Dissolution period. By this time, many were as much for decoration around new manor houses as parks for hunting. By the late 17th century, the deer gave way to the fox as the most common victim of hunting and there was a consequent decline in hunting parks.[5]

It is almost impossible to say when enclosure began. In west Cornwall and the chalk downs of Wiltshire, some of the oldest surviving fields in England date from the Iron Age.[6] The move towards open field farming in some parts of the country seems to have come later and was generally believed to have been introduced by the Saxons from what is now Germany. In the early 20th century, though, Frederic Seebohm suggested that it might well have been the Romans who developed the open fields since they also occupied parts of southern Germany where the pattern of agriculture closely mirrored that of the English open-field system.[7] The thorny question of the origins of the mainly three-field system has since been largely laid to one side while attention has been directed more to its demise.

As Thirsk believes, following the Black Death in 1348–9 and the consequent fall in the population, it made good sense to convert much of the existing arable land into sheep pastures.[8] With the number of farm workers in a community sometimes halved, there was not enough labour to work the open arable fields. Even if there had been, there was a much reduced demand for grain. Therefore in the 15th century, a form of enclosure—conversion to pasture—became common, particularly in the Midland plains where many manorial lords put their demesne farm down to grass. Conversion to pasture was not universally popular, however. Records from the pre-Tudor period are not abundant and we have to rely principally on the writings of John Rous, a Warwickshire chantry priest who had a special interest in enclosure and depopulation.[9] It is clear from him that conversion to pasture had led to considerable depopulation of hundreds of villages across central England. This had been to the detriment of the cottager class, many of whom were now opposing further enclosure with whatever means they had at their limited disposal.

From the findings of a later inquiry and the evidence of Rous, it is known that, especially in the period prior to 1485, a number of landlords forcibly depopulated villages by evicting the cottagers. This enabled them to engross and enclose the demesne farm which was put down to sheep. The inquiry heard evidence of a number of villages where the lord of the manor had waited until the harvest was in and then evicted the cottagers, many weeping, from their homes and small-holdings. Some of them, it was claimed, would have perished during the long winter months with nowhere to live.[10]

While such incidents no doubt represented the minority of cases, their notoriety would have spread and fear of conversion to pasture was inevitable. The way in which conversion to pasture led to depopulation was usually more subtle. In villages with already depleted populations, enclosure and the conversion of arable land to permanent pasture often proved to be the last straw. The sudden imbalance towards pastoral farming as opposed to mixed husbandry led first to high unemployment amongst wage-earning agricultural workers and then, ultimately, to the death of the community and the desertion of the village. Ecclesiastical landowners were as guilty as secular lords and attracted criticism from the mid-15th century onwards. In Warwickshire, a list was drawn up of 62 villages and hamlets which, to some extent at least, had been depopulated by conversion to pasture.[11] In Berkshire, in the period 1485 to 1517, approximately a quarter of all enclosures were on ecclesiastical land. This was equally so for both conversion to pasture and enclosure of land which remained arable.[12]

Why was there suddenly a drive towards enclosure and conversion to pasture? Within a hundred years of the Black Death, the population began to rise steadily again and by the more prosperous years of the late 15th and 16th centuries there were renewed pressures on the land.[13] On the Isle of Axholme, in north Lincolnshire, 100 new cottages were built at Epworth in the period 1590–1630.[14] While this may have been an extreme example, it was generally accepted that the population country-wide was rising steadily and, with it, there was a comparable increase in the numbers of farm animals and the demand for grazing.

Tudor governments seem to have been genuinely concerned by depopulation, engrossing and conversion to pasture, although they may not have fully understood the complex relationship between them. In 1488, under Henry VII, an Act of Parliament was passed to deal with engrossing on the Isle of Wight where landowners were drawing large numbers of farms into a few hands and turning them into sheep pastures. This Act was the first of more than a dozen to be passed over the next century or so. Some tried to deal with engrossing, some with maintaining arable land as opposed to pasture, and some attempted to control the number of sheep owned by any one farmer. Few were ever successful in solving the problem of depopulation. Apart from the Acts themselves, there were also periodic Proclamations, ordering enclosers and engrossers to obey the new laws. Pleas from such contemporary luminaries as Sir Thomas More[15] led Cardinal Wolsey, in 1517, to form what was to be the first of a number of Royal Commissions of inquiry. Its remit was to investigate, for the first time, depopulation, conversion to pasture and hunting parks throughout England with the exception of the far north.

Following Wolsey's enquiry of 1517, a number of landowners were charged with illegal enclosure and depopulation and brought before the Court of Chancery. In 1518 a Decree was issued which ordered that all those brought before the court and applying for a pardon were to be allowed 40 days to pull down all enclosures erected since 1485 unless they could prove that they were for the benefit of the commonwealth. Illegal enclosers continued for many years to be brought before the Courts of Chancery and King's Bench.

The Tudor period saw a number of uprisings and revolts whose causes were a complex combination of factors including depopulation, enclosure, engrossing, corn shortages, religious changes and the social problems caused by the Dissolution of the Monasteries. In 1536, trouble broke out in the North of England in what became known as the Pilgrimage of Grace—a reference to the mainly spiritual element of their complaints. The abolition of the monasteries disturbed local economies and caused great distress to cottagers who relied on the religious houses for trade and charity. Enclosure was also an issue, but not as important as disputes between the cottagers and their new, secular landlords concerning tenants' rights. The troubles began in North Yorkshire, Cumberland and Westmorland but spread further south to East Yorkshire and parts of Lincolnshire. The rebellion was put down and some of the leaders executed. Although no new legislation followed immediately, there was an attempt to deal with some of the grievances in the North by a more rigorous enforcement of existing laws to protect the cottagers' rights. This method of dealing with disputes became the pattern for late Tudor England. An uprising, often based on legitimate complaints, was ruthlessly put down, followed by executions and then belated action to redress the original causes.

More troubles followed during the time of Edward VI's minority but on this occasion it was partly triggered by a government sympathetic to the cottagers' concerns and complaints. Headed by the King's Protector, Somerset, a new Commission of Inquiry was inaugurated along the lines of Wolsey's. Dispatched to the Midlands first and then to other counties, the Commission was to investigate abuses and violations of the laws introduced to prevent enclosure, engrossing and depopulation.[16] By the next year, there were widespread troubles and Proclamations were issued to warn against riotous assemblies and anti-enclosure disturbances. Although the troubles had begun before the Inquiry had started its work, it was seen as antagonising an already difficult situation. The ensuing disturbances began in Hertfordshire but quickly spread across Southern and Central England—from Sussex to Warwickshire and from Gloucestershire to Norfolk. A major uprising in the West Country was blamed on unrest caused by religious changes, high prices and enclosure. In East Anglia, Robert Ket led a significant rebellion of farmers and agricultural workers who complained of lords who denied them common rights as well as committing other abuses of the agricultural system. Both rebellions were crushed and, as before, the leaders executed. In the Midlands, there were complaints of conversion to pasture, enclosure and depopulation. There was no organised rebellion in the Midlands but there was an order for the execution of rebels in Berkshire, Buckinghamshire, Northamptonshire and Oxfordshire.[17]

Despite a Depopulation Act in 1597,[18] continuing bad feeling led to an uprising in the Midlands in 1607 that bordered on rebellion. According to a contemporary account, the revolt broke out in Warwickshire but soon spread to Northamptonshire and Leicestershire. Moving through the three counties, the mob of upwards of 3,000 tore up new enclosure hedges and fences and filled in new ditches.[19] It was said that, wherever they went, they were welcomed by the ordinary folk who supplied them with food and drink and tools for their destructive work. The protesters called themselves Levellers or Diggers and blamed enclosure for a lack of corn and for the depopulation of rural areas. At Newton near Corby in Northamptonshire, which had been enclosed two years previously by the Tresham family,[20] about 1,000 rioters were confronted by a mounted body of the local gentry and their servants. The Levellers were routed and between forty and fifty killed, including their leader, John Reynoldes.[21] Many more were arrested, hanged and quartered, their quarters being put on public display in the local towns.[22]

Subsequently, a pardon was issued and in August 1607 another Commission was ordered to investigate the complaints of enclosure in Bedfordshire, Buckinghamshire, Huntingdonshire, Leicestershire, Lincolnshire, Northamptonshire and Warwickshire. The survival of the returns for each of the six counties is patchy—none at all surviving for Lincolnshire. The remainder were summarised earlier this century and published by Professor E.F. Gay.[23] It is clear that the county most affected by enclosure was Northamptonshire where over 27,000 acres of land were found to have been enclosed in the 30 years since 1578. This affected 118 townships in the county.[24] Bedfordshire, Leicestershire and Lincolnshire each also contained 10,000 acres of new enclosure during the same period. It is clear that the final straw which caused the revolt was the high grain prices that were prevalent. No doubt it seemed natural for the cottagers to turn their anger towards the enclosing landlords and farmers.[25] The period after the 1607 enquiry saw a number of actions in the Court of Star Chamber for illegal enclosing and depopulation. Prosecutions and fines followed but they were not punitive and did little to halt the trend. A contemporary document from this period is examined later.

By the end of the 16th century, enclosure was being carried out in a number of ways. Informal means included the assarting of woodland or the lord of the manor's collecting all the tenancies into his own hands either by buying out existing tenants or by not issuing new tenancies. This latter method was found by K. Gilbert at Ashley in Hampshire[26] but it continued into the late 19th century at Fordington in Dorset. The open fields of Fordington had formerly surrounded the town of Dorchester, strangling its expansion and development beyond the borough boundary. Their demise came when they were finally brought into the hands of the landowner, the Duchy of Cornwall, which set out a number of new, enclosed farms. These in turn later provided development land for the expansion of Dorchester throughout the latter years of that century.[27]

More formalised agreements were also being used from the end of the 16th century. In 1585, at Maidford in Northamptonshire, the mesne lord of the manor entered into a formal agreement with 12 other farmers in the village following alleged disputes concerning common of pasture in the open fields. An award was drawn up by four Arbitrators which had the effect of withdrawing the demesne farm from the open fields and cancelling virtually all the lord's rights of grazing in the open fields. Enclosure of adjacent heathland by the lord was also included in the agreement and some old enclosures were also confirmed.[28]

Agreements such as this were in the interests of the major landowners involved in the enclosure and were no doubt a response to their fear that their title to the land may have been otherwise unsound. It was this fear, rather than the desire for fair play, which influenced the changes in enclosure processes throughout the rest of the enclosure period. The registering or enrolling of such agreements from the 17th century onwards further strengthened the legal title to the land being enclosed. This might consist of no more than an entry in the minute book of the manor court such as at Sparsholt in Hampshire[29] or, more commonly, by having the agreement enrolled in one of the Courts of Record, thus bringing a private agreement into the public domain. The Courts of Record included the Courts of Chancery, Exchequer and Common Pleas but, of these, Chancery was the most commonly used and a sentence or two concerning the issuing of a decree from that court was usually added into the agreement towards the end.

In 1979, M.W. Beresford listed a total of 260 enclosure agreements enrolled by the Court of Chancery during the period 1547–*c*.1700 as shown overleaf. This list is the tip of the non-parliamentary iceberg and may even also be so for Chancery enclosures because, whereas Beresford was unable to find any for Hampshire, Professor J. Chapman and S. Seeliger claim that altogether, of the 209 villages still open field in 1700, 93 were subsequently enclosed entirely by informal means and a further 37 by formal agreement. Still more were enclosed by a combination of informal means, formal agreements and Acts of Parliament and this was for open-field systems alone.[30] Chancery records are notoriously difficult to use. Whereas enclosure may have been only part of the reason for an enrolment, the question of title might also have been of equal importance, particularly in the case of old enclosures.

In attempting to trace a non-parliamentary enclosure, a researcher might find Chancery records of a collusive action which were fascinating pieces of legal theatre. For a landowner

Distribution of Enclosure Agreements by Counties

County		County		County	
Bedfordshire	3	Herefordshire	2	Shropshire	3
Berkshire	4	Hertfordshire	1	Somerset	5
Buckinghamshire	7	Huntingdonshire	7	Staffordshire	9
Cambridgeshire	12	Kent	2	Suffolk	2
Cheshire	0	Lancashire	1	Surrey	1
Cornwall	0	Leicestershire	30	Sussex	5
Cumberland	1	Lincolnshire	24	Warwickshire	19
Derbyshire	5	Middlesex	2	Westmorland	1
Devon	5	Norfolk	16	Wiltshire	8
Dorset	5	Northamptonshire	26	Worcestershire	0
Durham	1	Northumberland	1	Yorkshire	23
Essex	2	Nottinghamshire	3	Montgomerieshire	1
Gloucestershire	10	Oxfordshire	8	Monmouthshire	2
Hampshire	0	Rutland	2	Uncertain	1

[Source: Beresford, M.W., 'The Decree Rolls of Chancery as a Source of Economic History, 1547–c.1700', Ec.HR, 2nd Ser. 32 (1979), p.8.]

to establish his claim to land which had perhaps been enclosed earlier by informal means, it sometimes became necessary to have it made the subject of a legal action with the outcome recorded by the court. If title to the land in question was in genuine dispute, this could have proceeded via a law suit to be settled by Chancery. If, in effect, no one was either able or willing to act as plaintiff (actions in Chancery were expensive and beyond the financial means of cottagers) then a collusive action was resorted to. In this sort of action, the landowner accepted the role of defendant and someone else, usually a lawyer in his pay, pretended to be the plaintiff claiming that the defendant had no rights to the land in question.

There was much protestation and posturing but the essence of the fake plaintiff's case would depend on a number of supporters not present in court. These central witnesses usually included characters with names such as John Doe, Richard Roe and Hugh Hunt. There were variations but, usually, the case would swing back and forth until eventually, and usually through the failure of the plaintiff's witnesses to appear, his case collapsed and the court found in favour of the defendant. His title to the land thus established, it was entered into the court rolls and was thereafter beyond dispute. The entire proceedings, while expensive at the time, make entertaining reading today but, for the first-time researcher, may appear a little confusing.

Although Beresford's list of Chancery enclosures is incomplete, making it difficult to draw comparisons between counties of differing sizes, trends for the use of Chancery are apparent. First, there is a top league of champagne counties where Chancery Decree was commonly used for enclosure of open and common fields. The prominent counties in this group were Leicestershire, Lincolnshire, Northamptonshire, Warwickshire and Yorkshire. Then, there is a second league of counties where enclosure by Chancery Decree was slightly less common. These include Cambridgeshire, Gloucestershire, Norfolk, Oxfordshire, Staffordshire and Wiltshire.

Typical of the early formal agreements are those from small parishes where there were only a few landowners. Sometimes these agreements evolved over many years, beginning perhaps with a simple, written agreement between the rector and the lord of the manor. Later, when circumstances changed, a new agreement confirming the arrangements in the original one were drawn up and this was then enrolled in Chancery. In some cases, the decree makes the dubious claim that all the tenants and inhabitants of the manor or parish were in agreement with the arrangements.[31] Chapman has noted that most of these enclosure agreements are for relatively small but discrete areas of land, unlike the parliamentary enclosures which often dealt with entire parishes.

Enclosure of open fields and some wastes by Chancery Decree remained the prevalent method throughout the 17th century and beyond but, in 1604, an Act of Parliament was passed to enable an enclosure at Radipole in Dorset. The principal aim of this action was to erect a new church and parsonage on the wastes. Although it was not necessarily an important enclosure in itself, nor typical of later enclosures, it was the method employed that was to become so crucial in the next century.

The processes as well as the product of enclosure attracted much contemporary criticism. In the more populous villages, the problem of consensus was an important issue and, under some of the earlier, less regulated enclosures, no formal notice was given of the intended changes. It was conceivable that an agreement between the principal landowners could be negotiated, agreed and implemented without the minor landowners and cottagers having any notice of it at all.

Perhaps Parliament, steeped in procedure and red tape, represented a more open and measured approach to what was a controversial and politically sensitive procedure. Alternatively, as with the introduction of Chancery and Exchequer enclosures, it may have been seen as no more than a means of strengthening title to the land. This latter reason for the increased use of Private Acts of Parliament in mid-18th-century enclosure is the most likely since many of the first Acts did no more than confirm earlier non-parliamentary enclosures, in the same way that some Chancery Decrees were used to confirm earlier enclosures by private agreement.

Herein lies one of the problems for the researcher: differentiating between the forms of enclosure. Where an earlier enclosure by agreement is later confirmed by a Private Act of Parliament, it is usually (and perhaps spuriously) classed as the latter form. In such a case, the Act will usually refer to the earlier agreement and there will be no map and, often, no separate award.

Conversely, Chapman found that in southern England, after the onset of parliamentary enclosure, the form of some non-parliamentary agreements was modified so as to resemble more closely the new Acts. This mimicry was even made explicit in some cases such as the Imber enclosure in Wiltshire, where the agreement actually ordered that the process of enclosure should proceed just as if a Private Act of Parliament had been obtained.[32]

With the joint pressures of a rising population, agricultural improvement and wars, there was increasing pressure on the countryside throughout the 18th century. Enclosure by Private Act of Parliament peaked in the late 1770s coincident with the American War of Independence. Parliamentary enclosure gave rise to a new professional body of enclosers headed by the commissioners who were appointed by Parliament to oversee the demise of the open fields, wastes, heaths, commons, fens and moorland. Among them was an important enclosure commissioner, the Rev. Henry Homer from Birdingbury in Warwickshire. On two counts, he could be called the first and most important of the professional parliamentary enclosers in that he served on countless commissions throughout all the Midland counties[33] and more importantly published instructions on enclosure. More will be said about him later.

Homer was not alone in working outside his county boundary; many commissioners travelled long distances for meetings in inns that sometimes lasted for several days. J. Crowther found that, in the East Riding of Yorkshire, many commissioners also worked in the other ridings or in completely different counties. Some were outsiders, like Cuthbert Atkinson, Peter How and Thomas Nicholson from Cumberland who came as commissioners to enclose Warter in 1794–5. John Tuke of York worked as a commissioner and surveyor in Derbyshire and Nottinghamshire as well as in his own county.[34] Another surveyor, John Goodman Maxwell of Spalding in Lincolnshire, was engaged for the parliamentary enclosure of Henlow in Bedfordshire, a distance of approximately 60 miles.[35]

After a second, smaller peak in parliamentary enclosure which coincided with the Napoleonic Wars in the early 19th century (during which time, non-parliamentary enclosure had also continued), the post-war agricultural depression brought a decline in activity. Throughout the previous century, parliamentary enclosure had developed from its early, clumsy beginnings with large commissions and bulky Awards to more streamlined bodies of three or only two commissioners who produced slimmer Awards which were accompanied by maps or enclosure plans. Although some isolated areas were not finally enclosed until the early 20th century, the bulk of the work had been completed by 1820. As a slight variation on the parliamentary process of enclosure, General Acts of Parliament were passed, mainly in the first half of the 19th century, to allow enclosures to proceed, without the cost of a Private Act. Nevertheless, many such enclosures by Private Act of Parliament continued to be implemented. Many of the later Acts were tidying up measures, enclosing small areas of land which had been bypassed by earlier non-parliamentary enclosures. There was also some disafforestation of the inland crown forests when they were found to be no longer capable of producing timber fit for the Navy.[36]

A.G. Parton[37] has looked at enclosure of land on the fringe of developing urban areas. Here the motives for enclosure were not the same as in wholly rural areas where agricultural improvement was one of the prime considerations. Instead, enclosure of open fields could have been seen as a necessary first step towards selling the land for building or, as in the case of London, it may have been a method of preserving open spaces.

Parton found that the Surrey land had been enclosed during the 19th century and was mainly heath and common land of little agricultural quality, which had been ignored by the enclosers of the 18th century. In the 19th century, there was a new awareness of the value and potential value of this land. However, in some cases in the London area, the earlier 18th-century assessments of land values proved accurate when some developers became reluctant to build on the poorly drained open areas. Much of this coincided with a growth of interest in retaining open spaces for recreational and conservational purposes. This helped to lead to the pattern of London parks that we know today.

So, the enclosure of all types of land in order to allow the adoption or expansion of farming in severalty has a long history. Of the several methods used to implement enclosure, ranging from mere verbal agreements or unilateral actions through to the passing of a Private or Public Act of Parliament, all came to be regarded as controversial. Associated with this was the large-scale conversion of common arable land to pasture and large sheep walks. In turn, this became synonymous with depopulation and was one of the factors which caused a number of uprisings and rebellions in the Tudor period. Before the early 17th century, there were many attempts by the Crown and central government to prevent the process of enclosure but these were mostly unsuccessful.

The increasing use of Acts of Parliament from the mid-18th century onwards suggests a greater degree of equanimity on behalf of the enclosing community although, as we shall see later, the cottager class continued to suffer to greater or lesser extents. It is now accepted, though, that non-parliamentary enclosure, and particularly that from before the beginning of the 18th century, is much more important than was once believed.

Chapter 1

Non-Parliamentary Enclosure

Enclosure by Informal Agreement

At one extreme, parliamentary enclosure generated a wealth of documentary evidence, much of which is extant today. Even enclosure by formal agreement can be investigated through surviving documents such as maps and Awards but informal enclosure, almost by definition, rarely generated any documents to begin with and so is the most difficult method of enclosure to research.

Often, as with some of the formal agreements, the informal enclosures initially involved only a few people. In cases of claiming from wastes such as mountain and moorland, which were not being used by anyone else, the process could involve a single person. In areas of declining populations, the enclosure might only affect the last two or three landowners who were well able to arrive at an acceptable, but only verbal, agreement. Even if correspondence was entered into, it may not have been enrolled in the records of an official organisation such as the Court of Chancery.

There are exceptions to this problem. A little-used source are the findings of the Tudor enclosure and depopulation commissions and subsequent prosecutions for illegal enclosures. Some work was carried out at the end of the 19th and the beginning of the 20th centuries, first by I.S. Leadham[1] who re-presented the extant Chancery Returns and then later by E.F. Gay who added to the original list with fresh discoveries.[2] Leadham's work in two volumes is an excellent printed primary source, but some readers may be dismayed to find that the transcriptions of the original documents are in Latin. However, because there is no problem of palaeography, those with a little medieval Latin should be able to make reasonable sense of them. The *Domesday of Inclosures* should not be confused with the later *Domesday of English Enclosure Acts and Awards* compiled by W.E. Tate and edited by M.E. Turner, which will be looked at later.[3]

Following the Midlands Revolt in 1607 and the subsequent enquiry, a number of enclosing landlords and farmers were brought before the Court of Star Chamber. Among them was Danyell Ward of Little Houghton in the worst affected county—Northamptonshire. Ward held the joint manors of Little Houghton and nearby Brafield-on-the-Green and had clearly been offending the enclosure and depopulation laws. His case came to light in 1998 when a Royal Pardon of 1608 was deposited with other documents at the county record office.[4] There are some records of the Court of Star Chamber held by the Public Record Office at Kew but they are mostly incomplete. There are 312 bundles of papers concerning proceedings from the early Stuart period[5] and there is also a set of Fee Books for writs covering the period 1580 to 1633[6] but there are no surviving decrees or orders.

Shown at just under half size, Figure 1 is a photographic facsimile of the original pardon granted to Danyell Ward and it is followed by an abstract which excludes the unnecessary repetition. It will be remembered that the purpose of the photographic facsimiles in this book is not to present the reader with a palaeographical exercise but to offer an impression of the documents. In this case, however, because the original hand was so neat, it is possible, with a magnifying glass, to read most of Squire Ward's pardon. Apart from the text, there is also a Great Seal of England attached to the bottom of the document, just out of view. The handwriting is very good and clear for the period but a newcomer may need to spend the first 20 minutes or so just looking at the page. There are two main areas of difficulty with transcribing documents such as this one: the capital letters and the abbreviations or contractions. Both of these problems can be helped by any good book on palaeography.[7]

Danyell Ward's pardon is couched in early 17th-century legal jargon, many phrases being repeated several times. For the inexperienced researcher, it is sometimes difficult to make sense of such documents even once the palaeographical problems have been overcome. For this reason, it is usually best to attempt a full transcription of the document and produce a typed version. It will be found that there is little or no punctuation and modern rules for sentence structure are completely ignored. Emphasis on certain words, usually the first word of a new section, is denoted by the use of bold characters. Thus, even in the reduced facsimile, Figure 1, it is possible to pick out words and phrases such as **and**, **knowe ye**, **and further** and **In wytness**. Because documents such as this are wide, sometimes up to 24 inches, and because they have been folded, it is easy to skip a line. Weights are usually provided in record offices to help with this problem and sometimes also long steel or plastic rulers. If you intend to use your own ruler, first ask the archivist on duty for permission. They may also provide sheets of transparent acetate for you to lay on top of the document to protect it.

Once a complete transcription of the document has been made and typed out, its purpose and message become clearer. You may wish to cut the document down by removing unnecessary repetition, as in the abstract of Figure 1, by producing a synopsis of it in your own words, or you may simply extract the basic information that you need such as names, dates, acreages or whatever.

From the abstract of Figure 1, we can see that Danyell Ward had been brought before the Court of Star Chamber for the violation of one or more of the crimes of depopulation; decay of houses; severing of land from farm houses; or converting arable land into pasture. The pardon does not say which of these crimes were actually committed, nor exactly where or against whom. It also allows for the crimes to have been committed either by Ward himself or by others permitted by him to do so on his land.

It may seem surprising to read on and discover that the pardon was not absolute. Ward, having admitted his guilt, had humbly thrown himself on the court's mercy. For his crime, he was fined £30 but there are no explicit instructions that he should right the wrongs committed by him or on his behalf. Further, the cottagers received no compensation and the fine was paid into the Exchequer. Clearly, this procedure did little to help the worse off and became no more than a revenue-raising scheme for the Government.

Even where no official documentary record of an informal enclosure exists, some information might be obtained from other sources. Beresford has pointed out the usefulness of glebe terriers as indicators of early enclosures.[8] These records of the extent and location

Figure 1   Royal Pardon: Danyell Ward of Little Houghton

Abstract of Danyell Ward's Pardon (Figure 1)

James by the grace of God Kinge of England Scotland France and Ireland defender of the faith et[c]. **To** all to whom these p[re]sent shall come Greetings; **Whereas** we have by our comission under our Great Seale of England given authority to our Privie Councell and some others to treate with such as havinge offended in depopulacons and decay of howses and habitations severinge of land from howses wherewith they were wont to be occupied and used in husbandry, or converting of arrable ground into pasture ...

And whereas Danyell Ward of Houghton Parva in the county of Northampton Esquier being lately at the suite of Sir Henry Hobart Knight our Attorney Gen[er]all called unto our Court of Starr Chamber to answer for and conc[er]nynge divers of the said misdemeanors and offences And fyndinge himself and his case subiect to the censure and punishment of our said court hath voluntarily in all humylity submitted himself to be ordered by our said comissioners accordinge to theire wisdome and the quality of his case ...

Knowe ye therefore that we for the consideracons aforesaid and also for and in consideracon of the some of thirty pounds of lawfull Englishe money to be paid into the receipt of our Exchequer to our use by the said Danyell Ward... for a fyne... absolutley p[ar]don remitt and release unto the said Danyell Ward... and everie... tenant and farmer of ... the p[re]misses, ... and all manner of depopulacons decayinge and ruynatinge of howses buylding t[enem]ent and habitacon severing deviding and sep[er]ating of land and ground from howses t[enem]ents or farms by him them or any of them ... and all converting of arrable ground from tillage into pasture

And further we doe by these p[re]sent ... p[ar]don remitt and release unto the said Danyell Ward ... all ayding helping comfortinge and abbetting of ... And also all suit in our Court of Starre Chamber or in any other our court ... against the said Danyell Ward ... or his ... farmers at will or by demyse for yeares ... in respect of the p[re]misses before by these present p[ar]doned ... our firme peace ... we grante ...

In Wytnes whereof we have caused these our tr[eat]es to be made patent; **Wytnes** ourself at Wes[minster] the twentith day of June in the sixt yeare of our Raigne of England France and Ireland and of Scotland the one and fortith

[Source: Royal Pardon: Danyell Ward of Little Houghton, 20 June 1608 (Davidge MSS), Northamptonshire Record Office. Reproduced by permission of Christopher Davidge.]

of the glebe farm appear in parish records after the English Reformation in the 16th century. Their need arose from concern that the Church could become impoverished through the loss of land dispersed in small plots across the open fields. The income of a parish incumbent, or living as it was called, came from four main sources. First were the dues of passage—the fees obtained from marriages, christenings and burials. Second was the proceeds from the Easter Offering or collection. Then there were the two main sources of income—tithes and glebe. The first was by way of a tax on the other farmers in the village who paid the incumbent a tenth of their crop. In the case of a rector who was entitled to the Great or Rectorial Tithes, this meant a tenth of their crops of hay and grain. A vicar was only entitled to the lesser or vicarial tithes which included, variously, eggs, fruit, dairy products—

all according to the local custom. The tithes were originally paid in kind with a tenth of all the other farmers' crops being brought by cart to the incumbent's tithe barn at the appropriate time of the year. Later, this was often replaced by a modus or cash payment in lieu; later still, in some parishes enclosed by Act of Parliament, the tithes were replaced by a one-off grant of land.

The other main source of income was the glebe farm which, in effect, made the local cleric a farmer. In many cases, the glebe farm had historically been land donated by the lord of the manor as an act of piety. If the parish was open field, the glebe farm, like most farms of its size, could have been scattered amongst 30, 40, or perhaps as many as 70 plots of land, each of half an acre or an acre in size. Thus the terriers were necessary to keep track of this land, particularly at times when the incumbent did not farm it himself, owing to age, infirmity or disposition. The surveys and consequent terriers were made throughout the late 16th and 17th centuries.

There are two ways in which a series of glebe terriers helps to track early, informal enclosures. First, as the glebe farm itself becomes more compact with the drawing together of the individual plots following an enclosure, the actual terrier becomes shorter as it records fewer plots of land but each of a larger size. Secondly, in the open fields, the terriers list the individual plots according first to the furlong and then to the field where they can be found, beginning with a description of the incumbent's house, barns and other buildings. In some cases, this description is in fine detail; in others, not so. The main business of the terrier, though, is to list each individual plot of land together with its size, location and information about neighbouring plots. Where some of the plots occur in new enclosures, this will also be mentioned. If earlier terriers make no mention of land in enclosures but later ones do, it may be possible to deduce the approximate time of the enclosure and its purpose. Usually, the best that can be found from this source is the latest date for such an enclosure. For example, the glebe terriers for Shifnal in Shropshire show that there had been an early enclosure long before the first terrier which was compiled in 1612.[9] Not only had at least 40 acres of glebe pasture been enclosed to the south east of the town but the terriers indicate that the surrounding pastures were also enclosed. S. Watts found that the remaining open fields were relatively small and the old enclosed land was greensward, which might suggest evidence of an early conversion to pasture. There is also a reference to a deer park on the demesne farm.[10] The remaining open fields were enclosed by Parliament in 1793.

In Northamptonshire, D.N. Hall made extensive use of glebe terriers in his survey of the open fields. He found, for example, that they provided the only evidence of an enclosure that had taken place at Chipping Warden, close to the Oxfordshire border. The glebe terriers show that this must have occurred in the decade 1726–36.[11] Conversely, if glebe terriers are unable to supply evidence regarding early enclosures, they can, in open-field areas, supply details of the survival of the common fields.

ENCLOSURE BY FORMAL AGREEMENT

The most valuable source for formal, non-parliamentary enclosures is the agreements and Awards drawn up for the parties involved in the scheme. These agreements, usually between the lord of the manor and perhaps the incumbent or other principal farmers and landowners, were usually drawn up by a local solicitor. Sometimes they were followed some years later by either another agreement or by a parliamentary enclosure. In either case, there might be a reference in the second set of documents to the original enclosure. Sometimes, these agreements were enrolled in the Court of Chancery or one of the other recording courts. Many such agreements can be found in county record offices and, in some rare cases, more than one original can be found or perhaps a later copy may exist. Each of the original parties received their own copy and it is these which have descended through family manuscript collections.

Figure 2 is an example of the private enclosure agreement for Maidford in Northamptonshire (1585).[12] The Maidford agreement was a bipartite agreement between the mesne lord of the manor on the one part and 12 other farmers on the other. There is no suggestion in the agreement of its being enrolled in any court of law. The original copies of the agreement were, therefore, the only record of the transaction to enclose.

As before, the abstract of Figure 2 contains much of the original phrasing but unnecessary repetition has been excluded and some limited punctuation added, sufficient only to help the modern reader make sense of the document. By sifting through the abstract and deciphering the Elizabethan legal language, we can find out much about what was happening. The mesne lord of the manor was William Tryst, who lived in the village. Of the other 12 farmers, nine also lived at Maidford. One of them, Ralph Ravenscroft, described himself as a Gentleman and two more of them were widows—Katherine Tue and Elizabeth Fretter. Richard Butler of nearby Preston also described himself as a Gentleman but Edward Whitmell of the hamlet of Dagnell in Wicken and Henry Bird of Greens Norton, like the Maidford farmers, referred to themselves as husbandmen.

The need for an agreement arose because there had been '… divers controvosies and striffes …' between all the parties to the agreement concerning the use of common of pasture for cattle and sheep in the open fields. Four arbitrators were appointed consisting of two men from Northampton—Henry Baylye and James Chamberlayne—and two from neighbouring villages—William Watts of Blakesley and Francis Wyrley of Farthingstone. These were, broadly, the equivalent of the commissioners used in the later parliamentary system and, whereas in that system a commissioner was sometimes nominated to represent the interests of one of the groups in the proposed enclosure, so it may have been that Wyrley or one of the other arbitrators was appointed to represent the interests of William Tryst.

Both sides of the action established their position in writing to the arbitrators who questioned all of the parties involved and then considered the evidence. They were working within a tight timetable, the arbitration process having begun officially on 18 July 1585; they were to report back by the end of August and final arrangements were due by Michaelmas—29 September. By 23 August, they had drawn up their Award which, while not giving acreages, was clearly intended to enclose the demesne farm and allow it to be farmed in severalty and distinct from the open fields. Altogether, Watts and the other arbitrators made several decisions. First, they awarded Tryst the right to continue to farm in severalty a number of grounds and copses that he had already enclosed. Second, he was to be allowed to enclose two other areas—an area near to the village known as Duncroft and another, on the Heath, called Effley End (both old English names). These were to be

Figure 2 The Maidford Enclosure Agreement, 23 August 1585

Abstract of the Maidford Enclosure Agreement (Figure 2)

To all Chrispen[1] People to whom this presente wrytinge indented of worde shall come, be shewen or reade. William Wattes of Blakesley in the County of Northampton gentleman & Francis Wyrley of Farthingston in the County aforesaid gentleman, Henry Baylye of the town of Northampton gentleman and James Chamberlayne of Northampton, gentleman Senden gretynge in our Lord God everlasting.

Whereas William Tryst of Meaydforde in the County of Northampton gentleman of th one part And Richard Buttler of Prescon[2] in the County of Northampton gentleman, Raphe Ravenscroft of Maydford gentleman, William Seaton of Maydford husbandman, Thomas Pill of Maydford, Edward Witmell of Dagnell in the parish of Wicken in the County aforesaid husbandman, Henry Tue of Meaydforde husbandman, Hughe Mayo of Meaydford husbandman, Henry Birde of Grenes Norton in the County aforesaid husbandman, Robarte Smythe of Maydforde husbandman, John Brown of Meaydforde husbandman, Katherine Tue of Meaydford wydowe and Elizabeth Fretter of Maidforde widowe of the other parte by their two severall wrytinges obligatories bearinge date the eightenth day of Julye in the seaven and twentith year of the reyne of our sovaigne Lady Elizabeth the Quenes Majestie that nowe ye are and standen bounden either parte to other in two hundred poundes of good and lawfull money of England with condicions indorsed in effecte as followeth

that whereas divers controvosies and striffes weare at that present depending Betwene the said parties for and concerninge the intereste and use of comon of pasture for beaste and shipps within the fields of Maydforde for the appeasinge whereof the said parties willingly of their owne voluntarie and free consente and assente submitted them selves and every of them to the ordenance, awarde, order, rule and determination of we the aforesaid arbitrators indifferently named and chosen as well on the parte and behalf of the said William Tryst as also on the parte and behalf of the others to arbitre, awarde, order, determine, deeme, and judge of and uppon all manner of matters variances quarrels and trespasses whatsoever betwene the parties before the date of the said wrytinges to be delivered or published before the last day of August then next comynge As by the said two severall wrytinges obligatories with their severall condicons indorsed more at large appeareth

Whereupon know ye that we the said Arbitrators takinge uppon we the charge and burthen of the same awarde and having called before we the said parties and diligently hearde their allegations answers and replies and deliberately perused and considered the same do make an awarde of the premisses in manner and forme followynge. That is to say first, we the said Arbitrators do awarde **that** he the said William Tryst and his heirs at all tymes hereafter shall and may quietly and peacably have hold, use, occupy, possesse and enioye in severall, all his groundes, wardes, and copps nowe already inclosed and encopsed lyenge and beynge in the towne parishe and fields of Maidford without any lett, interruption, vexacon, evintion, evection, encumbrance or disturbance of the said other party

And further, we the said arbitrators do order That it shall be lawful for the said William Tryst and his heirs at his and their will and pleasure at any time hereafter to inclose all that one peece of ground called or knowen by the name of Duncrofte as also that one other peece of ground called Efeley end accordinge to such markes and bondes as are already by the above named parties sett downe and appointed and the peece of ground called Duncrofte and the other peece of ground called Efeley end so inclosed to have and keepe severall and inclosed for the said William Tryst and his heirs for their perpetual use

and that he, the said William Tryst and his heirs and assignes for ever may quietly and peaceablie have use and enioye free and quiet passage in convenient tymes of the yeare with his carriages, cattell and other necessaries whatsoever into and from his groundes lyenge or beynge within the town parishe and fields of Maydford through a peece of ground called Watergall Slade also lyenge and beinge in the parish and field of Maydford without any deniall, lett, vexacon, interruption or disturbance of them the said other party

In consideration whereof we the said Arbitrators do order that the said William Tryst and his heirs nor any of them at any tyme after the feast of Saint Michaell th archangell next comynge[3] shall not have use within the comon fieldes of Maidford (other than in the groundes already inclosed and to be inclosed before menconed) any comons for horses, mares, geldings, beaste, kine, ship or any other cattell whatsoever for the said Farme or mannor with the landes there belonging & which he nowe holdeth enioyeth and dwelleth in for and in respecte of any the grounde before menconed Except and alwaes reserved unto the said William Tryst and his heirs and assignes for ever, comon of pasture ratable for two landes lyenge on the furlong called the Town Leyes and all his wade, underwade, bushes, thorns and fyrrs nowe growing uppon one peece of ground called the Heath and one other peece of ground called Grenehill lyenge and beynge in the parishe and fielde of Maydford Togeather with free and quiet ingresse, egresse, and regresse at all tymes hereafter at his pleasure for the haveing, takeing, fellinge, cuttinge downe and carriage awaie of the said woode, underwoode, bushes, thorns and firs before excepted

And further we the said arbitrators do order that the said William Tryst and his heirs hereafter shall leave to the said other party a Dryfte way for cattell and other necessaries whatsoever betweene one peece of ground called Efeley Coppes and the foresaid peece of ground called Efeley end which Drifte Waie shall contene in Breadth thirtie foote of assisse at the least

and finally we the said arbitrators do order That if the said William Tryst and his heires do not at all tymes for ever peaceably and quietly occupy and enioye all the said recited ground in severalltie without any deniall, lett, eviction, troble, vexacon or incumbrance of the said other party then at all tymes thereafter the said William Tryst and his heirs to be at their libertie, this awarde or any thinge herein conteyned to the contrary not withstanding

In witness wherefore we the said Arbitrators to enter parte of this our presente wrytinge indented of awarde & have sett our hands and seales to Dated the thyrd and twentieth day of August in the seaven and twentieth yeare of the rayne of our soveigne Lady Elizabeth by the Grace of God of England France and Ireland Quene Defender of the faith etc.

William Wattes   Francis Wyrley   Henry Baylie   Jas. Chamberlayne

---

[1] This contraction represents the word *Christian*.
[2] Preston, Northamptonshire.
[3] Michaelmas, the third Quarter Day – 29 September.

[Source: Private Enclosure Agreement, Maidford, 23 August 1585, Grant (Litchborough) MSS (in X 5265), Northamptonshire Record Office. Reproduced by permission of Captain R. de C. Grant-Rennick and his heirs.]

farmed by Tryst and his heirs in severalty. As part of this enclosure process, he was also allowed a right of way across a furlong, Watergall Slade, to approach his land. In exchange, Tryst was to create a 30-foot-wide drift way alongside his new enclosure at Effley End in order to allow the other farmers access to their land. Further, with the exception of the equivalent of two lands in the Town Leys, his rights of grazing in the common fields were extinguished. His existing rights to wood and fuel on the Heath and Greenhill and to access there were unaffected and were confirmed by the Arbitrators.

The Maidford enclosure lacks any evidence of coercion by the mesne lord or that his neighbours suffered inconvenience following what seems to have been little more than his opting out of community farming. It seems likely that Tryst was able to present a logical argument in favour of enclosing the demesne land. Despite some of the poorer folk losing some of their gleaning rights, it is difficult to see how else they could legitimately have opposed the enclosure. Indeed, if there really had been 'diverse controversies', as the agreement claimed, the cottagers and others might have treated the departure of Tryst with a sense of relief.

If Tryst's withdrawal from the open fields was indeed amicable, there are a number of possible reasons for this—apart from the obvious one stated above, that of relief from feuds and disputes. First, Tryst actually lived in the village and was clearly central to the social and economic life of the community. Despite this, he was only the mesne lord of the manor. As such, he was a member of the lower or middle order gentry and did not move in the same social circles as say the Spencers of Althorpe. It would have been far more difficult for Tryst to turn away from any local dispute or misery caused by his enclosure than if he had been an absentee landowner. In short, he had a local duty. Second, the agreement Tryst made was not simply with other husbandmen but with two others, Ravenscroft and Butler, who, like Tryst, described themselves as Gentlemen. It is fair to assume that they could have taken legal advice and acquainted themselves with the rights and wrongs of the proposed enclosure. While Tryst may have been capable of manipulating a few local husbandmen or cottagers, he would not have found it so easy to dominate men from his own or near to his own social class.

The evidence from this early enclosure shows how, when the remainder of the parish was divided by Parliament in 1778, much of it was already classed as ancient enclosure. Also, in terms of the processes and procedures, we can see that there was at least an attempt at equity in the Elizabethan period and that the idea of independent commissioners, with the use of arbitrators, began at least as early as the 16th century.

Whereas the Maidford agreement was between two groups of interested people, the later enclosure agreement for nearby Dodford was a tripartite one—an agreement between three groups of people which was drawn up and confirmed by Chancery Decree in 1623.[13] It was more complex than that for Maidford 38 years earlier—the main differences being the third group; that tithes and glebe were involved; and that the use of professional and independent surveyors is mentioned. The three parties involved were: first, John Wirley of Dodford (mesne lord of the manor); second, Sir Arthur Throckmorton of Paulerspury (impropriate rector); and, third, a group consisting of Valentine Lane of Dodford (vicar), Thomas Lane (yeoman) of Great Linford and John Lane (yeoman) of Longton (both in Buckinghamshire) and Valentine Wirley of Dodford (gentleman).

John Wirley held the demesne farm, part of which had already been enclosed and farmed in severalty and part of which still lay in the open fields. Sir Arthur Throckmorton held the impropriate rectory consisting of the great tithes of grain and hay. He also held a farmstead with barns and home closes as well as the right of presentment to the vicarage of Dodford church. The vicar at that time was the Rev. Valentine Lane who occupied the vicarage house and over 150 acres of land—half in the common fields and half in severalty. John and Thomas Lane together leased just over 70 acres of pasture and arable land and Valentine Wirley held just over 80 acres in Dodford Meadow which, while common land, seems already to have been marked out and divided.

The reasons for the proposed enclosure were more refined than those of the Maidford agreement but set the pattern for the stereotyped phraseology of the parliamentary Bills of the 18th and 19th centuries. The agreement talks of the problems of the individual holdings being so intermixed and interlaced within the common fields that it was not possible to maximise individual profits (through increased efficiency) without doing so to the detriment of neighbours. Because of this problem, there had been a number of disputes and controversies between the owners and tenants. Also, because all the farmers wished to keep more cattle than the common meadows could support, there was constant over-grazing which, as the meadows were also used as a drift way, caused them to become a mire in wet and rainy weather. This in turn caused foot rot amongst the sheep and other disorders amongst the cattle. There is no mention in the agreement of any trial of stinting arrangements, but enclosure and farming in severalty seem to have been considered as the only solution.

Thus, independent surveyors had marked out 100 acres of land for Sir Arthur Throckmorton in lieu of his rectorial tithes. Fencing and hedging of this land was to be the responsibility of the lord of the manor. The vicar was awarded an extra 60 acres in lieu of the glebe and the lesser tithes and half the cost of his fencing and hedging was to be met by the lord of the manor. The remaining farmers received allotments in proportion to their holdings in the open fields and the lord of the manor received whatever was left. The land was tithe-free but the cost of mounding, fencing and hedging was to be the farmers' responsibility. Roads, rights of way and accesses were agreed, marked out and protected by the agreement. The entire agreement was submitted for enrolment to the Court of Chancery and so became embodied in law.

The Dodford enclosure was of a broad type common across England throughout the 17th and 18th centuries. Where the agreements are extant, much can be learned from them, but the researcher must be aware of stylised phrases and arguments. These occur throughout all enclosure agreements and may not carry much meaning.

Not all enclosures were authorised in long and formal agreements. Figure 3 shows a relatively short document—a licence to enclose. Closer inspection will reveal that this is quite a difficult document to read. The handwriting is untidy, there are several corrections and there remain a number of mistakes. It may also be that there was another document pertaining to a third parcel of land since, as can be seen from the transcription, parcels of

---

Figure 3 *(opposite)*   Licence to enclose Gwain Cygorwen, Glamorgan

[Source: D/DE 210, Licence to enclose, Glamorgan Record Office. Reproduced by permission of the County Archivist.]

Transcription

Manor of Cygorwen   2· 7ber   1713

~~Whereas~~ Whereas Watkin Aubrey father [ ] Thomas Aubrey a customary ten[an]t did form[er]ly inclose a parcel of ground parte of the Comon of the s[ai]d. Manor called Gwain Cygorwen containing by estimacon one acre (be the same more or less) I hereby [empower] the s[ai]d Thomas Aubrey (as far as in me lyeth) to enclose nine acres more of the s[ai]d Comon adjoining to the s[ai]d two acres the whole making tenne acres to hold the same to him his Exeds & Amids [Executors and Administrators] for the terme of 99 years if the lives I hold the s[ai]d Manner by lives for longe yeiding and paying to me Exeds & Amds [Executors and Administrators] the y[ear]ly Rent of five shilings payable att Micha[elmas]s y[ear]rly provided I my agents & substitutes Exeds & Admds [Executors and Administrators] shall may from time to time during the s[ai]d terme have hold enjoy all Mines of Coal and quarries of stone & all other Royalties being in the s[ai]d demissed Parishes with free liberty of Ingress & Egresse ~~& egresse~~ to dig for sink & carry away the same which is always saved & Excepted out of thy grant In Wittnesse whereof I have hereunto putt my hand the day & y[ear]r above s[ai]d

                         Thomas Awbrey

.. Gri Jenkins
Anthony Maddocks

one, two and nine acres are referred to but the total area is given as only 10 acres. Because of the palaeographical difficulties of sources such as this, as full a transcription as possible might be necessary in order to interpret the contents; one is given below the original. Even so, the reader will be forgiven if the full meaning is still not immediately apparent. Words which are still missing from a document are usually denoted by a line; new words inserted or existing words altered, both to assist with the meaning, appear in square brackets.

In this particular transaction, dated 2 September 1713 (note that 'September' is abbreviated here to '7ber'), Thomas Aubrey, a customary (copyhold) tenant of the manor of Gwain Cygorwen in the Glamorgan parish of Llangiwg, was granted permission to enclose nine acres of common. From the transcription, it would seem that Thomas Aubrey's father, Watkin Aubrey, had already enclosed approximately one acre (this may be the same piece of land later referred to as two acres or it may be another). The new enclosure was to be attached to this on a 99-year lease. The rent was five shillings per year, payable at each Michaelmas. The lease did not include mineral rights—coal and stone being particularly mentioned in the agreement.[14]

Similar non-parliamentary enclosures can be found in other parts of the country. A further example can be found in another 99-year lease dated 26 February 1728.[15] John Treffry esquire of Place in Cornwall granted a strip of land beside the public road from Fowey to Caffa Mill to Francis Goude, a Fowey shipwright. Goude paid four guineas and received the right to enclose the land on all sides, approximately 120 feet by 60 feet, but Treffry retained the right to take water from a nearby spring. The enclosure of small areas alongside public roads was not confined to Cornwall and another case history is given later.

Another important documentary source for enclosures by formal agreement is maps. These fall into three broad categories: maps which were produced specifically to accompany a non-parliamentary enclosure, estate maps and maps drawn to accompany the parliamentary enclosures in the late 18th century and onwards. The maps which accompanied the non-parliamentary enclosure agreements are extremely valuable as sources of information but are correspondingly rare. Where they exist, they may give information about patterns of husbandry, crops, names of fields, furlongs, wastes, heaths, commons, moorland and other local features. Fields and furlongs, for example, often took their name from the crops grown in them such as Ryehill Furlong, Woad Ground and others. Names such as 'Retting pits' betray a local flax and linen industry and so on. Most importantly, along with the Award or agreement, the maps give specific information about the enclosure, perhaps including the reasons for it, who was involved, the type of land and soil involved and much more.

The second type of map is the estate map, drawn on behalf of a landowner. In Norfolk, for example, Bruce Campbell found maps and surveys for several parishes, dating from the 1580s.[16] These allow a study of the demise of the common fields of the period and their eventual disappearance due to enclosure. In rare cases, maps or other documents may survive from more than one period, the earlier source showing or describing an open

Figure 4 *(opposite)* Brightling map, Sussex, 1788

[Source: Extract from Map of Netherfield Hundred in the Rape of Hastings, Sussex, AMS 6106, East Sussex Record Office. Reproduced with permission of the County Archivist, copyright reserved.]

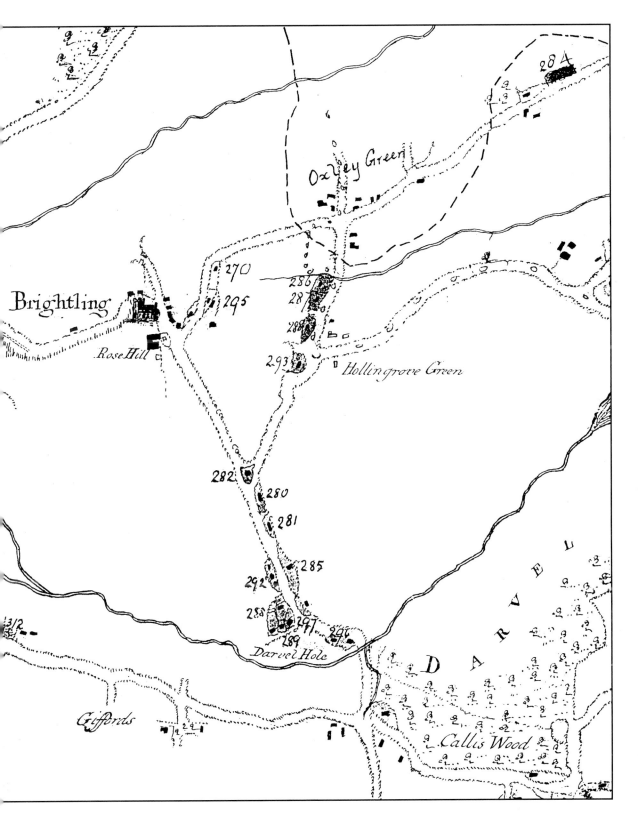

landscape and a later one indicating enclosures. At Wield in Hampshire, Professor Chapman found that a map from 1779 showed three open fields. Yet in 1821, a manorial surrender refers to some of the land as being formerly open but, by then, enclosed.[17] At best, cases like Wield suggest the approximate period when a lordship was enclosed and direct attention towards a wide variety of other documentary sources for further evidence. At Wield, Chapman was unable to find any further information so concluded that the enclosures had either been introduced by a formal agreement no longer extant or were perhaps the partial result of another, unrecorded enclosure.

Enclosure of small plots alongside roads has already been referred to. On rare occasions, estate maps can offer information on this unusual form of non-parliamentary enclosure. A good example can be found in the archive of the Pelham family of Stanmer, the Earls of Chichester.[18] The earls were lords of the manor of the Rape of Hastings, part of the county of Sussex. They seized small areas of land alongside highways and let them out on leases mainly for the erection of cottages with gardens. Many of these plots amounted to no more than a wide grass verge and the buildings erected on them were almost on the highway. Apart from the evidence of such enclosures contained in the estate maps, there is further information in accompanying rentals. Figure 4, for example, shows the village of Brightling on a small section of the map of the Netherfield Hundred. The small roadside enclosures are shaded, the buildings being shown in black. Each has a number which corresponds to an entry in the rentals. Thus we can learn that in 1788 a yeoman, John Cullenden, rented a cottage and garden numbered 282 on the map. The total area of the plot was 2 roods 30 perch (just under three-quarters of an acre) at 6d. per acre. The plot had originally been granted to Alex Roff in 1598 on a 200-year lease.[19]

B. Tyson has studied the piecemeal enclosure of a Cumbrian common field in the mid-18th century using a combination of maps and other documents.[21] Because there had been very little parliamentary enclosure in Cumbria, earlier writers had assumed that common arable fields had never been important in that area. Following his own study, Tyson claims that this was not the case and that it was informal enclosure and enclosure by formal agreement that had eradicated the open fields.

The final category of maps which provide useful data on early enclosures is that of the maps produced especially from the late 18th century onwards to accompany parliamentary enclosure Awards. These will be looked at in more detail in a later chapter but their usefulness for the student of non-parliamentary enclosure requires immediate mention.

Non-parliamentary enclosure was, as we have already seen, often concerned with parts of a manor or parish. Only rarely was a complete lordship enclosed and, where this did happen, it was usually because either the manor was a small one or there were only a few landowners. Otherwise, the partial enclosures were usually followed by others and, in many parishes in Central England, a parliamentary enclosure was introduced to mop up the remainder of the open and common fields. In such cases, 'ancient enclosures' are often mentioned in the Award or entered on the map. Sometimes, these old enclosures were respected by the new Act, but in others they were thrown back into the melting pot with the open fields, wastes and commons for re-allotment. Whatever the case, reference to them is evidence of earlier enclosure. Such early enclosures are often named on later parliamentary maps but must not be confused with the ring of small home closes and orchards that surrounded an open-field village, each being associated with a particular farmstead fronting one of the village streets.

OPPOSITION TO NON-PARLIAMENTARY ENCLOSURE

A complete section on opposition to parliamentary enclosure appears in a later chapter but what of non-parliamentary enclosure? Researchers sometimes have to dig deep to find any evidence of opposition but where the enclosure was non-parliamentary, which was invariably adopted to avoid confrontations with opposing groups, this is even more so. Therefore, survival of documentary evidence is rare. Figure 5 then, whilst being no more than a letter, is an unusual find. It is concerned with a dispute which arose in Bovey Tracey, Devon in 1826 over a very small area of land which had become the subject of a late, non-parliamentary enclosure.[21]

From this and accompanying documents it is possible to discover that the story had begun some 10 years earlier when the good folk of Bovey Tracey on the north-eastern edge of Dartmoor began to complain about the town pound where stray cattle were temporarily housed until their owners could collect them. Situated in the middle of the town, the people claimed that the pound was inconvenient and ought to be moved. They levelled their complaints at Mr. Pidsley, a local solicitor and steward to the lord of the manor, Lord Courtenay of Powderham Castle, which sits on the west bank of the Exe estuary. As a result of the complaints, the pound was removed in November 1816 and rebuilt on the edge of the common called Bovey Heathfield near to the rear of the *Dolphin Inn*, which was also owned by Lord Courtenay but occupied by one John Lamble. Lamble was given permission by his lordship to extend his garden on to a small part of the common adjoining the new pound. No complaint was made about this encroachment nor indeed about a further enclosure near the pound which had been requested by the town so that it could be used to grow vegetables for the inhabitants of the local poorhouse. The cost of moving the pound came to £11 5s. of which Lord Courtenay contributed £11.

The matter of the slowly diminishing common lay idle for some years until Mr. Pidsley was approached by John Lamble, who wished to extend his pub garden still further. It was only 'twelve or fourteen feet wide and in length about twelve or fourteen cloth yards' but it was apparently too much for local opinion. Mr. Pidsley, though, had given his permission as steward for the enclosure to go ahead and a wall was erected around it. Soon after, John Lamble received the letter in Figure 5. It was from John Hearn Mugland, the Portreeve of the Borough of Bovey Tracey. There had been a public meeting held at a rival public house, the *Union Inn*. They objected to the new wall and were determined to pull it down if Lamble refused to. Hence the Portreeve's letter! The meeting at the *Union Inn* was of local inhabitants but, strangely, they included all or most of the Manor Court Jury, thus placing the Steward, Pidsley, in a dilemma. Pidsley replied to Mugland, telling him that he had given permission for the erection of the new wall and warned him against rash behaviour. The lord claimed the right to take the land since he owned adjacent parkland and, further, there was a surplus of common.

On 5 June 1826, however, the wall was still standing—but not for long. In the afternoon of that day, some two to three hundred people, headed by the Portreeve and some of the

Figure 5 Letter to John Lamble

[Source: Courtenay MSS, 1508/M/London, letter, 31 May, 1826 to John Lamble, Devon (Exeter) Record Office. Reproduced by permission of the Earl of Devon.]

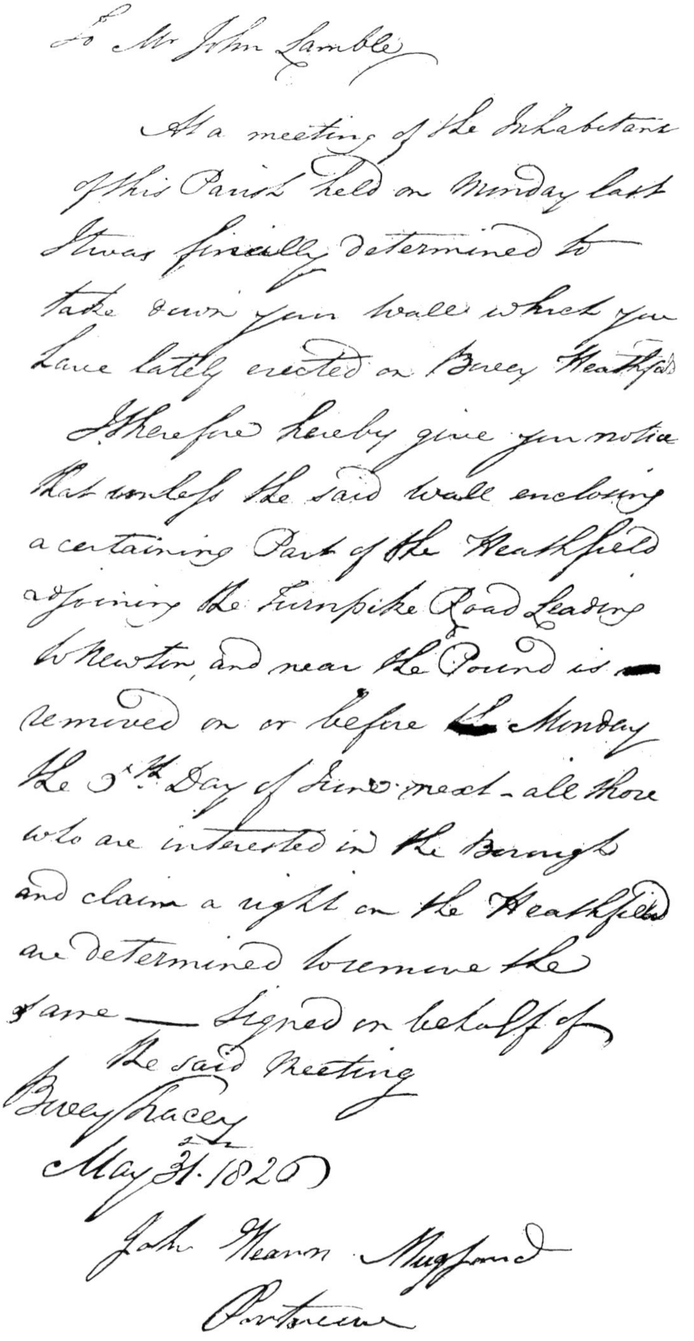

Transcription

To Mr John Lamble

At a meeting of the inhabitants of this parish held on Monday last It was finally determined to take down your Wall which you have lately erected on Bovey Heath

I therefore hereby give you notice that unless the said Wall enclosing a certaining Part of the Heathfield adjoining the Turnpike Road leading to Newton and near the Pound is removed on or before Monday the 5th Day of June next – all those who are interested in the Borough and claim a right on the Heathfield are determined to remove the same – Signed on behalf of

the said Meeting

Bovey Tracey

May 31st 1826

John Hearn Mugland

Portreeve

jurors accompanied by the constables of the borough with their staffs of office, appeared. Armed with picks, iron bars and a barrel of cider, they set to work on the wall. Working silently, except for the noise of the bars on the stone, they systematically dismantled the wall until, three hours later, almost nothing was left of it.

Lamble himself was not at the scene, being confined to his bed by a leg injury, but he sent three spies along to watch events, details of which were passed in due course to the steward. Mr. Pidsley took legal counsel, seeking to have the Portreeve, the constables and the jurors indicted for riot and conspiracy. Apart from Lord Courtenay's right to claim the land due to the sufficiency of the commons, Pidsley also felt that the commoners' actions were not concerned with establishing their rights since, in order to do so, they did not have to remove all of the wall, but only a section of it, to allow access to graze it or remove turves (for fuel).

A list of 24 commoners, headed by Mugland the Portreeve (who was a shoemaker by trade), was drawn up. They were taken before a Justice of the Peace, the Rev. George Gregory, who bailed them £20 to appear before the Devon Lent Assizes in 1827. At some point, Pidsley seems to have been advised by counsel that the wall could be said to have encroached on a highway in that it impeded access to the new pound. In a sudden change of emotions, his lordship became concerned for the 24 defendants and their families should they be convicted and, as a result, a mutual agreement was arrived at for which no details are currently known and the matter was allowed to rest.

Summary

The introduction, then, of enclosure by non-parliamentary means was much more common and hence important than was once believed. Although we know much more about these methods, they are characterised by their diversity and much more research needs to be conducted in order to place non-parliamentary enclosure more firmly in the overall picture. In particular, comparatively little is known about the methods and effects of enclosure before the Tudor period. There is a wide range of sources available at the Public Record Office, local record offices and libraries which may help the amateur as well as the professional historian to investigate either a single enclosure or a series of them. The palaeography is often challenging in the early documents but serious researchers should not allow this to put them off. Before starting work in the record office, though, the student of non-parliamentary enclosure is recommended to study the works of Leadham, Gay, Beresford and Chapman, all of whom are cited above and in the bibliography.

Chapter 2
Processes of Parliamentary Enclosure: Stage I

In the Introduction, a brief outline of the onset of parliamentary enclosure was given. How was this form of enclosure implemented and how easy was it? Further, is it possible to use surviving records to examine the nature of support and opposition to it? These and other questions are looked at in this chapter.

MOTIVES AND THE EARLY STEPS

The ways in which a parliamentary enclosure might have begun are as various as the reasons for doing it. As the processes in the early stages depended to a certain extent on the motives of the enclosers, a brief examination of them is appropriate. There was as broad a range of motives for introducing enclosure by Act of Parliament as there was earlier for introducing it by a private agreement. There was also the extra motive—that of a loss of confidence in earlier enclosures by agreement.

As we have already seen, many of the early Private Acts of Parliament were introduced to confirm earlier enclosures carried out by formal or informal agreement. These secondary actions would have been instigated by the main parties to the original agreement—for example, the tithe-holder or the lord of the manor.

Other espoused motives for introducing an enclosure might centre on agricultural improvement. This entire topic is examined in detail in a later chapter. For now, suffice to say that the preamble to many Enclosure Acts includes phrases such as, 'And whereas the said lands and grounds lie intermixed and for the most part inconveniently situate, are in their present state, capable of but little improvement ...'. This constitutes a vague claim that the *improvement* had been prevented by the dispersal of the individual farms in lands (or strips) across the open fields. Some of the larger farms could be divided into as many as 60, 70, 80 or more parcels, each of no more than an acre and often only in half acres or less and so the prima-facie case for enclosure looked a strong one.

In other examples, enclosure might have been seen as the vehicle of improvement by allowing drainage or scrub clearance. In Westmorland, in the enclosure of Strickland Roger, Whinfell and Helsington in 1837–8, the Act declared that low-lying land and marshes on the north side of the river Kent were of little value and should be effectively drained and precautions taken to prevent flooding.[1] As we shall see, many of the Acts included provisions for the management or improvement of drainage and water courses. At Poole in Dorset, the enclosure in 1805 was seen partly as a means of reclaiming mud and marsh lands for agriculture.[2]

Other reasons for an enclosure might arise following a dispute over tithes. At enclosure, tithes could be commuted to land or a corn rent. By this means, a source of local trouble and strife could largely be eliminated. In *The Yearly Distress, or Tithing Time at Stock in Essex*, the poet William Cowper described the annual trauma of the local cleric who, by tradition, invited his tithe-payers to the parsonage to pay their dues and partake of a meal with him at his table. The farmers took the opportunity to tell him of their woes, problems with the weather, poor crops and all the myriad of other reasons why they felt that they really should not be paying so much in tithes. As tithing time drew near, said Cowper, the priest became,

> ... full of fright and fears
> As one at point to die,
> And long before the day appears,
> He heaves up many a sigh.[3]

But there were many other reasons for introducing enclosure. Long-running disputes about boundaries could be permanently settled. The problems of establishing boundaries in the open fields and more particularly on wastes and moorland are no more clearly seen than in the 1835 enclosure of Heathfield Common in Devon. This enclosure involved land in four parishes and Heathfield Common, sometimes known as Brent Heathfield, which consisted of Week Common, Kilworthy Common and Brentor Common. Like most late enclosures, there was only one Commissioner, Henry Cornish of Tavistock, who, following his perambulation of the commons, recorded that he had heard 'a good deal of conflicting evidence as to the boundary between Hardwick and Brentor Common'. In the event, it was found that one of the proprietors, William Batten, had claimed more land than there was on the entire common. He was persuaded to change his claim from 155 to just 53 acres.[4] Abuses of common rights, particularly stinted pastures where some proprietors grazed more than their share of beasts, could also lead to an enclosure where the matter was settled by the planting of quickset hedges or the building of stone walls.

There were also the less usual enclosures, such as the early and apparently unsuccessful proposal in 1662 to enclose Ashdown Forest and Broyle Park in Ringmer, Sussex. The reason given was that the forest and park had been laid waste, the deer and other beasts killed and the fences pulled down during 'the late troubles and distractions', reference to the English Civil War period.[5]

In Cumberland, C.E. Searle found that one and perhaps the principal motive of the enclosers, who were the copyhold tenants themselves, was the change to freehold status that enclosure brought them.[6]

Although groups of enclosures over time shared common similarities, all were largely individual. The driving forces behind them dictated the nature of events during the incubative stages. It can be surmised, though, that all enclosures began with an idea following a spoken or written word. Perhaps this was between the lord of the manor and his steward, the cleric and his bishop or through the writings of Arthur Young and the other agricultural writers for the Board of Agriculture.[7]

There are very few existing records of these early steps, when the germ of the idea to enclose was still forming. County record offices hold collections of estate documents which may contain correspondence between landowners and their stewards. Solicitors' collections may hold similar documents because part of their work often included acting as steward for an absentee landowner. The process of enclosure was as much a legal process as a physical operation of erecting hedges, fences and walls. From at least the late 18th century onwards, the provincial legal profession realised that enclosure had become a gravy train and so actively promoted it. In some rare cases, the lord of the manor's steward could benefit almost directly from enclosure. A small area of only 120 acres at Beer Hackett in Dorset, enclosed under a General Act between 1836 and 1853, was conducted by a single commissioner, originally Edward Percy, a local surveyor.[8] He was appointed by the lord of the manor's stewards, Messrs. Fooks, Gooden and Fooks. Upon his appointment, Percy appointed a commissioners' clerk; he chose William Fooks from the same practice.[9]

Once the prime mover or movers in an enclosure were set on their course, their next step was to elicit support. This could be done formally through a meeting of the proprietors or informally through local lobbying. In practice, they probably used both. Occasional records survive from this period of an enclosure. On 8 December 1802 Phillip Gell, for example, wrote to John Cruso, the clerk of the Kirk Ireton enclosure in Derbyshire. In the letter he agreed to the proposed enclosure and also made enquiries about obtaining a bulldog to counter six men and a large dog who were making incursions on to his land—possibly to poach game.[10]

The document shown in Figure 6 seems to relate to the enclosure of 7,000 acres at Kilham on the Wolds in the East Riding of Yorkshire in 1771. It is in the form of preliminary notes which set out the proposals. First, they make it plain that only land agreed between the commissioners and the proprietors shall be enclosed. Second, the vicar and the owners of rights on the commons will receive land in lieu. New roads will be laid out. There is also an impropriate rector or rectors. Such lay persons held the great or rectorial tithes which had passed into secular hands at the time of Henry VIII's religious changes in the 16th century. The impropriators at Kilham were to receive 15 shillings for every oxgang of land—tax-free. They were also to receive one half tithe in kind or, alternatively, an eighth of all the land not already taken as compensation for the vicar and the commoners or for new roads.

The parish clerk was to have three pence per oxgang instead of the annual payment of one sheaf of barley per oxgang that he had hitherto received. Finally, each proprietor should receive enclosed land in lieu of oxgangs in the open fields, but from the same part of the township.[11]

By such documents the initial intentions of the enclosers were made clear. This was especially important where there were many proprietors or other people involved in the project. At Kilham, the principal landowners, the vicar, the impropriator, the commoners and even the Parish Clerk were involved. All would have held views and the finished proposals may well have differed markedly from the original ideas. Nevertheless, the project had to start somewhere.

Earlier in the 18th century, when enclosure by Act of Parliament was still getting under way, some potential enclosers entered into formal agreements. These were not

---

Figure 6 *(opposite)* Kilham enclosure, 1771

[Source: Note, 'Proposals for an Enclosure at Kilham', DDIN 190, East Riding Record Office. Reproduced by permission of the County Archivist.]

Proposals for an Inclosure at Kilham.

That such Fields only be Inclosed at present as the Commissioners or Proprietors shall think proper & the residue laid in Slatts to be inclosed at pleasure.

Land to be allotted in lieu of all Common rights and to the Vicar as a compensation for what he may suffer by the Inclosure proper Roads to be laid out by the Commissioners.

Impropriators in lieu of the Tyth of Corn Grain Hay Wool Lambs and all other Rectorial Tyths whatsoever to have Fifteen Shillings for every Oxgang of Land clear of Taxes (to be assessed by the Commissioners having regard to the value & quality of each Oxgang) and one half Tyth in hand, or if that be not agreeable, then the Impropriators to have Fifteen Shillings per oxgang and one Eighth part of the Land after the above deductions, for Common rights, the Vicar & Roads.

The Parish Clerk to have three pence per oxgang in lieu of one Sheaf of Barley per oxgang, which he now Enjoys

That each persons Land be allotted on the same side of the Township as the Oxgangs in respect of which such Allotment is made now lyes. ——

Transcription of Figure 6

Proposals for an Inclosure at Kilham

That such Fields only be Inclosed at present as the Commissioners or Proprietors shall think proper & the residue laid in Flatts to be inclosed at pleasure.

Land to be Allotted in lieu of all Common rights and to the Vicar as a compensation for what he may suffer by the Enclosure proper Roads to be laid out by the Commissioners.

Impropriators in lieu of the Tyth of Corn Grain Hay Wool Lambs and all other Rectorial Tyths whatsoever to have Fifteen Shillings for every Oxgang of Land clear of Taxes (to be assessed by the Commissioners having regard to the value & quality of each Oxgang) and one half Tyth in kind, or if that be not agreeable then the Impropriators to have Fifteen Shillings per Oxgang and one Eighth part of the Land after the above deductions for Common rights, the Vicar & Roads.

The Parish Clerk to have three pence per Oxgang in lieu of one Sheaf of Barley per Oxgang which he now Enjoys.

That each persons Land be allotted on the same side of the Township as the Oxgangs in respect of which such Allottment is made now lyes.

agreements to enclose in the old sense but an agreement to seek an Act of Parliament to enclose. Thus it was that, following the apparently failed plans of the 17th century to enclose Broyle Park in Sussex, in June 1766 an agreement was drawn up between the Duke of Dorset who was the lord of the manor of Ringmer and the owner of Broyle Park on the one side and, on the other, the Bishop of Durham and 10 others. The two parties agreed to apply for an Act in the next parliamentary session to permit the enclosure of the Park, dividing it between the lord of the manor and the tenants. The agreement set out precisely the manner in which this was to be conducted. First, it decreed that an accurate survey was to be made. It also specified that there were to be two arbitrators, a term harking back to the early days of non-parliamentary enclosure, and it also named them. They were set a deadline of 1 October in the same year for delivering their judgements. Further, in the event that they disagreed, they were to nominate another person to make the judgement on their behalf and he was to be given another month to do this. If necessary, the arbitrators could apply to the Attorney General for assistance.[12]

In the event, the arbitrators, Thomas Jackman of Guildford and Abraham Baley of Halland, did disagree. The first deadline was not met and the matter was handed to Robert Palmer of St George's, Bloomsbury, who also failed to deliver his verdict on time and so was granted a new deadline of 1 February the following year. When this date also came and went, a further date of 5 March was set and the verdict was achieved on the 4th, with one day to spare.[13]

In the light of parliamentary enclosures that were to follow, this was an unusual procedure, because the work of reaching an agreement and then an Award was completed before Parliament was even approached. As we shall see, the method became to obtain an Act first, which then authorised the enclosure in law and, from this, the commissioners and their surveyor drew up an Award—not the other way round.

By the 19th century, it became necessary to give notice that an Act to enclose was to be sought or, more properly, that permission to submit a Bill was to be petitioned for. This was an attempt to prevent the major landowners conducting the process in relative privacy without reference to the smaller farmers and commoners. As parliamentary enclosure developed over the 100 years from the mid-18th century, the idea of public notices for each and every stage was developed and expanded. After 1774, Parliament required that public notice of an intended enclosure should be given, either by fixing a paper notice to the door of the parish church where the enclosure was to take place or by publishing a notice in the local press. Sometimes the Act specified exactly in which newspapers the notices were to appear.

It is unlikely that many of the original notices fixed to church doors survive, although the myriad of small pin-holes bear testament to these and many other parish notices, posted in the same way. File copies of the notices occasionally come to light in solicitors' collections. In the Etton (Yorkshire) enclosure notebook is a draft of the Notice issued by Messrs. Lockwood and Shepherd explaining the intention to seek an Enclosure Act in 1817.[14] The Act in the following year led to the enclosure of over 2,800 acres.

At Morland in Westmorland, the draft notice in Figure 7 was drawn up in September 1802 by solicitors based in Appleby. Intending to enclose an estimated 600 acres of the common and waste grounds in the manor of Reagill, this notice gave a warning of the application to Parliament for a Bill. The subsequent Acts—one was also introduced for the manor of Sleagill in the same parish—were passed in 1803. In some cases, the copy notice will have a postscript to the effect that the original was fixed to the church door; in other cases a more formal affidavit appears wherein someone, usually the steward's assistant, swears that he has seen the notice fixed in place.[15] The survival of evidence of such notices is rare.

The use of newspapers for publishing notices was rare for the early and comparatively informal stages of introducing an enclosure. Where newspapers were used, however, their survival is very good. Many county record offices and local studies libraries now have microfilms of local newspapers dating back to the 18th century. Another source is the solicitors' collections in local record offices. At the time a notice was placed in the local press, the solicitor concerned may have been acting either as the lord of the manor's steward; as legal representative to any of the major landowners; or, if later in the process, as clerk to the enclosure commissions. Lawyers often kept a copy of the edition bearing their notice. As in Figure 8, they frequently drew attention to their entry by the use of a pen or blue crayon. The entire newspaper was then folded small enough to fit into a metal deed box along with the other enclosure papers. The notice for the proposed Ruthin enclosure in Denbighshire is a late one and this may account for the use of the newspaper to publish the intended project.[16]

Having given notice of the intention to seek a Parliamentary Bill, a meeting of all the proprietors was usually called. The term 'proprietors' is usually used to include freeholders

Figure 7   Reagill, notice to enclose, 1802

[Source: Reagill Enclosure Papers, WQ1/R, Cumbria Record Office (Kendal). Reproduced by permission of the County Archivist.]

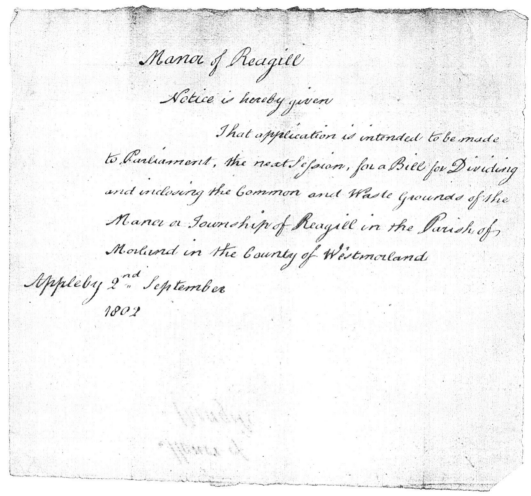

Transcription

Manor of Reagill

Notice is hereby given

That application is intended to be made
to Parliament, the next session, for a Bill for Dividing
and inclosing the Common and Waste Grounds of the
Manor or Township of Reagill in the Parish of
Morland in the County of Westmorland

Appleby 2nd September

1802

Figure 8 Ruthin enclosure, newspaper notice, 1850

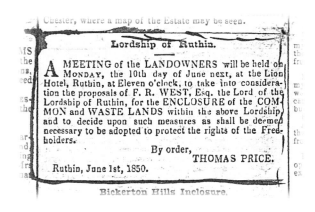

[Source: *Chester Courant*, 5 June 1850 in QSD IDS/2/9, Denbighshire Record Office. Reproduced by permission of the County Archivist.]

and copyholders. Copyhold or customary tenure was finally abolished in the early 20th century. The law surrounding this method of holding land was complex and varied from district to district and manor to manor. Basically, it was a system whereby the lord of the manor was recognised as the ultimate landowner but, on the payment of an entry fee, the copyhold tenant enjoyed most of the freedoms of a freeholder. In exchange, he owed the lord of the manor certain things. By the 18th century, this mainly consisted of a small annual payment—called by various names, for example, quit rents—and annual attendance at the lord's manor court, where he approached the court to pay suit or homage to the lord. Any transfers of copyhold land, even within a family, had to be via the manor court. In some manors, the term 'surrendering by the rod' was used to describe the termination of a copyhold lease and 'receiving by the rod' for the entry of a new tenant. Originally, a wooden rod was used by the lord's steward to symbolise land transfers to and from tenants. Denis Stuart gives a brief introduction to copyhold tenure in *Manorial Records* together with an explanation of some of the documentary records.[17]

One other important group, at least numerically, comprised the holders of common rights. Where an enclosure was concerned only with dividing the open arable fields, common rights were not so important, although there might have been local issues such as gleaning that were capable of causing controversy. Where large wastes, woods, heaths, fens, mosses and moorland were the subject of enclosure, common rights were certainly important. Of the common rights, without doubt the principal one was common of pasture. The nature and relevance to the enclosure debate of common rights is looked at in detail later. In the initial stages of an enclosure, the researcher may regard the commoners as another potential group with a coarse-edged axe to grind. As we shall find later when investigating an actual enclosure, the waters become very muddied for those trying to compare the motives and interests of the different groups. This is because, in most cases, discrete groups did not exist. Many farmers held both freehold and copyhold land. In some parishes the commoners with right of pasture also held some land in the arable fields; in other parishes they did not. Thus it was quite possible for some people to have apparently conflicting interests when enclosure was being discussed; for others, it was not.

Present at the first meeting were the lord of the manor, the parish incumbent, the impropriate rector (if there was one), or their representatives. There may also have been representatives from absentee landlords. The meeting may have been comparatively small or there may have been 50, 60 or more present. Most of those attending were men, the only possible exceptions being widows and spinsters who held land in their own right. Land which had passed to married women, usually through inheritance, was held by their husbands.

The first meeting was almost always in the parish where the proposed enclosure was to take place and usually at the inn. It was of the utmost importance. As the enclosure period wore on, it became evident that it was in the enclosers' interests to take everyone along with them. Expensive measures to defeat opposition to the proposed project had to be avoided. Thus, apart from the statutory notices, there was also a great deal of unofficial lobbying; in a large enclosure, this was very time-consuming.

For example, when in 1807 a number of proprietors of lands at Irthlingborough in Northamptonshire decided that an enclosure of the six open arable fields was in their best interest, they engaged a Northampton solicitor, Richard Howes, to act on their behalf. In July of that year, Howes travelled by horseback to Higham Ferrers to talk to John Allen, steward to Earl FitzWilliam of Milton Hall near Cambridge, who was the impropriate rector. Then he turned to the local incumbent, the Rev. G.W. Malim. Irthlingborough contained two ecclesiastical parishes: FitzWilliam held the rectorial tithes for one, Malim held the tithes of the other. There were also two manors: the larger of the two was held by the Dean and Chapter of Peterborough Cathedral and the other lordship was held jointly by Thomas Pirkins of Eastcote in Northamptonshire and William Flack of Ware in Hertfordshire.

Of the four principal parties, then, only one was a local resident; there were also other important landowners who were absent. Howes visited the Rev. Robert Outlaw who lived at Brockton near Shrewsbury, W.Z.L. Ward who lived at Guilsborough in north Northamptonshire, and William Freer of Wymeswold in Nottinghamshire. All of this was in preparation for the first meeting of the proprietors. In the event, 60 letters giving notice of the Irthlingborough meeting to be held at the *White Horse* were dispatched.[18]

Whether the first meeting of proprietors was a large affair like the Irthlingborough one or an almost private conference as in some of the smaller parishes with only a few interested parties, a number of business items needed attention. First and foremost was the moving and passing of a resolution to seek a Bill to enclose. So, when the initial meeting of 18 Etton proprietors or their representatives assembled in the *Beverley Arms Inn* on Wednesday, 17 September 1817, their most important business was to pass a unanimous resolution to proceed with the enclosure. In a second resolution, they asked that the subsequent Act should mention that there were two claims to the manor—both Robert Belt Esq. and the Rev. John Gilby aspired to be manorial lord.[19] The preamble to the Acts always identified the lord of the manor because he enjoyed certain rights which had to be dealt with by the enclosure process. In some enclosures, a dispute regarding the manor was not uncommon. In some enclosures it was found that, as at Irthlingborough, there was more than one manor, albeit one of them was very small with no record of manorial courts.

The Etton proprietors also agreed at their first meeting that the manorial lords should receive one-eighteenth of the commons and waste lands in lieu of their rights to the soil. At some point, the minutes of this meeting were signed by everyone present and we notice that, of the 18 present, all were men, the three female proprietors at Etton, Mary Grasby, Mrs. Watson and Sarah Thompson, being represented by men, none of whom were their husbands.

Having settled the agreement for the manorial lords, most initial meetings might have gone on to discuss tithes and perhaps commissioners. The Etton proprietors, though, called it an evening and met again three weeks later in early October. The rector had made a number of requests. First, he asked that some of the land he was to be allotted should be situated near to his rectory rather than in another part of the parish. Second, he requested a corn rent in lieu of his glebe. Third, he asked for the other proprietors to pay for ring-fencing his allotments. Fourth, he asked that a modus (a money payment) that he was already receiving in lieu of tithes should continue. Fifth, he was anxious that an existing scheme of charging surplice fees for the church and the Easter Offering (which he received) should be unaffected by the enclosure and, lastly, that he should have the right of nominating a commissioner for the enclosure.[20] The Etton enclosure, as much as any other, shows us the extent and breadth of the enclosure process and how it could embrace much more than the dividing and sharing of land.

Some initial meetings of proprietors conducted more business than others, depending on how much work had already been done during the informal stages and on how much work was to be left to the commissioners. At some meetings, the commissioners were chosen first. In the early days of parliamentary enclosure, commissions were large. The 17th-century attempt at enclosing Broyle Park in Sussex was to be by a commission of 24 which included a baron, two baronets and two knights.[21] In Northamptonshire, the first enclosure commission for which data is available was for Chipping Warden in 1733 where 11 commissioners presided. Ten years later at Great Brington there were ten. From the mid-1740s onwards, five commissioners became the norm for many years. After the Towcester enclosure in 1762 the number dropped to three, falling to two in the early 19th century, when the average size of Northamptonshire enclosures had correspondingly dropped. By the end of the main period of enclosure activity in that county, only one commissioner served the enclosures at Higham Ferrers (1838), Ringstead (1839) and Stoke Bruerne with Shutlanger (1840).[22]

The final and most important work of the initial meeting of proprietors was either to examine a draft Bill, if one had already been drawn up or, more likely, to draw up a petition to Parliament, requesting permission to submit a Bill for their consideration. By this stage documents, such as this first petition and even perhaps the notice of intention to seek an enclosure, might already include some of the stylised phraseology that would eventually appear in the Act itself. In open field arable enclosures, the scattering of the strips of land might be mentioned as a bar to improvement. Where waste and moorland was under consideration, its *present state* might simply be given as the reason for its lack of use or value. When the Pennine community of Dufton came together in the late 1820s, they drew up the draft petition to Parliament shown in Figure 9. In view of the poor hand, a transcription follows.[23]

Figure 9 *(overleaf)*   Dufton draft petition to enclose, c.1826

[Source: Dufton draft petition to enclose, WD/HH/53, Cumbria Record Office (Kendal). Reproduced by permission of Lord Hothfield.]

To the Honourable the Commons of the United
Kingdom of Great Britain and Ireland
in Parliament assembled

The Humble Petition of the —
several persons whose names are
presents subscribed on behalf of
themselves and other owners of
Cattlegates in the several Common
Stinted pastures called respectively Dufton
Pike Dufton Fell pasture and Flascow —
of Dufton in the
within the Parish Township of Dufton and
in the County of Westmorland

Sheweth

That there are within the said township
of Dufton certain Common Stinted pastures called
respectively Dufton Pike Dufton Fell pasture and
Flascow containing altogether by estimation
Two thousand three hundred acres — or thereabouts

That if the said Common Stinted pastures
were divided and allotted unto and amongst the
several persons interested therein according to
their several and respective rights and interests
and such allotments inclosed they would be
rendered of much greater value and might be
much improved

Your Petitioners therefore humbly pray
that leave may be given to bring in
a bill for dividing allotting and —
inclosing the said several Common —
Stinted pastures in such manner and
under such regulations as to this
Honourable House shall seem meet

And your Petitioners will ever
pray &c —

Transcription of Figure 9

To the Honourable the Commons of the United Kingdom of Great Britain and Ireland in Parliament assembled

The Humble Petition of the several persons whose names are hereunto subscribed on behalf of themselves and other owners of Cattlegates in the several Common stinted pastures called respectively Dufton Pike, Dufton Fell Pasture and Flascow within the township of Dufton in the Parish of Dufton and the County of Westmorland.

Herewith

That there are within the said township of Dufton certain common stinted pastures called respectively Dufton Pike, Dufton Fell Pasture and Flascow containing altogether by estimation Two thousand three hundred acres · or thereabouts.

That if the said Common stinted pastures were divided and allotted unto and amongst the several persons interested therein according to their several and respective rights and interests and such allotments inclosed they would be rendered of much greater value and might be much improved.

Your Petitioners therefore humbly pray that leave may be given to bring in a Bill for dividing, allotting and inclosing the said several Common stinted pastures in such manner and under such regulations as to their Honourable House shall seem meet.

And your Petitioners will ever pray etc —

AT THE HOUSE

And so, with petitions such as the Dufton one, the process moved on to another and wider stage. The passage of a petition to Parliament can be followed through the pages of the *Commons Journal*, copies of which are kept in the Commons Library and the House of Lords Record Office. A random glance at the *Journal*'s entries for 26 January 1778 shows that all five petitions dealt with on page 600 were concerned with enclosure. This was the first peak of Parliamentary enclosure activity affecting the open arable fields across the Midland Plain. Throughout the *Journal* entries, familiar phrases abound concerning lands and grounds of petitioners which lie intermixed in open and common fields and being incapable of further improvement in their present state.[24]

Not all petitions were for new enclosure projects. Earlier enclosures by agreement were also still being reviewed. As the *Journal* shows, Little Berkford (Barford) in Bedfordshire had been enclosed by private agreement in December 1764. The petition which appears in Figure 10 was from the incumbent, the lord of the manor and three other proprietors. Small numbers of proprietors often made use of private agreements. They recite the background to their earlier agreement but then request a Bill to confirm and establish the enclosure by the authority of Parliament.

After hearing a petition for leave to introduce an Enclosure Bill, the Commons usually ordered that permission should be given and the county MPs were instructed to prepare it and bring it to the House. In practice, of course, the members themselves did not prepare the Bill; this was done locally by the solicitor acting on behalf of the enclosers. Nevertheless, the support of the county MPs was essential for the passage of the Bill but, since most were landowners themselves, this was usually a matter of course.

One other stage in the process of enclosure needs to be mentioned here: the obtaining of consents. As Professor Mingay points out, in order for Parliament to accept it, a Bill had to be accompanied by a document which listed the consents.[25] On this document—and there was no standard form of layout—all the proprietors of the land affected by the enclosure were listed together with the size of their holding. They were also entered as supporting

Figure 10

Extract from *Commons Journal*, 1778

> A Petition of the Reverend *John Blakiston*, Clerk, Rector of the Parish of *Little Berkford*, in the County of *Bedford*, *Henry Tingey*, *Thomas Adams*, and *Richard Saunders*, on Behalf of themselves, and *Thomas Lee*, Esquire, Lord of the Manor of *Little Beckford* aforesaid, was presented to the House, and read; Setting forth, That the Petitioners, together with the said *Thomas Lee*, Esquire, are Owners and Proprietors of all the Lands and Estates within the Manor and Parish of *Little Berkford* aforesaid; and that, by Articles of Agreement, bearing Date the 20th of *December* 1764, the Petitioners *Henry Tingey*, *Thomas Adams*, and *Richard Saunders*, together with the said *Thomas Lee*, and the Reverend *Thelwall Salusbury* (then Rector of the said Parish) covenanted and agreed to divide and inclose all the Common Fields, Common Meadows, and Common Pastures, within the said Parish, upon certain Conditions therein mentioned, and appointed Commissioners for dividing the said Fields, Meadows, and Pastures, and allotting the same amongst the Parties entitled thereto, according to their respective Rights and Interests therein; and also impowered the said Commissioners to make Exchanges of Lands for the Convenience of the several Owners and Proprietors; and that, on or about the 16th of *May* 1766, the said Commissioners did (in pursuance of the said Articles) divide and allot the said Lands and Grounds, and also made several Exchanges, to the mutual Satisfaction of the Parties interested; and the said Allotments and Exchanges were accordingly accepted by them, and have been inclosed with Quickset Hedges and other proper Fences, and cultivated, by the respective Owners, at a very great Expence, who find that their Estates are greatly improved by the Divisions, Exchanges, and Inclosures, made as aforesaid, and are desirous to have the same confirmed and established by Authority of Parliament: And therefore praying, That Leave may be given to bring in a Bill for confirming and establishing the said Divisions, Inclosures, and Exchanges, in such Manner as to the House shall seem meet.
>
> *Ordered,* That Leave be given to bring in a Bill, pursuant to the Prayer of the said Petition: And that the Lord *Ongley* and Mr. *Dickinson* do prepare, and bring in, the same.

Little Berkford Inclosure.

[Source: *Commons Journal*, 26 January 1778, p.600.]

the enclosure, opposing the enclosure, or 'neuter'. This latter description included those who abstained and those who, like the Quakers, simply refused to sign on principle. Documents such as the one shown in Figure 11 are examples of these consents. In this copy from the Pennine enclosure of Mickleton Moor and the Town Fields, only the proprietor's name and amounts described as 'Old Rate for Mickleton' and the 'Pasture Grass' are given. This was an Act to amend an earlier Award which omitted measures to deal with tithes. The names in the document are set out in two columns, 'Signed' (for) and 'Not Signed' (against), and appear in order of social position—Lord Strathmore being at the top. Pencil notes in the margins suggest that this may have been a draft copy.[26]

Figure 12 is another draft copy of consents. Here, the names of the proprietors have been arranged in geographical order. From this, we can see that only nine of the 32 proprietors lived at Kirk Ireton. This pattern of absentee landownership continued to develop throughout the 18th and 19th centuries. This particular list gives only names. In front of each name is a mark. In the case of those consenting to the enclosure, a cross appears. For those who either did not sign because they objected, like Joshua Kiddy and Robert Wrighton, or were unable to sign, like Mrs. Williamson (who was in gaol), a circle appears.[27] It shows that, of the four objectors, three were from the village itself (the fourth being Mrs. Williams). As a draft, this may not have been the final state of play when the Bill was accepted. Indeed, attempts to coax and cajole support for an enclosure could go on for many years, the lobbying continuing up to and including the eleventh hour.

The obtaining of consents was important, since Parliament considered that those requesting the enclosure should hold at least 75 per cent of the land in terms of its value. Because the proportion of land by value was considered and not the actual number of proprietors, miscarriages were both possible and common. Later, a proportion in value and number was introduced in order to overcome this injustice.

OPPOSITION MOVEMENTS

Just as the *Commons Journal* records the receipt of petitions from enclosers, so it also records counter-petitions from groups opposed to a particular enclosure, although many of these did not appear until the Bill stage. Just as there were many motives and reasons for pursuing an enclosure, there was an almost equal number for opposing it.

A large proportion of the complaints about enclosure were associated with common rights and were borne by the lower economic classes or commoners. Who were commoners? Quite simply, anyone who enjoyed common rights, rights which tended to vary from parish to parish and from manor to manor. Their legal standing also seems to have been variable. There are two differing interpretations of the legal basis of many of the common rights. The late Professor Chambers and Professor G.E. Mingay described them as illegal. Alternatively, the late E.P. Thompson talked about *lex loci*—local laws based on established custom. It is true that no Act of Parliament awarded the 18th-century farmers of a particular village the right to graze cattle in the common pasture but nobody seriously disputed that they should or should not do so. And we are quite familiar, even today, with local laws—bye-laws. Perhaps Chambers and Mingay were only syntactically incorrect: common right may not have been *within* the law, but it was certainly not *against* the law.

Figure 11 Mickleton enclosure: Consents

[Source: Consents to Mickleton enclosure, D/St/E3/19/11(2), Durham Record Office. Reproduced by permission of Lord Strathmore.]

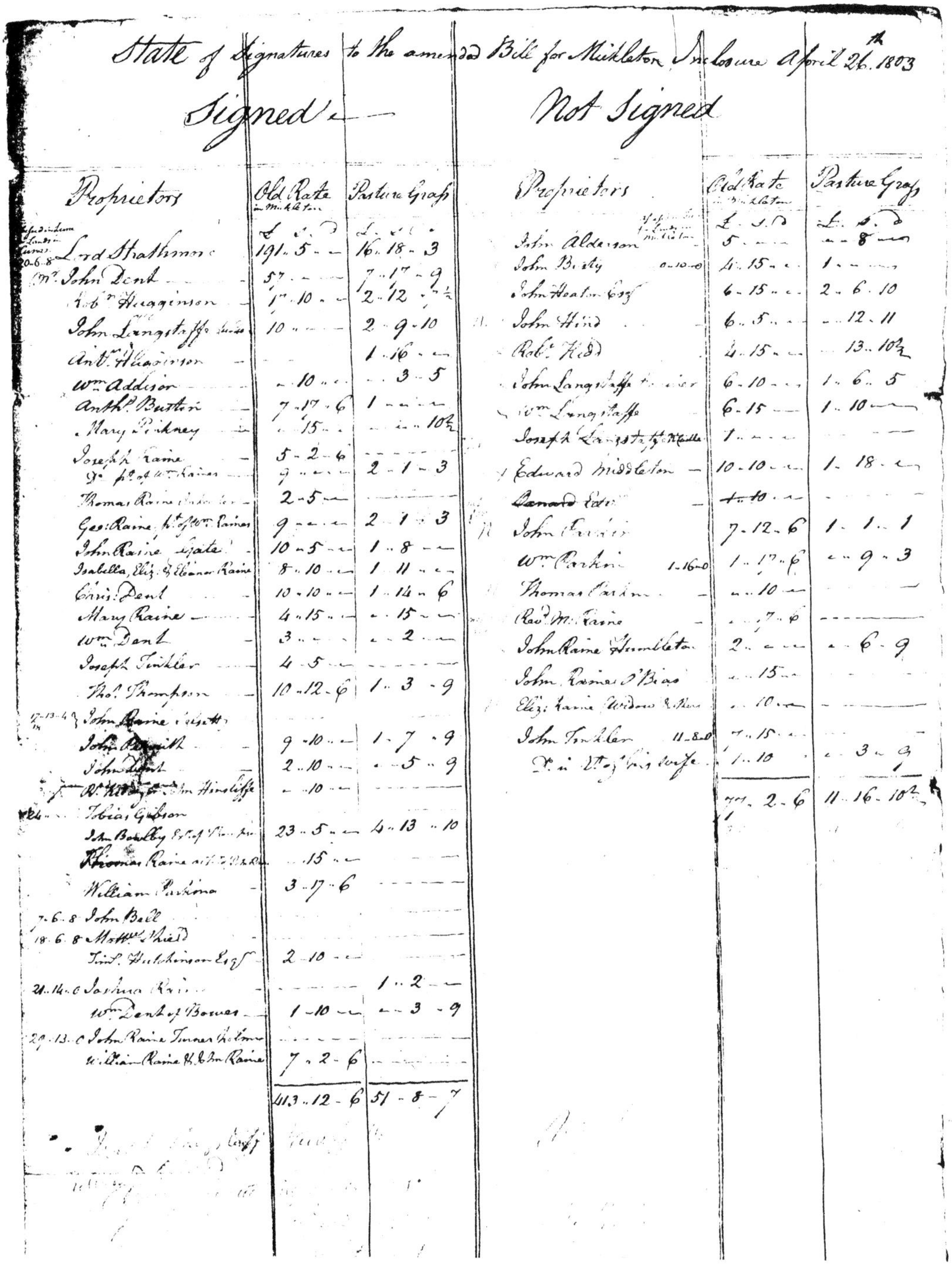

State of Signatures to the amended Bill for Mickleton Inclosure April 26th 1803

Signed

	Proprietors	Old Rate in Mickleton	Pasture Grass
		£ s d	£ s d
0-6-8	Lord Strathmore	191-5--	16-18-3
	Mr John Dent	57--	7-17-9
	Robt Heaginson	1-10	2-12-½
	John Langstaffe	10	2-9-10
	Antw Harrison		1-16
	Wm Addison	-10	-3-5
	Anthy Buston	7-17-6	1--
	Mary Pinkney	-15	--10½
	Joseph Raine	5-2-6	
	Do [illegible]	9	2-1-3
	Thomas Raine [illegible]	2-5	
	Geo: Raine [illegible] Raine	9	2-1-3
	John Raine Gate	10-5	1-8
	Isabella, Eliz. & Eleanor Raine	8-10	1-11
	Chris: Dent	10-10	1-14-6
	Mary Raine	4-15	-15
	Wm Dent	3	-2
	Joseph Tinkler	4-5	
	Thos Thompson	10-12-6	1-3-9
17-13-4	John Raine [illegible]		
	John [illegible]smith	9-10	1-7-9
	John [illegible]	2-10	-5-9
	[illegible] Hinsliffe	-10	
	Tobias Gibson		
	John Bowlby [illegible]	23-5	4-13-10
	Thomas Raine [illegible]	-15	
	William Parkinson	3-17-6	
7-6-8	John Bell		
18-6-8	Matthw Shield		
	Tims. Hutchinson Esq	2-10	
21-14-0	Joshua Raine		1-2
	Wm Dent of Bowes	1-10	-3-9
29-13-0	John Raine Tinner [illegible]		
	William Raine & John Raine	7-2-6	
		413-12-6	51-8-7

Not Signed

Proprietors	Old Rate in Mickleton	Pasture Grass
	£ s d	£ s d
John Alderson	5	-8
John Bisky 0-10-0	4-15	1
John Heaton Esq	6-15	2-6-10
John Hind	6-5	-12-11
Robt Kidd	4-15	13-10½
John Langstaffe [illegible]	6-10	1-6-5
Wm Langstaffe	6-15	1-10
Joseph Langstaffe Middle	1	
Edward Middleton	10-10	1-18
~~Bernard Ede~~	~~4-10~~	
John Fraser	7-12-6	1-1-1
Wm Parkin 1-16-0	1-17-6	-9-3
Thomas Parkin	-10	
Revd Mr Raine	-7-6	
John Raine Hunbleton	2	-6-9
John Raine [illegible]	-15	
Eliz: Raine (Widow [illegible])	-10	
John Tinkler 11-8-0	-15	
Do [illegible] his wife	1-10	-3-3
	71-2-6	11-16-10½

Figure 12 Kirk Ireton enclosure: Consents

[Source: Consents to Kirk Ireton enclosure, Record Office D4459/1/1/14, Derbyshire Record Office. Reproduced by permission of the County and Diocesan Archivist.]

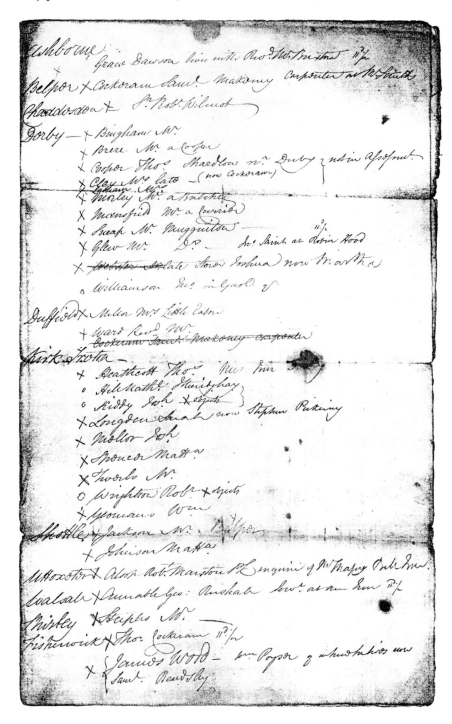

Common Rights under Threat

What were these common rights? The right of pasture has already been mentioned. The right to graze cattle and sheep in the common pasture or cow meadow was the most important and usually the most closely guarded and highly regulated. Known as cow commons in some parts of the country, cattle gates in others, they were originally attached to a farm or property and were sometimes called cottage cow commons. Thus the inhabitant, on taking the property, also gained the right to graze one, two or however many cows the deeds allowed. The same went for sheep. Other cow commons or cattle gates could be bought and sold.

In some manors, the common pastures were divided by lottery and others by auction. In some, problems arose with over-pasturing and stinting arrangements had to be agreed where the number of grazing animals had to be reduced.

In 1838, the Wellingborough historian, John Cole, witnessed an occurrence at Higham Ferrers, which was becomingly increasingly rare, but had been in frequent use in many East Midlands' villages throughout the medieval period:

> On returning through Higham, I was much struck with the appearance of all the cows of the parish, about 100, which were feasting on the Common, where they are from 4 o'clock in the morning until 6 in the evening, and being there at that time—I witnessed the pleasing scene of their retirement for the evening: up the whole length of the town, preceded by a boy blowing a horn, in order that those who had cows might be on the look out.[28]

Pasturage, or perhaps more properly grazing, was not confined to the common pastures. Other important rights arose out of the stubble fields after harvest, the fallow field and any wastes, moors, heaths or commons.

The rights to graze in the stubble fields and the fallow field were often agreed and embodied in field orders produced by the manor court. For example, one Midlands village came together at a manor court in 1724 and agreed that the mares and colts be 'flit' (grazed) in the pease field and not the corn field until the harvest was finished. Hogs and pigs of more than six weeks old were allowed into the fields but had to be ringed. Cattle had to leave the common cow pasture by 20 March to allow the hay to grow. Following hay-making, they were allowed to return after 10 May but their horns had to be tipped.[29] Rams had to be excluded from the common fields between Bartholomus-tide and St Luke's. Quite often, such arrangements were timed with the religious feasts and festivals, in this case, the period from the middle of August to the middle of October.

In many villages with wastes and heaths, pigs were not allowed in the common fields at all because of the mess and disturbance they caused. Along with geese, they were driven out each day to the wastes on the edge of the parish and then returned to their respective homesteads in the evening. Forest and woodland sometimes provided rights of pannage where animals such as pigs could feed on beech mast, acorns or browse.

Not all rights were concerned with animals and not all villages possessed heaths, commons or wastes but, where they did, a variety of materials and other resources became available to the cottagers. Fallen wood and sticks, thorn faggots and broom and gorse could all be collected for use as a fuel for the cottage fire. The winters of the 18th century were really cold. Gilbert White records that on New Year's Day in 1785 there was much snow on the ground and that the ponds were frozen up and dry. The following year, there was a fierce frost on 3 January and at 8 o'clock in the evening a Captain Lindsey's hands were frozen whilst journeying.[30] He suffered pain all night and the following morning his fingernails had turned black. There was an average of six inches of snow on the ground and meat was frozen so hard that it could not be spitted for cooking. Many wild birds were frozen to death. Fuel for the cottager's fire was a necessity but he was in competition with local brewers, wheelwrights and bakers who all used large quantities of faggots and firewood. In the early 1720s, an East Midlands victualler, William Coleman, was presented at the manor court of one of his neighbouring villages for making off with 10,000 faggots from their heath. These would have been worth an estimated £65.[31]

Not a necessity but a luxury was a supply of clean sand for the cottage floors, most of which were earthen. Food such as rabbits, wildfowl, berries, crab apples and fungi could also be gathered from the wastes and commons at the appropriate time of the year—a task done mostly by the women and children. Enclosure made poachers of many of these people.

The right of gleaning occurred in most, if not all, villages. At Rempstone in Derbyshire, gleaning survived as late as the mid-19th century.[32] After the harvest was complete, the gleaning began:

> The village crier, having proclaimed the Queen, nearly a hundred gleaners assembled at the end of the village. Women with their infant charges, boys with green boughs, and girls with flowers, the whole, wearing gleaning pockets. Children's carriages and wheelbarrows dressed in green and laden with babies etc, were in requisition.
>
> [A] royal salute was shouted by the boys and the crown brought out of its temporary repository. This part of the regalia was of simple make; its basis consisting of straw-coloured cloth, surrounded with wheat, barley and oats of the present year. A streamer of straw-coloured ribbon, dependant on a bow at the crown, hung loosely down; a leaf of laurel was placed in front, while arching over the whole was a branch of jessamine ... The ceremony of crowning was now performed; after which the Queen, enthroned in an armchair decorated with flowers and branches, moved ... [to] the first field to be gleaned. Then her proclamation was read and it was announced that the gleaning bell would be rung each morning at 8-30 to call everybody together to be led to the fields by [the Queen].

Enclosure, of course, rang the 'bell of doom' for such occasions as it did many others. The effect that enclosure had on household finances—in particular, cottage finances—was marked. J. Humphries has identified the subtle way in which enclosure hastened the proletarianisation of the poor.[33] She points to the usefulness of the commons which were exploited mainly by the women and children who produced a vital component of the family income. This was certainly the case with the Rempstone gleaners. At enclosure, when the commons were lost, the industry of this group was added to the mainly male wage market. This represented a gradual shift towards a wage-earning economy and a more elastic supply of labour.

Little wonder, then, that the commoners were often wary or perhaps even in open revolt against enclosure. Because Northamptonshire was one of the counties most densely enclosed by Act of Parliament (approximately 50 per cent of its surface area), opposition movements seem to have been common. For this reason, Dr. J.M. Neeson based much of her work on commoners, common right and enclosure on this county.[34] She found that, in many cases, the opposition started long before the petition to seek a Bill was lodged with Parliament and that, in some cases, it continued long after an Act was passed.[35] Probably the most effective means of opposition was not riot or other high-profile methods, but by local argument, refusing consent to the Bill, a necessary requirement as we shall see later, and spreading false rumours. During the early, informal stages, an enclosure project was at its most vulnerable. The threat of parliamentary opposition or even attacks on property could be effective in either causing modifications to a Bill or stopping it altogether. For the local historian, few of these methods produced documentary evidence which can be studied today. Indeed, in cases where such opposition was so successful that the enclosure project failed to get off the ground, we may not even know that there was an effective opposition movement. 'Stubborn non-compliance, foot dragging and mischief were common', Dr. Neeson found.[36]

At Long Buckby, Neeson found that the largest landowner received an anonymous poem threatening him and other enclosers not to go out at night. Shortly afterwards some of his trees were pulled down and two summer-houses destroyed. Long Buckby was, however, enclosed three years later, in 1765. Some years later, at Pattishall, alongside the Watling Street, rumours and counter-rumours were spread by both enclosers and opponents, trying to win the support of the Duke of Grafton as part of a six-year period of discussion. Neeson found that this 'Grumbling' stage, as she calls it, was the first stage of opposition. It allowed people of a like mind to band together and prepare for more effective steps, the next one often being the refusal of consent.

In Buckinghamshire, Professor M.E. Turner found that opposition to parliamentary enclosure increased after 1774 when it became necessary to issue public notices of proposed enclosures. Here, too, one of the frequent forms of opposition was refusal to sign the Consent although, as Turner suggests, many refused to sign despite having no personal objections to enclosure. They may, he suggests, have refused to sign in deference to friends and neighbours.[37]

In Northamptonshire, as in other counties, another measure was to raise a counter-petition. As we have seen, the group wishing to introduce an enclosure Bill first submitted a petition to the Commons to request permission. Equally, opposers of the scheme could submit a counter-petition. If the scheme was still in its early stages, the counter-petition could be addressed directly to the local landowner. Neeson found two examples of letters or petitions of this nature, one to the Duke of Buccleuch from the commoners of Brigstock

Figure 13 *(opposite)*   Ravenstonedale enclosure: Counter-petition

[Source: Ravenstonedale enclosure, counter-petition, WDX 76, Cumbria Record Office (Kendal). Reproduced by permission of the County Archivist.]

Transcription

To the Right Honourable the Lords spiritual and temporal of Great Britain in Parliament assembled.

The humble petition of the several persons whose names are hereunto subscribed

Sheweth

That your petitioners are Customary Tenants Owners and Occupiers of diverse Messuages Lands and Tenements in the Manor and Parish of Ravenstonedale in the County of Westmorland and in right thereof are intitl'd to Common of Pasture and Turbary in and throughout all the Commons and Waste Grounds situate and being within the Manor and Parish aforesaid.

That a Bill is intended to be brought into or is now depending in this right honourable House for dividing and inclosing the s[ai]d Commons and Waste Grounds which will be greatly prejudicial to your Petitioners several Rights and Properties.

Your petitioners therefore humbly pray that they may be heard against the s[ai]d Bill by themselves or Counsel,

And your Petitioners shall ever pray etc ...

and one to the Duke of Montagu from commoners opposing the enclosure of Benefield in Rockingham Forest.[38]

If the scheme had already been passed to Parliament for consideration, it was necessary for the opposition to submit their counter-petition to the House, giving their reasons and requesting that the Bill or Act should be not allowed. At Newport Pagnell in 1794 Turner found that a powerfully represented counter-petition attacked the enclosure plans on a wide range of issues including the lord of the manor's rights to the soil, the selection of the commissioners and so on. Overall, Turner found that counter-petitions were not often used: only 16 for the whole of Buckinghamshire out of a total of 120 enclosures. Counter-petitions were unlikely to halt an enclosure and, if they did, it might not be for long. Nevertheless, Turner believed that, where they were used, they were able to delay the process and in some cases cause the enclosers to amend their Bills.[39]

Counter-petitioners expressed a wide range of objections to Enclosure Bills, but sometimes the petition lists only a simple objection. Figure 13 is a copy of the top half of the petition that opposers to the Ravenstonedale enclosure drew up. The lower half contains all the signatures of the counter-petitioners. It can be seen that the petition is addressed to the Lords; this indicates that the opposers were afraid that the Commons had already dealt with it and that it had now been referred to the Upper House.[40] In other cases, the opposers of an enclosure sent counter-petitions to both Houses.[41]

In other parts of the country, similar counter-petitions had already appeared. In Sussex, the counter-petitioners of Ringmer and neighbouring villages were also concerned about the Bill currently before the Lords to enclose Broyle Park. Their counter-petition of 1767 appears in Figure 14.[42]

Amongst the signatures at the bottom is that of F. Read, the doctor who, along with five others, was recorded as signing both for and against the enclosure. Herein lay one of the problems for either camp, as it was not uncommon for some people to sign both the consents and then also a counter-petition. It may be that they had been persuaded by argument during the intervening period or that one or other petition was signed out of deference to the folk hawking it around the proprietors. It may be as likely that, while they were not opposed to the enclosure *per se*, as the Broyle Park counter-petition suggests, they objected to certain aspects of it covered by the clauses mentioned in the counter-petition.

When reasoned argument failed to halt or amend an enclosure, the opposers were left with only one other course, riot and insurrection. These disturbances were comparatively rare and in the period of parliamentary enclosure, they usually only occurred either during the later stages or even after it had been completed. J.W. Anscomb found details of such an uprising at West Haddon in Northamptonshire which was enclosed in 1765 when approximately 800 acres of common heathland were taken out of common use.[43] An advertisement appeared in the *Northampton Mercury* on 29 July 1765, shortly after the enclosure (see Figure 15). It invited gentlemen players to attend a game of football which was to be held at West Haddon on the following Thursday, 1 August. The advertisement seemed innocent enough. A good prize of considerable value was offered and another on the following day, Friday 2 August. Being a block advertisement it was not a cheap entry. The gentlemen players were invited to attend any of the public houses in the village on

Figure 14 Broyle Park enclosure: Counter-petition, 1767

[Source: Broyle Park enclosure, Counter-petition (1767), GLY 3174, East Sussex Record Office. Reproduced with permission of the County Archivist, copyright reserved.]

To the Right Honble the Lords Spiritual and Temporal in Parliament Assembled —

The Humble Petition of several Owners Proprietors and — Occupiers of Ffarms and Lands lying within the respve Parishes of Ringmer Framfield Glynd Glyndbourne and Southmalling in the County of Sussex

Sheweth

That Your Petitioners are informed an Act is depending for dividing & Inclosing the Park or Common called the Broyle Park in the Parish of Ringmer & Framfield in the County of Sussex

That Your Petitioners are apprehensive that the said Act or several Clauses therein contained will if the same should pass into a Law be — very Injurious to your Petitioners

Your Petitioners therefore humbly pray your Lords. that they may have leave to be heard by themselves or their — Council against such parts of the said Bill as may Affect Your Petitioners or have such other Relief as to Your — Lordsh shall seem meet —

1 Wm Kempe	✓ 6 John Willard	2 15 Wm Gaston
— Fra.s Wheler	2 ✓ Jno Fugwell	— S. Goldsmith
2 Rich.d Comber	✓ 7 Tho: Wacklyn	16 The Mark of Eliz Gudsby
— Tho: Hards	— John Natly	2 — The Mark of Rob. Hooper
3 John Jenner	8 John Elphick	17 The Mark of Elizth Wright
— John Moon	9 James Bryant	18 — Christian Norris
✓ 4 F: Read the Doctor	2 — Willm Rother	— John Goring
— Steph: Filder	10 Rob.t Plumer	19 John Tarrant
— Eliz.a Filder	— Jos: Martin	20 Fra.s Melner Newton
2 Joseph Glozbrook	11 Henry Pocock	in all 42 —
— Edw.d Gadsby or Mrs Eliz	— John Pocock	
✓ — Wm Rice	12 John Barnard	
5 Rich. Hill	13 John Martin	
— John Blundell	— Tho: Laurence	
— The Mark of Tho.s Smith	— The Mark of Mary Elphick	
— John Potter	14 Mary Heaver	
	2 John Gaston	

Those with this Mark ✓ Signed both for & against ————   &c.

Transcription of Figure 14

To the Right Honorable the Lords Spiritual and Temporal in Parliament Assembled–

The Humble Petition of several Owners Proprietors and Occupiers of Farms and Lands lying within the respective Parishes of Ringmer, Framfield, Glynd, Glyndbourne and Southmalling in the County of Sussex.

Sheweth

That Your Petitioners are informed an Act is depending for dividing & Inclosing the Park or Common called the Broyle Park in the Parish of Ringmer & Framfield in the County of Sussex

That Your Petitioners are apprehensive that the said Act or several Clauses therein contained will if the same should pass into a Law be very Injurious to your Petitioners

Your Petitioners therefore humbly pray your Lords[hi]ps that they may have leave to be heard by themselves or their Council against such parts of the said Bill as may Affect Your Petitioners have such other Relief as to Your Lordships shall seem meet.

either day between 10 and 12 o'clock in the morning when, '… they would be joyfully received and kindly entertained'.

The next mention of the event appeared in the *Mercury* of Monday 5 August when it was reported that the large crowd who had gathered for the football match had formed themselves into a tumultuous mob and torn up the new enclosure fences and committed other acts of criminal damage. Dragoons under General Mordaunt had been sent for from Northampton to quell the disturbance. A week later, a further advertisement was published stating that a reward of 10 guineas was offered for information regarding the placing of the first advertisement. Two weeks after this, a further notice appeared which included the information that enclosure fencing to the cost of £1,500 had been destroyed in the riots. The notice reminded the readers that this particular crime was one of felony and the guilty parties, when identified, could risk execution without the benefit of clergy.

Figure 15 *Northampton Mercury*

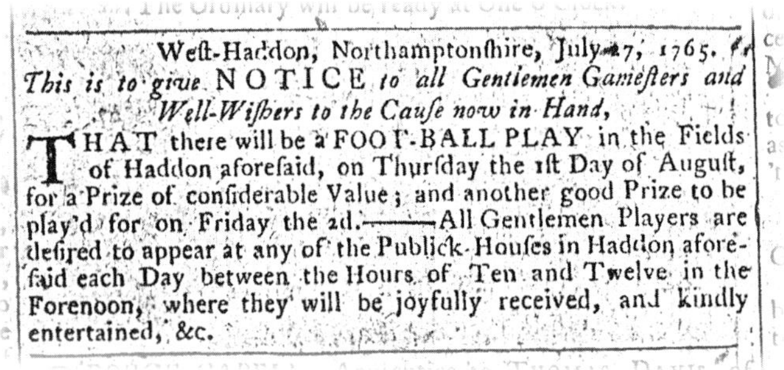

West-Haddon, Northamptonshire, July 27, 1765.
This is to giue NOTICE to all Gentlemen Gamesters and Well-Wishers to the Cause now in Hand,
THAT there will be a FOOT-BALL PLAY in the Fields of Haddon aforesaid, on Thursday the 1st Day of August, for a Prize of considerable Value; and another good Prize to be play'd for on Friday the 2d.———All Gentlemen Players are desired to appear at any of the Publick-Houses in Haddon aforesaid each Day between the Hours of Ten and Twelve in the Forenoon, where they will be joyfully received, and kindly entertained, &c.

[Source: *Northampton Mercury*, 29 July 1765.]

The reward for information leading to the conviction of one of the offenders had been increased to £20 and suspicions were being harboured that the affair had not been planned by mere labourers but that a person of property was behind the scheme. It would certainly seem that the placing of the original advertisement and its payment were beyond the means of even a small group of commoners. In September, William Caldecott of Rugby inserted another advertisement offering a £20 reward for the arrest of Francis Botterill of East Haddon and John Fisher the younger of West Haddon. The former was accused of placing the advertisement for the football match and the latter of helping to finance it. Both were textile workers. In March of the following year, 1766, nine men were tried for their parts in the riots. Four men were acquitted but the remaining accused were sentenced to prison terms ranging from one month to a year. Botterill and Fisher were not amongst the nine and so are presumed to have fled the district to avoid more serious charges. (Almost the entire West Haddon story was extracted by using advertisements and news items from the local newspaper.)

Although such incidents were rare and details today are difficult to trace, there were other incidents across the country. Very often, as in the Tudor riots and uprisings, enclosure was seen as part of a wider source of complaint which often resulted in violence. This was no less true than for the period of long-term economic depression which followed the end of the Napoleonic Wars in 1815. In the 1820s, Poor Rates, unemployment amongst the labouring classes and the price of bread were all high. A bad harvest in 1829 led to even more agricultural workers being laid off.[44] In other parts of the country, anger was directed against the new threshing machines and in mid-1830 riots broke out. Apart from the agricultural workers, skilled craftsmen such as wheelwrights, carpenters, smiths, bricklayers and shoemakers all joined in the insurrection. Known as the Swing Riots after a *nom de plume*, 'Captain Swing', used in a series of threatening notes and letters, almost 2,000 participants appeared before special assize courts of whom 19 were executed and 481 transported to the colonies.

Although the troubles are mostly associated with southern England, John Cooper of Potterspury near Towcester, giving evidence to a Parliamentary Select Committee in 1837, claimed that there had been cases of arson in his area.[45] Other witnesses from across England shared Cooper's view that farmers at this time were paying labourers more than they could afford following threats and intimidation.[46] After the riots of 1830–1, sporadic outbreaks of arson and cattle maiming continued until the 1850s. These riots and disturbances can be traced through local newspapers and through the *Report from the Select Committee on Agriculture with Minutes of Evidence*, 2 August 1837, which is available in many university libraries or the British Library.

Whatever the nature and effectiveness of opposition to an enclosure, the balance of power inevitably lay with the enclosing faction. Only occasionally did an opposition movement stop enclosure in its tracks and, even when it did, the enclosers would pick themselves up, dust themselves down and then, within a few years, introduce another, more successful scheme. Even where opposition was moderately successful in securing better terms, ultimately, enclosure was inevitable as today's landscape easily testifies. Thus it was that, in nearly every case, the process moved on from the initial and informal steps outlined above.

Chapter 3
Processes of Parliamentary Enclosure: Stage II

FINAL PREPARATIONS

In the previous chapter, the process of parliamentary enclosure was traced as far as submitting a petition to the House of Commons requesting permission to draw up a Bill. Setting aside for the moment the possibility of a counter-petition, the next step—procuring or soliciting the Act—could become a period of sometimes frenetic activity. This was not, however, the case with smaller enclosures, particularly where there were only a few proprietors.

In the case of medium and large enclosures which involved more than, say, 10 proprietors, the process was characterised by countless meetings, journeys and correspondence. Usually, there were two spheres of activity running concurrently during this phase of the project. Locally, work would be continuing to obtain consents from as many of the proprietors as possible. Some, perhaps most, would at least have indicated their support for the project before the petition was submitted to the House. Many others would prove either intransigent, indifferent or just simply beyond reach. As we saw in the case of Kirk Ireton, less than half of the proprietors lived in that particular township about to be enclosed. Further, the absentee landowners were dispersed across a wide area. Table 1 shows the extent of this for Kirk Ireton.

Table 1   Kirk Ireton enclosure: Absentee Proprietors

Place of Residence	Number of Proprietors
Ashbourne	1
Belper	1
Chaddesden	1
Derby	11
Duffield	2
Shirley	1
Shottle	2
Uttoxeter	1
Walsall	1

[Source: Draft Consents, D 4459/1/1/14, Derbyshire Record Office. Reproduced by permission of the County and Diocesan Archivist.]

In May 1803, the commissioner's clerk for the Kirk Ireton enclosure received a letter from John Blackwell (Figure 16). Putting aside any questions regarding Elizabeth Sutton having a different surname to her father-in-law, the letter reminds us of two things. First, as Bedford is over 70 miles from Kirk Ireton, the travelling expenses were inevitably large. Second, in this case at least, it seems that some absentee proprietors could easily be temporarily forgotten in the heat of the project.

Figure 16   Letter from John Blackwell of Bedford, 1803

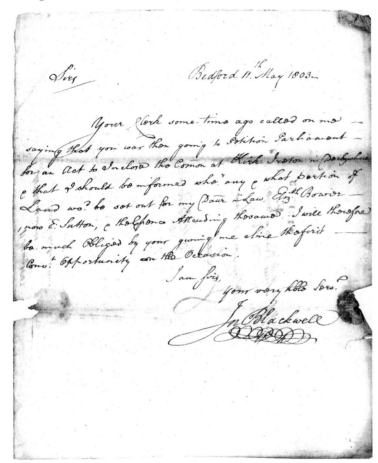

[Source: D 4459/1/1/35, Derbyshire Record Office. Reproduced by permission of the County and Diocesan Archivist.]

Transcription

Sirs   Bedford 11th May 1803

    Your Clerk some time ago called on me saying that you was then going to Petition Parliament for an Act to Inclose the Common at Kirk Ireton in Derbyshire & that I should be informed whe[n] any and what portion of Land wo[ul]d be set out for my Dau[ghte]r in Law Eliz[abe]th Bower now E: Sutton & the Expense Attending the same. I will therefore be much Obliged by your giving me a line the first conv[enien]t Opportunity on the Occasion.

    I am Sirs,

        Your very h[um]ble Servant

        J[oh]n Blackwell

When the clerks to the enclosure commission submitted their final account, all of the journeys were listed, and with some it is even possible to learn how they travelled. Some rode, some took a mail coach, others a chaise and others even a chair.

This local and sometimes not so local lobbying for consents was not only time-consuming and wearying, it could also be frustrating. Many proprietors needed time to consider the proposals which indicated more than one visit. Some were completely hostile to enclosure and vented this on the visiting clerk whom they saw as the agent of the enclosing movement. At Westbury in Wiltshire, Mingay found that many of the proprietors were unwilling to give their consent to the proposed enclosure. Their reasons varied and it took the solicitor, charged with initiating the scheme, eight years before an initial meeting of proprietors could be held. A year later, he was still amending the draft Bill and obtaining consents.[1]

STATE OF PROPERTY

Allied with the process of obtaining consents was the task of compiling the State of Property. This statement described the area of land to be enclosed and the degree of consent. It will be remembered that, at least in theory, there had to be a considerable majority in both number and value of proprietors who consented to the enclosure. Later, the promoters of the scheme would be questioned about this by a parliamentary committee and it was necessary that they were in possession of the facts; information from the State of Property was also used in the preamble to the Bill and Act. However, there were problems in compiling the State of Property, the main one being that accurate totals for the area of land in statute acres were not always available. Arable land was often measured in yardlands or oxgangs (depending on the region) or other local units.

Historically, a yardland had represented a single farm but the actual size varied from manor to manor. Even within a single county, it could range from 18 to 40 acres or more. In the absence of an accurate survey, which did not usually take place until after the passing of the Enclosure Act, only two courses were open: the State of Property, the Bill and the subsequent Act could all use a round estimate or the area of land could be given using the local units—yardlands or oxgangs. Estimates in particular were notoriously inaccurate. The 1809 Act for enclosing Shobdon, Lingen and Kingsland, and Aymestrey, all in Herefordshire, estimated the area to be 900 acres when, in fact, the subsequent survey found only 622—a deficit of just over 30 per cent.[2] At Kington in Worcestershire, the Act of 1781 was based on an estimate of 1,000 acres but only 575 were Awarded—a deficit this time of over 40 per cent.[3]

The discrepancy between areas of land claimed in Acts and that subsequently Awarded has attracted much debate in recent times, particularly by writers trying to assess the total area of land enclosed by parliamentary Acts.[4] One important factor in some enclosures is the amount of land taken out of agriculture for road construction. The Act for enclosing Wootton in Northamptonshire in 1778, for example, claimed that there were 1,884 acres but only 1,688 were Awarded. Part of the deficit could be the 53 acres used for roads.[5] Another possible reason for differences between the area claimed in the State of Property, the Bill and the Act could lie in parishes where there had already been a considerable level of non-parliamentary enclosure. Sometimes the old enclosures were left, but on other occasions they were included in the new enclosure scheme. To use another example from Northamptonshire, Hannington was enclosed in 1803. The Act claimed that there were 800 acres but over 1,200 were subsequently Awarded. This represented a discrepancy of 52 per cent but, if the ancient enclosures in the Award are excluded, this leaves a more acceptable difference of less than 14 per cent.[6]

While there were problems in assessing the amount of arable land to be enclosed, it was as bad or worse for pasture, meadows and wastes. Here, areas were often expressed in terms of the amount of animals that could be grazed by common right. South of the Danelaw area, the terms cow common, cottage cow common and sheep common are found. In the north, gates, cow gates, cattle gates or sheep gates are more often found. This was simply a reflection that, especially where the grazing was poor, acreage was unimportant; farmers were more concerned with how much stock they could pasture. Because of these problems, the preamble in some Bills and Acts expressed the area to be enclosed in the old units of yardlands, oxgangs, commons, stinted commons or whatever local terms were used.

Procuring the Act

The comparatively local activity was concerned with obtaining signatures for the consents form and compiling the State of Property. As this drew near to completion, the project was entering a new phase—the Procuring of the Act. The term 'Procuring the Act' was often used by solicitors when charging for their legal expenses incurred during this part of the formal process of introducing an enclosure scheme by Act of Parliament. It was that part of the process whereby the two houses of Parliament considered the enclosure project. It too could involve much travel, correspondence and negotiation.

Before 1801, procuring the Act began as soon as the petition had been granted and leave given to submit a parliamentary Bill. A Bill is a draft Act and in its final, printed form looks almost the same, except for the front page. The front page of the Bill to enclose over 400 acres of moor and common in 1777 at Kings Meaburn in the Cumbrian parish of Morland appears in Figure 17. The format for enclosure Bills and Acts became standardised by this time. The preamble on the front page gives details of the location of the proposed enclosure project and the need for an enclosure is explained in stylised phrases. Sometimes an estimation of the quantity of land under consideration was given where this was known; even where this was given, the amounts were only very approximate. The Bill then contained a long introduction to all the key personalities involved in the proposed enclosure. The lord of the manor usually headed the list but then other proprietors in descending order of social position were given along with the tithe-owner, whether clerical or impropriate.

Very occasionally, a handwritten draft of the Bill can be found but these are usually copies of earlier Bills, sometimes with blank spaces left for the new details. In most cases the draft Bill was sent to a Parliamentary Agent to be checked. George White, writing from the Commons on 16 March 1803, set out the procedure from that point. First, he gave instructions about the consents which were to accompany the Bill. Once the draft Bill had been agreed by all the parties, a fair copy was to be made. This was to be offered to the lord of the manor for his signature and then to all the other proprietors—a witness to these

Figure 17 Bill to enclose Kings Meaburn, *c*.1777

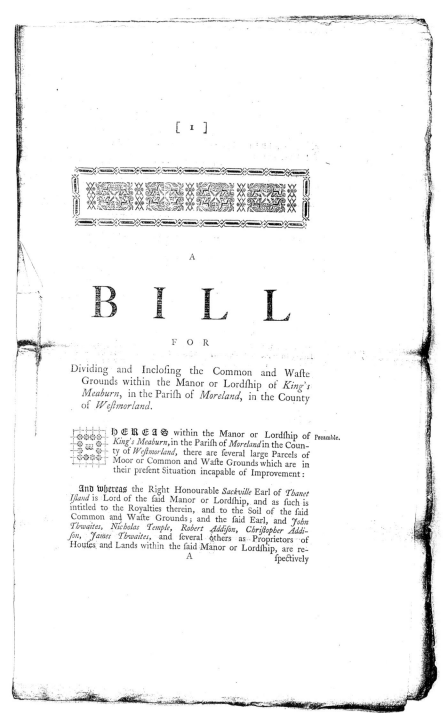

[1]

A

BILL

F O R

Dividing and Inclosing the Common and Waste Grounds within the Manor or Lordship of *King's Meaburn*, in the Parish of *Moreland*, in the County of *Westmorland*.

WHEREAS within the Manor or Lordship of *King's Meaburn*, in the Parish of *Moreland* in the County of *Westmorland*, there are several large Parcels of Moor or Common and Waste Grounds which are in their present Situation incapable of Improvement: **Preamble.**

And whereas the Right Honourable *Sackville* Earl of *Thanet Island* is Lord of the said Manor or Lordship, and as such is intitled to the Royalties therein, and to the Soil of the said Common and Waste Grounds; and the said Earl, and *John Thwaites, Nicholas Temple, Robert Addison, Christopher Addison, James Thwaites,* and several others as Proprietors of Houses and Lands within the said Manor or Lordship, are respectively

A

signatures was to present their evidence to the Committee of the House of Commons and the Committee of the House of Lords. If someone refused to sign, he was to be asked to give his reasons and these were to be written down. 'Every person,' instructed White, 'let his property be ever so small, must be applied to for his consent.'

The parish incumbent had to explain the contents of the Bill to his bishop at least as far as they affected the church. (Usually, this was by way of tithes, glebe and perhaps a settlement towards the upkeep of the fabric of the parish church.) The bishop was then to be asked for his approval and signature—again, in front of a witness.

A witness had also to be found to produce a list of everyone with an interest in the wastes and commons with details of the extent of their property. This could be expressed in terms of the area of his land, the amount of Land Tax he paid on it, or the amount of Poor Rate for which he was liable. White explained that the purpose was to show Parliament that anyone with a legitimate interest in the enclosure had been consulted so that it could be shown what proportion of them in value had assented, dissented, were neuter or, as he put it, 'not to be met with'. Finally, White advised that the completed Bill could be sent on and it would be kept until the Committee day when it would be necessary for the solicitor and any witnesses representing the enclosers to be present.[7] For enclosures in the north of England especially, it was a long journey to London to appear before the Parliamentary Committees. Apart from the local solicitor dealing with the preparations for the enclosure (who was quite often the lord of the manor's steward), there might also be one of the principal proprietors involved in the scheme. In London, they might be met by legal counsel from one of the inns of court and they would attend Parliament together.

The stay in London while the Bill completed its passage through Parliament might last several days. There was always a possibility that more information might be required by the Committees, although in practice, by the late 18th century, most Bills were little more than rubber-stamped. Amendments were made to some Bills, mainly to overcome opposition and dissension. In projects with only a bare minimum of support, clauses in the Bill which were either unusual or perhaps unfair were particularly vulnerable. At some point, for example, the Bill for the Yorkshire enclosure at Etton was changed. The Bill contained a large section headed 'For Regulating Assessment'. This clause was an attempt to prevent disputes between the commissioners and required them, in effect, to produce their own survey and valuation of property before they began. This rather clumsy regulation was omitted in its entirety from the Act when it was passed in 1818.

Nor could the promoters of the Bill be absolutely certain of its successful passage. While most proceeded without serious difficulty, others faced with a counter-petition had a less secure future. As we have seen, some of the counter-petitions only went as far as to express concern about certain clauses within the proposed Act and they probably stood a greater chance of being heard.

The journey from the provinces by coach might have taken several days and the visitors would have been dusty and travel weary. Therefore, the local representatives visiting the capital would have to stay at one of the city's inns for several days. This visit from the country on full expenses was not necessarily an onerous affair. Apart from the social advantages of inn life, it also enabled visits to absentee landowners who might be staying at their London homes. For example, at the beginning of April 1808, two solicitors, Richard

Howes from Northampton and John Hodson from Wellingborough, travelled to London to see the enclosure Bill for Irthlingborough through both Houses of Parliament. Altogether, they spent 18 days at the *White Horse Inn* and the Exchequer Coffee House. On their return to Irthlingborough, they met immediately many of the tenants and proprietors. After many months of planning, the sudden prospect of the parish being turned upside down must have been charged with excitement and apprehension and the news of the successful passage of the Bill into an Act received more than passing interest.[8]

Many of the enclosure records accumulated by the House of Commons, along with other documents, were lost in the fire that destroyed the Houses of Parliament in 1834. However, where an original copy of a Bill or an Act does not survive locally, the House of Lords Record Office may be able to provide photocopies from one or more of the original documents. One of the most valuable parliamentary sources is the *Commons Journal* mentioned in the previous chapter. This is the official record of the business conducted each day by the House of Commons. Sometimes, two versions of these events survive, the original, handwritten account and the printed volume produced later. They are usually identical in content.

Earlier in the process, we saw how the *Journal* recorded the receipt of the petition requesting permission to submit a Bill. Later, when the Bill was received and read, this was also minuted by the *Journal*. The Commons heard the Bills three times and referred them to a Commons committee. If, after the third reading, there were no major problems with the Bill, its name was confirmed or altered and it was carried to the Lords. There, it would be referred to a Lords Committee. If, after this, there were still no objections, it would be carried back to the Commons where it would be passed as an Act. The new Act first appeared in a handwritten form and then later a number of printed copies would be produced. Enclosure Acts found in county record offices are usually printed versions.

Apart from the entries in the *Commons Journal*, minutes from the Lords' Committee may survive and so might the original, handwritten Act. The latter, although an attractive document, will once again be no different in content to the later printed versions. The Parliamentary Committee minutes on the other hand are unique, although many show the perfunctory way in which most enclosure Bills were processed by Parliament.

The Nocton (Kesteven, Lincolnshire) enclosure of 1776 offers a simple example of the way the parliamentary system worked. The enclosure involved only two proprietors. The Honourable George Hobart was lord of the manor, patron of the vicarage and impropriate rector of two-thirds of the great tithes. Hobart also owned most of the land to be enclosed which altogether was estimated at 4,500 acres. The other proprietor was the vicar, the Rev. Peregrine Harrison Curtois. The vicar was proprietor of the glebe farm, certain rights of common, the lesser or vicarial tithes and the remaining one-third of the greater or rectorial tithes. Both proprietors consented to the enclosure.[9] The *Journal* entry for 11 March 1776 appeared as below after the Bill had had its third reading before the Commons:

> An ingrossed Bill for enabling the Honourable George Hobart to enclose the Heath Lands and Low Commons or Fen Grounds in the Parish of Nocton in the County of Lincoln, and for vesting the Glebe Lands, Vicarial Tithes, and Right of Common, belonging to the Vicarage of Nocton aforesaid, in the said George

Hobart, and for making a Compensation to the Vicar of the said Parish in lieu thereof, was read the third time.

[Source: The *Commons Journal*, 11 March 1776, p.644.]

After the Bill had been read, the *Journal* tells us that the House agreed a resolution to pass it. They also approved a complete title for it which ran to 70 words. It was then ordered that Lord Brownlow Bertie carry the Bill to the Lords and 'desire their concurrence'. This was done and on 14 March, just three days later, the Nocton Inclosure Bill came before the Lords Committee chaired by Lord Scarsdale, the minutes of which appear in Figure 18.

Figure 18 Minutes of the Lords Committee meeting

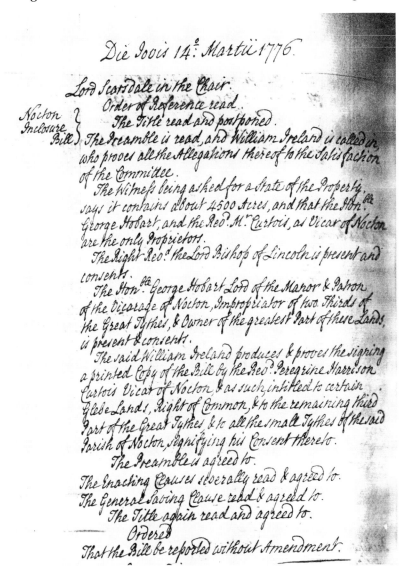

[Source: Lords Committee Minutes of Meeting 14 March 1776, House of Lords Record Office. Reproduced by permission of the Clerk of the Records.]

Transcription of Figure 18

Die Iovis 14º Martii 1776

[Thursday 14 March 1776]

Lord Scarsdale in the Chair.

Nocton   Order of Reference read.

Inclosure   The Title read and postponed.

     Bill   The Preamble is read and William Ireland is called in who proves all the Allegations thereof to the Satisfaction of the Committee.

        The Witness being asked for a State of the Property says it contains about 4500 Acres, and that the Hon[ora]ble George Hobart and the Rev.d Mr Curtois, as Vicar of Nocton are the only Proprietors.

        The Right Revd. the Lord Bishop of Lincoln is present and consents.

        The Hon[ora]ble George Hobart Lord of the Manor & Patron of the Vicarage of Nocton, Impropriator of two Thirds of the Great Tythes & Owner of the greater Part of these Lands is present and consents.

        The said William Ireland produces & proves the signing a printed Copy of the Bill by the Revd. Peregrine Harrison Curtois Vicar of Nocton & as such intitled to certain Glebe Lands, Right of Common, & to the remaining third Part of the Great Tythes & to all the small Tythes of the said Parish of Nocton, signifying his Consent thereto.

        The Preamble is agreed to.

The Enacting Clauses severally read & agreed to.

The General Saving Clause read & agreed to.

        The Title again read and agreed to.

          Ordered

That the Bill be reported without Amendment.

Despite there being just the two interested parties in the Nocton enclosure, the Act ordered that a survey should be made and an Award drawn up. However, when, in the 1960s, W.E. Tate was compiling the data for his domesday of English Parliamentary Enclosures, he could find neither.[10]

PARLIAMENTARY ACTS

At this point, something needs to be said about the Acts themselves. Over time, there was a complex array of different Enclosure Acts. In Chapter One, the enclosure at Radipole in Dorset in 1604 was mentioned. This, though, was a Public Act. Public Acts were usually sponsored by the government of the day and dealt with matters in the national interest. When parliamentary enclosure took off in the 18th century, Private Acts were used. These were sponsored by individuals or groups of individuals. They were numbered like the Public Acts but in a different series. Until 1798, Private Enclosure Acts were listed in the annual volume of statutes but, unlike the Public Acts, they were not printed. Their survival is patchy but there are good collections in some county record offices and the House of

Commons Library. After 1798, copies of all Enclosure Acts were sent to the local Clerk of the Peace. These copies have usually been transferred to the local record office. Further copies often appear in solicitors' collections.

From 1801, another change took place with the passing of the first General Enclosure Act. It was realised by this time that the parliamentary procedure in introducing a Private Act was unnecessarily time consuming and expensive. There were other factors: the country was at war and there had also been a succession of poor harvests. Along with the need to produce more grain, influential landowners wanted to be able to introduce enclosure projects more cheaply. Since, by this time, Private Enclosure Acts had become almost entirely standardised, the new General Act contained those clauses which had been used and approved by Parliament over a long period of time. A small Private Act was still needed to take care of the fine, local detail, but overall much time and effort was saved. A Private Act passed after 1801 will have a reference in it to the General Act, so tying the two halves of the legislation together. For example, the front of the Act for enclosing lands in the parishes of Tavistock, Milton Abbot, Brentor and Lamerton in 1835 mentions:

> And whereas an Act was passed in the Forty-first Year of the Reign of His Majesty King George the Third, intituled *An Act for consolidating in One Act certain Provisions usually inserted in Acts of Inclosure, and for Facilitating the Mode of proving the several Facts usually required on the passing of such Acts ...*[11]

In comparison, Private Acts, such as that for several Westmorland townships in the parish of Kirkby in Kendal (1823) which did not draw on the powers of a General Act, include only the dates of the parliamentary session and the Royal Assent (Figure 19).

In 1836, another General Enclosure Act was passed in order to deal solely with the enclosure of open arable land. In 1840, a further Act widened the scope of the 1836 Act so that not only open field arable could be enclosed but also common meadow and pasture. Land enclosed after this time is said to have been enclosed under the 1836 and 1840 Acts. Together, they allowed local proprietors to carry out enclosures without making specific reference to Parliament, provided that two-thirds in number and value agreed. Commissioners would be appointed by the proprietors to carry out the enclosure as before, unless the proportion in favour was seven-eighths, in which case the proprietors were able to carry out the division and allotments themselves.

The last important development was the passing of the 1845 General Inclosure Act. Intended to prevent further abuses and to protect small areas such as village greens, the new Act provided for the formation of a permanent, national enclosure commission in London. Local assistant commissioners and surveyors acted as valuers and held local enquiries into each proposed new enclosure project. The Commission would make recommendations to Parliament on this basis and, if the enclosure was approved, the local officials would be responsible for implementing it.

Figure 19 *(overleaf)*
Front of Act, Whitwell and Selside, Skelsmergh and Crook, 1823

[Source: Front page of Act for enclosing land at Whitwell and Selside, Skelsmergh and Crook in the parish of Kirkby in Kendal, Westmorland, WDB/35, Box 17, Cumbria Record Office (Kendal). Reproduced by permission of the County Archivist.]

4 Geo. IV.——Sess. 1823.

A N

A C T

FOR

Inclofing Lands within the Townſhips or Diviſions of *Whitwell* and *Selſide, Skelſmergh* and *Crook,* in the Pariſh of *Kirkby in Kendal,* in the County of *Weſtmorland.*

[Royal Assent, 23 *May* 1823.]

𝕎𝕙𝕖𝕣𝕖𝕒𝕤 there are within the ſeveral Townſhips or Diviſions of *Whitwell* and *Selſide, Skelsmergh* and *Crook,* in the Pariſh of *Kirkby in Kendal,* in the County of *Weſtmorland,* ſeveral Commons and Waſte Lands or Grounds: **Preamble.**

And whereas the Honourable *Fulk Greville Howard* is Lord of the Manor of *Fawcet Foreſt,* in which the Townſhip of *Whitwell* and *Selſide* is ſituate, and is alſo Lord of the Manor of *Skelsmergh,* with its Members, in which the ſaid Townſhip of *Skelsmergh* is ſituate; and the ſaid *Fulk Greville Howard* is, or claims, and the Right honourable *William* Earl of *Lonsdale,* Knight of the Moſt Noble Order of the Garter, is, or claims to be, Lord of the Manor of *Crook,* in which the ſaid Townſhip of *Crook* is ſituate: **Manorial Lords.**

And whereas the ſaid Honourable *Fulk Greville Howard, Daniel Wilſon, Ralph Riddell, Arthur Shepherd, James Hoggarth Long,* Eſquires, and ſeveral other Perſons are Owners and Proprietors of divers Meſſuages Lands and Hereditaments within the ſaid ſeveral Manors Townſhips or Diviſions, or ſome or one of them, **Proprietors of Common Right.**

48.   A   and

Because the contents of the Bills and Acts were mainly determined by precedent—and this certainly applied to the general headings—it is necessary to look at only a few to obtain an overall picture of the information that can be derived from them. In addition to the general layout, much of the detail was also part of a general pattern which developed over the course of the 18th century.

AN EXAMPLE OF AN ENCLOSURE ACT FROM SHELTON, BEDFORDSHIRE

The enclosure of Shelton in Bedfordshire in 1794 provides a good example of a Private Enclosure Act.[12] The original estimate of the area to be enclosed was 1,000 acres but in the event only 807 acres were found, which took two years to complete.

The first part of the Act is the preamble in which a brief description of Shelton is given. There then follows the 'Who's Who' of the parish. Brampton Gurdon Dillingham Esq. was given as the lord of the manor and also a proprietor of part of the open and common fields. Usually, the lord of the manor also claimed the right of soil of any commons or wastes. He received land in the new allotments specifically in lieu of these rights.

Two people, the Right Hon. Henry Beauchamp Lord St John Baron of Bletsoe and the Rev. George Freeman DL jointly held the advowson of the parish church—the right to nominate the incumbent. They divided this privilege, Beauchamp having the right of nomination twice out of every three and Freeman exercising his right the remaining once out of every three. Freeman not only owned part of the right to present the incumbent but the Act tells us that he himself was actually rector. As such, he received the great and small tithes or a modus or composition (money) in lieu of them. Also, as rector, he had the glebe farm of 45 acres in the open fields. The rest of the land to be enclosed was held by Beauchamp, the Corporation and Wardens of Barnwell Hospital, John Collett and others. By 'others' the implication from the Act is that they had comparatively smaller landholdings. Next, the Act recognised that some of the cottagers at Shelton possessed cottage commons and as such were entitled to common of pasture for their cattle.

The Act named the three commissioners who had been nominated earlier in the process. First was Edward Hare from Castor near Peterborough. He was to become a very experienced commissioner, and adopted a hands-on approach when he later became a commissioner at Irthlingborough, making many site visits. Charles Marion Welstead of Kimbolton, then in Huntingdonshire, also served on other enclosure commissions and finally there was John Venn, from Norton near Daventry in Northamptonshire. Later in the Act, the commissioners' allowances were set at two guineas per day and full allowance for travelling from home. Later in the enclosure period, in an effort to reduce the costs, a further clause was often added to introduce a time penalty. After a given period of time, the commissioners' expenses were reduced on a sliding scale. They were only paid for the days they worked and the length of a working day for winter and summer was specified in hours by the Act. Many Acts also included a copy of the form of oath to be sworn by the commissioners when they took office. The Shelton Act also ordered that a surveyor was to be appointed by the commission. The Act did not name a surveyor but serving commissioners were barred from the post.

Road construction, as we shall see later, was also an important aspect of some enclosure projects. The Shelton Act ordered that there was to be a surveyor of roads and that the roads dividing parishes should be 40 feet wide. Carriage roads were to be fenced on both sides by the proprietors and no gates were to be erected across them. Trees alongside the road were to be at least 60 feet apart. This was possibly to deny footpads and highwaymen cover from which to strike at passers-by.

The Act demanded that up to five acres of land was to be set aside for public stone quarries and gravel pits. This was to be used for repairing the roads in Shelton only. A clause to this effect was common in the larger enclosures; usually it was tied in with the requirements for building new roads rather than their subsequent repair. The Shelton Act also allowed for stone to be used for erecting buildings and walls. This was less common, as was the setting aside of up to three acres for public mortar pits which, again, was for the benefit of Shelton only but was to be available for anyone to dig mortar for repairs or new buildings.

No pasturing was to be allowed on the highway for seven years after the execution of the Award. The Act laid down the following penalties for anyone found guilty of doing so: 10 shillings for every beast (cow or steer) or horse and one shilling for every sheep. These were quite severe punishments. In other parishes, the Enclosure Act allowed the grazing of herbage on the roadside verges, the income from it going to the Surveyor of Highways.

The rector was to receive an allotment for his glebe. This was perfectly normal—the glebe was just another farm in the manor. It was held by the rector who in this respect was also a farmer. It was usually a large farm and in some cases was one of the two largest farms in the manor—the demesne farm belonging to the lord being the other. In this case, one allotment for his glebe was to be near the rectory house but the glebe farm was to be fenced at the expense of the other proprietors. Many Acts used the phrase 'ring-fenced', meaning that only the outer perimeter was fenced or hedged by the others. If the rector wanted to subdivide his allotment into smaller fields, he had to pay for the extra boundaries himself. The rector of Shelton was to be allowed to lease out his allotments provided the diocese and the patron (of which he was one-third) consented.

The rector's other source of income was the tithes and the Act decreed that these were to be replaced by a yearly rent at the rate of one-fifth of arable land and one-ninth of all such other lands. (Otherwise, had the rector been awarded land in lieu of his tithes, he might have expected new allotments to represent these proportions of the total land being enclosed.) The rent, known as a corn rent, was to be calculated by the enclosure commissioners after checking the prices of a Winchester bushel of wheat in Bedfordshire over the previous 21 years. The rent was to be paid at the Rectory House in half-yearly payments on 5 April and 10 October each year. The rector was to become exempt from keeping a bull and boar for the services of the other farmers in the manor. Again, this was a common clause in Enclosure Acts.

The lord of the manor was to be allowed an allotment for the wastes. In some Acts, this allotment, usually relatively small, was described as being in lieu of the lord's right to the soil. The implication was that although commoners often had certain rights on the wastes, ultimately, the soil itself belonged to the lord. The lord also claimed the trees and scrub on the wastes and so the Act allowed him 12 months to remove them.

The lord of the manor was also to receive some land in lieu of Quit Rents, the small annual payments made in some manors by the copyholders, which allowed them to retain their title to the land. As the lord received land instead of these payments, the implication is that the copyhold was effectively being bought out in favour of freehold. This in turn would have sounded the death knell for the manor court whose two purposes by this time were the regulation of the open fields (which were now being enclosed) and the control of the copyhold land market (which was also being dismantled).

The Act required that each proprietor construct the hedges or fences laid down in the Award and, if any failed to do this, they were to be presented to a Justice of the Peace. The Act recognised that it might not be possible to make a fair allocation of the fencing, in which case anyone with an undue proportion was to receive compensation from the commissioners. The Shelton Act then went into specifications for the boundaries, ditches, post and rail fencing and the new quickset hedges. Not all Acts entered into such fine detail. New fences and hedges need not be erected where there was an existing boundary marker such as a fence, mound, brook or rivulet. In such cases, existing hedges were to be left in place. (Clauses dealing with hedges are examined in more detail in the Epilogue.)

By way of a disclaimer, the Act declared that it did not serve to cancel or alter any will. However, leases on land which was to become subject to the enclosure were to become void on 10 October 1794.

The Shelton Act then dealt with the powers and responsibilities of the commissioners. Much of these were in the form of standard clauses. The commissioners were to direct the course of husbandry during the period of enclosure. The enclosure process could take a year or more (sometimes many years) and, during this difficult time, the farming year had to proceed as best it could. Land would need to be ploughed and seeds sown. The commissioners were charged with making these arrangements. In some Acts, these duties were set out in detail, particularly where arable land formed a large part of the enclosure. In particular, the commissioners were concerned with the agriculture in the open fields prior to their division and enclosure. Some Acts required the commissioners to be responsible for the stocking of the fields with cattle, and the sowing of cereals, grass seed or clover. They were also to be responsible for ploughing; sometimes a ploughing book kept account of the costs of tillage. On the wolds in the west of Northamptonshire, one enclosure commission in the 1770s was ordered by the Act not to allow any existing meadow, pasture or common land to be ploughed before the new enclosures were completed.[13]

The Shelton Act also empowered them to construct land drains and to raise revenue to defray all their expenses. The most common ways of financing an enclosure were either by levying a rate against the proprietors or by selling some of the land which was being enclosed. At Shelton, the enclosure was financed by a rate payable by all the proprietors with the exception of the rector. If any of the proprietors had put up money to get the scheme off the ground, they were to receive it back with interest. The commissioners were to produce an Award of their allotments and both they and the surveyor to the enclosure were to have right of access to the land being enclosed. At the time of executing the Award, the commissioners were to present the proprietors with a copy of their accounts for the cost of the enclosure.

New allotments were to be made in lieu of all former rights and proprietors were expected to accept the allotments that they were awarded. The Shelton Act, like others, allowed for appeals to be heard by Quarter Sessions.

The final two clauses were also standard entries. One was in the form of a saving for the lord of the manor who retained his title and whose rights remained unaffected by the Act. The second was a general saving which protected any existing interests, in what was to become the new enclosed lands, held by the crown or anyone else other than the proprietors to whom they were to be allotted. This, then, was the Act for enclosing Shelton.

At different times or in different parts of the country other clauses were included in Enclosure Acts. There are many examples; some were rarely used, others were very common. Some Acts allowed for commissioners refusing to act. In a few, rare cases this happened. At Llanidloes in Montgomeryshire, Professor Chapman found that the Act of 1816 named three commissioners but all refused to accept the post and were replaced by three more. Of these, one, George Nuttall of Leominster, died and had to be replaced by John Dyer after John Maughan had been elected but removed following court action.[14] If that situation seemed complex, another Welsh enclosure, that of Llangynfelyn in Caernarfonshire, was even more so. The Act of 1813 to enclose 10,000 acres (the actual total was only 4,505 acres) appointed two commissioners—Thomas Hassall and Richard Jones. Thomas Hassall of Cilrhiw unfortunately died and was replaced by Charles Hassall of Eastwood, who also died. He was replaced by David Joel Jenkins of Lampeter who failed to take up his appointment and so was removed. He was replaced by Richard Griffithes of Bishops Castle. Meanwhile, the other original commissioner named in the Act, Richard Jones of Pantirrion, had resigned. He was replaced by Robert Williams who failed to take up his position and so was removed from office. He was replaced for a time by Thomas Jones the Younger of Penbryn. In 1845 a new commissioner, Thomas Jones Griffithes, also of Bishops Castle, was made sole commissioner.[15]

To a student of one single enclosure, the full impact of the death of a commissioner is not always apparent. When the Rev. Henry Jephcott, Rector of Kislingbury in Northamptonshire, died on 9 November 1776, he was a member of six enclosure commissions in that county alone. In total, he had served on 41 known enclosure commissions in his own county plus others in Oxfordshire.[16]

Sometimes, Enclosure Acts specified how a vacancy for a commissioner was to be dealt with. Usually, if the vacancy arose for a commissioner nominated by a particular party to the enclosure, such as the lord of the manor or the rector, they also had the right to nominate his replacement. If the commission consisted of three or five men, the surviving commissioners might be empowered to replace their colleague. Where there was only one commissioner, as in some of the later enclosures, the clerk to the commission placed a newspaper notice advertising the vacancy. This happened during the Beer Hackett enclosure in Dorset when, under the General Act of 1836, Edward Thomas Percy, a local surveyor, was appointed commissioner.[17] He died before the enclosure was completed and so Messrs. Fooks, clerks to the enclosure, advertised the vacancy. William Haggett of Sherborne, another surveyor, was appointed to replace Percy since, as he claimed in his letter of application, he already had all of Percy's papers and maps. They had no doubt been in partnership or a similar business relationship.[18] Not all changes were as smooth as this. At Kidwelly St Mary in Caernarfonshire, the original commissioner, William Hand of Molleston, was removed for neglect and incompetence. Two rival groups each elected a replacement for him, Dr. Thomas Evans and a Mr. Parry. Parry began work but was challenged by Evans and the group who had tried to appoint him. Eventually, they were both effectively replaced by the appointment of David Davies as a valuer.[19]

Another clause which appeared, particularly in the 1770s, was one concerning qualitymen or qualiteers, as they were sometimes called. These were more common where the enclosure was primarily one of arable land, particularly during the 30-year period from the mid-1760s onwards. At least in theory, the importance of quality as well as quantity was realised when re-allotting land to the proprietors and most Acts acknowledged this. One of the advantages of the open-field system was that, with dispersed holdings, everyone held a fair share of the good and bad land in the township. After enclosure, it may not have been easy to achieve this. By consolidating holdings into larger parcels, some would have to be in the poorest part of the field system and some in the better. Therefore, it was recognised that those receiving the poorest land ought to have correspondingly more of it. Similarly, if a proprietor in the open and common fields occupied land which was either predominantly poor or predominantly good, this too had to be recognised in the re-allotment after enclosure.

A study of Northamptonshire qualitymen found that the first appeared in 1765 with the Act to enclose Syresham. Two local men, John Watts of Sulgrave and William Gibbons of Canons Ashby, were appointed. (Watts also served as an enclosure commissioner in at least four counties.) It was the qualitymen's duty to advise the surveyor on matters affecting the quality, and hence value, of the land he was re-allotting to the Sulgrave proprietors. Qualitymen and their role in enclosure is examined in more detail in Chapter 5.

The Acts often made provision for two small allotments. One for the poor of the parish (to help subsidise the Poor Rate) and the other for the parish church towards the upkeep of the fabric of the building. This was usually vested in the churchwardens and was quite separate from the land received by the rector or vicar in respect of glebe land or tithes. Depending, of course, on the size of the enclosure, neither the Poor Land nor the Church Land usually amounted to much more than an acre apiece. There are notable exceptions, especially in Wales. Chapman found that, in 1837, the Llanymynech (Denbighshire) Enclosure Act resulted in the Overseers of the Poor of Ruabon receiving 244 acres.[20] This was a large enclosure, however, of 22,770 acres of open field, common and waste dispersed across 13 parishes, some of which were in Shropshire. Similarly, at Gwyddelwern in Merionethshire, the enclosure of 13,498 acres in 1810 left the poor of Llanraiadr with 344 acres.[21] Crude comparisons of the fortunes of the poor at enclosure are not possible though. The amount of land awarded to overseers depended on two factors. First, as we have seen in the last two examples, large enclosures of often inferior land might have led to large allotments for the poor. Second, the final amount depended on whether the overseers already held land in the open fields or wastes or whether they held any rights over them before the enclosure.

RIGHT OF SOIL AND MINERALS

The lord of the manor's right of soil has already been mentioned but there were many variations concerning the details. This was usually the right to the soils below the wastes, heaths, commons, mosses, fens, moorland or mountain, which had previously been open and enjoyed by the commoners for grazing or any of the other locally accepted common rights. At enclosure, these rights were extinguished and the open land enclosed and divided and a clause to this effect often appeared in Acts. The lord of the manor, who had previously claimed no more than the right of soil, usually surrendered this right in exchange for land in the new enclosures. As such, he took no further interest in what had been the old common land. There were, however, exceptions, particularly where there was at least a suspicion of some residual value in the soil itself. This usually took the form of minerals such as metal ores or coal. The Brentor (Devon) enclosure of the common in 1835 saw the lord of the manor retaining his mineral rights. Ores, metals, minerals, slate, lime and stone were all specified in the Act.[22]

On the North Yorkshire-County Durham border, the draft Bill for the enclosure of Mickleton Moor (1802) saw the lord of the manor claim new allotments in lieu of his rights to the soil, but he retained his rights of royalty (title of lord of the manor) and minerals. If he subsequently mined coal, lead, minerals or stone, however, the Act required him to compensate the new proprietors for making wagon ways, drifts, levels or watercourses across their land. They were also to be compensated for the lord's use of fire or other engines, pit rooms or heap rooms. By 'fire engines' the Act was referring to the still new-fangled steam engines being used to drain pits and mines at that time.[23] On the other side of the Pennines, an Act which covered several townships in the parish of Kirkby-in-Kendal also protected the lord of the manor's mineral rights but provided for compensation to be paid to the allotment owners for any inconveniences incurred during any searches for minerals as well as during the mining of them if they were found.[24]

The Shelton Act provided for the protection of new roadside hedging by preventing grazing on the verges for seven years; most Acts made similar rules regarding the new allotments. Although, given time, hawthorn makes an impervious barrier to sheep, they are not averse to grazing off the new growth, especially in times when grass is in short supply such as during a drought. Thus many Midlands enclosure Acts prohibited the grazing of lambs in the new enclosures for four years and sometimes seven.[25] In other parts of the country such as the Yorkshire Dales or in the south west, asses were also mentioned. These may have been bred or reared by farmers as pack animals used by local mineral extractors but, whatever their purpose, they were considered particularly injurious to the new quickset hedges.[26]

WATER AND DRAINAGE MATTERS

The Shelton Act and others recognised the usefulness of water courses and streams as natural boundaries; some Acts allowed commissioners to move or re-direct water courses. The Maidford Act of 1778 included a large clause under the heading, *Commissioners to direct water-courses*.[27] The aim of this section was to enable the commissioners to provide the new allotment owners with a supply of water where they thought it appropriate. This they were to achieve by diverting springs or other water courses as appropriate and to direct landowners to scour the ditches and springs that travelled through their allotments. Water at this particular village had a number of uses. At one end of the parish, earth tanks had been dug alongside the stream in which to wash sheep. Further downstream was a water corn mill and, further still, a fulling mill. Throughout the parish there were places for sheep and cattle to drink from the stream. In the East Riding enclosure at Etton, just over a quarter of an acre was to be set aside for a public watering place[28] and at Irthlingborough, in 1809, provision was made for bridge building and the construction of a weir on the River Nene.[29]

Some watercourses were beyond even the grasp of enclosure commissioners. When Alderton, near to the Northamptonshire-Buckinghamshire border, was enclosed by Parliament in 1819, the commissioners were ordered not to interfere with the Grand Union Canal property.[30] Similar conditions were made across the country regarding turnpike roads and the 1809 Act for enclosing Rothersthorpe (Northamptonshire) referred to the railway as a boundary, presumably a horse-drawn tramway.[31]

In the fenland and low-lying districts too much rather than too little water was the problem addressed by some Acts. The Skellingthorpe (Kesteven, Lincolnshire) Act of 1804 provided for banking, draining and improving land in the city of Lincoln and the Act for Friskney in the same county was also, primarily, for draining and banking.[32] At Lancaster in 1795 a Public Local Act covering just 210 acres authorised the draining and embanking of a common pasture and the extinguishing of the common rights. The profits from the enclosure were to be shared among the 80 oldest freemen of the town.[33] The 1838 Act for the enclosure of an estimated 6,000 acres in the three Lake District townships of Strickland Roger, Whinfell and Helsington also allowed for drainage. The Act claimed that there was low land or marsh in the parish of Levens on the northern bank of the River Kent. Also, in nearby Bradley Field and Underbarrow, there was another marsh known as Underbarrow Mosses. There was a third area in Helsington called Helsington Low Common. The Act further claimed that they were of little value but that it would be a great advantage if they were to be effectually drained and precautions made to prevent flooding.[34]

The Act appointed a number of commissioners. Anthony Battersby Tomlinson was appointed to oversee the enclosure of Strickland Roger and John Watson the younger was appointed for the enclosure of Whinfell. Two others, John Watson and William Turner, were appointed to oversee the enclosure of Helsington and also for the draining of the three marshes and mosses. Here an umpire was also to be appointed in case of a dispute. The two Commissioners of Drainage were ordered by the Act to produce a separate Award which was to make allowance for the long-term maintenance of the ditches, sluices, water courses or whatever else. The expense of this maintenance was to be borne by the proprietors, pro rata according to the value of their holding. The commissioners were to have regard to the different levels of benefit that each farm might receive from the drainage. After the execution of the Award, the proprietors were to appoint a superintendent who was to be responsible for the long-term care of the drainage scheme. The proprietors were to hold an annual meeting when they could fix the amount of money to be raised to carry out any necessary repairs and to appoint the superintendent. The Act allowed each proprietor to have at least one vote but those with more land could have as many as 10 votes on a sliding scale. There was also to be an annual audit and minutes kept of the meetings.

FINANCING THE ENCLOSURE

Most enclosures, no matter how small, were expensive and this was particularly so where drainage projects were also undertaken. A controversial enclosure in Oxfordshire, which subsequently led to riots and disturbances, was introduced by a Public Act in 1815. The project was dependent upon the drainage of a large, low-lying common called Otmoor. In total, the Act was concerned with an estimated 4,000 acres and it now seems that the project may have cost as much as £30,000.[35] Although these particular costs were exceptionally high, even small projects could not always be financed out of current reserves. Some enclosure Acts included a clause which allowed the commissioners to take out a mortgage to cover the costs of the enclosure. Evidence that many commissioners actually raised money in this way is rare but, in some enclosures financed by a rate levied on the proprietors, some individual proprietors used mortgages to finance their share of the costs. Where proprietors, for whatever reason, were not able to exercise control of their own estate, and this was carried out by others on their behalf, some Acts covered the eventuality with clauses which referred to the rights of 'husbands, guardians, trustees, committees, executors in trust, or attornies' to act on behalf of proprietors, being 'under coverture, minors, lunaticks, or beyond the seas[36] or otherwise incapable' of acting for themselves. They were specifically authorised to raise money by a mortgage on the land to be enclosed in order to pay for their share of the enclosure costs. In one typical case, the Act allowed a maximum of 40 shillings per acre to be raised in this way.

Fencing and Walling

The Shelton Act examined above went into detail in describing the position of the enclosure fencing. Not unsurprisingly, information concerning the methods of creating boundaries in the new enclosures was dealt with by most Acts, although in varying detail. The ring-fencing of the incumbent's enclosures has already been mentioned as was the use of existing landscape features such as streams. New boundaries usually consisted of stone walls or quickset (hawthorn) hedging. In the latter case, post and rail fencing had also to be constructed for the first 15 or more years. By that time, the hedge had grown and had been laid in order to make a stock-proof barrier. Ditches and mounds were also specified in many Acts, the mound being the spoil from the ditch upon which the quickset hedge was often planted. In some Acts, there was also a deadline for the creation of these boundaries—12 months from the signing of the Award was the usual maximum. Where proprietors failed to complete their fencing, some Acts empowered local Justices of the Peace to compel them to.

In parts of the country where stone was plentiful, perhaps even where it had to be removed from the newly enclosed wastes in order to allow tillage, walls were preferred to hedging. Their construction required effort but the effects were relatively immediate. Thus in the uplands of England and Wales we see mile upon mile of walling that makes the local landscape so distinctive. For local reasons, though, some Acts did not require either a wall or a hedge. The Strickland Roger enclosure recognised that some boundaries need not be fenced. They were to be marked with stones.[37]

For a period defined in some Acts—usually a year—gaps were to be left in the new boundaries so that livestock and farm implements could be moved about as the farmers relocated to their new fields. Thereafter, the gaps were to be blocked.

Conclusion of the Second Stage

Armed with all the instructions set out above and with Parliament's authority, the principal landowners, proprietors and the solicitor, who would almost undoubtedly become the commission's clerk, set out for home. The often long and arduous journey did nothing but whet their appetite for the ensuing work and upheaval that faced them and the local community. As the second stage in the enclosure process drew to an end, the costs incurred during the procuring of the Act would have to be paid and plans drawn up for the first meeting of the commission. In many enclosures, opposition and obstruction could still be expected but this had to be weighed against all the plans for executing the Act. No doubt the euphoria which greeted the returning band by those in support of the scheme tended to diminish the potential problems that lay in wait.

Chapter 4

Stage III: The Commissioners Take Over

THE COMMISSIONERS

The process of enclosure entered a new phase with the passing of the Act. From this point, the local proprietors temporarily lost control of their farms and even the parish as the commissioners took over the course of husbandry during the period of executing the Act. As the 18th-century boom in parliamentary enclosure approached its zenith, a number of trends in the composition of the commissions developed as areas of responsibility and special skills were acquired. The commissioners mostly referred to themselves as gentlemen. Some had a connection with the land, a few describing themselves as graziers and others being clerics. One such commissioner, Rev. Henry Jephcott, rector of Kislingbury in Northamptonshire, has already been mentioned but another even more prominent enclosure commissioner was the Rev. Henry Homer of Birdingbury in Warwickshire.

Homer is one of the most important and possibly the first of the professional commissioners because he published work on the topic. His most important publication appeared in 1766 wherein he dealt with the background to enclosure, the economic and social arguments for and against, as well as the practical means whereby commissioners should proceed. He was particularly concerned with introducing professional standards by which enclosure commissioners worked in the execution of their duties.[1] He humbly recognised the immense power that the commissioners had in implementing an enclosure and how, unlike a land dispute dealt with by a court of law, there was, despite clauses in most Acts allowing for appeals, little or no recourse in practice for dissatisfied proprietors. It was, he felt, 'one of the greatest trusts, which is ever reposed in any set of men in the Kingdom; and therefore merits all the return of caution, attention, and integrity which can result from an honest, impartial, and ingenuous mind'.[2] Professor M.W. Beresford found that Homer served as a commissioner in all the Midlands counties.[3] Since Homer and Jephcott were, by their reliance on glebe land for their own income, already agriculturalists, it was entirely natural that they and others like them should have an interest in enclosure, just as any other farmer or agriculturalist of the time might.

Many commissioners in the late 18th century were virtually professionals, serving, as Jephcott and Homer did, on several commissions across a number of counties at the same time. John Davis of Bloxham in Oxfordshire is another example of this type of commissioner. Professor M.E. Turner found that he sat on 113 enclosure commissions across nine counties. This may have been a slightly conservative estimate as one more commission and one more position as umpire have since been found.[4] However, Davis, like other busy commissioners, seems not to have attended all the meetings. Turner found, for example, that Davis attended only half the meetings of the Buckinghamshire enclosure of Moulsoe.

Not all commissioners were like Davis and the other professionals. In Northamptonshire, of 166 commissioners who served between 1733 and 1841, approximately half served only once. Typically, these commissioners became involved with an enclosure in their own area.[5]

In the early parliamentary enclosures, large commissions were appointed. Enclosure was a sensitive operation and the presence of a large number of the great and good might have been necessary to put their stamp of approval on the scheme. As we saw earlier, though, with the 17th-century attempt to enclose Broyle Park in Sussex, not many of the commissioners would have been involved in the day-to-day operation of executing the Act. When parliamentary enclosure began to gather pace in the first half of the 18th century, commissions were still large, especially in Gloucestershire and Lancashire where 20 or more were appointed.[6] By the 1730s and '40s, most enclosure commissions were of 10 or 11, as we have seen, but almost immediately, as the cost of introducing enclosure began to spiral, this was reduced first to five then to three. Commissions of three men continued as the norm into the 19th century and then, particularly after 1815, this was reduced to two and often one. Sometimes an umpire or referee was also appointed, particularly where there were only one or two commissioners. Later, in the enclosures ordered under the General Acts of the mid-19th century, local commissions were not appointed; instead, a local valuer would act on behalf of the Inclosure Commission in London.

Whereas in the 1770s, when parliamentary enclosure was approaching its first peak of activity, it was typical for all the main parties involved to appoint their own commissioner, this was not possible later when there were smaller commissions. [So, a typical three-man commission in 1775 might have had members appointed by the lord of the manor, the incumbent and the other proprietors, and each was expected to protect the interests of the nominating party.] By the 19th century and the smaller commissions, it was no longer possible to do this and so it was more important to appoint a commissioner who could be respected by all the parties involved in the scheme.

This third stage in the introduction of enclosing by Act of Parliament could take varying amounts of time. In the 18th century, a typical enclosure of mainly arable land but perhaps with an area of waste or commons usually took one to two years from the passing of the Act to the reading and signing of the Award. In Worcestershire, the Act to enclose an estimated 864 acres (the actual area was 775 acres) in the parish of Grafton Flyford was passed in 1779 and the Award was read in 1780.[7] At Middlezoy in Somerset, an Act was passed in 1798 to enclose estimated areas of 500 acres in the open arable fields and 600 acres of pasture. The Award appeared two years later in 1800.[8] In 1814, an Act to enclose an estimated 900 acres of land which did not include open field arable in the Kent townships of Coxheath in Boughton, Monchelsea, Loose, East and West Farleigh, Hunton and Linton was presented the following year, 1815.[9]

Not all enclosures were performed so promptly and many seem to have taken much longer. Such enclosures are worthy of research. Among them are some from Bedfordshire where significant periods of time elapsed between the passing of the Act and the completion of the Award. They include those shown in Table 2 overleaf.

There are many other examples of apparently long processes of executing an Enclosure Act. In Berkshire, the Aston Act was passed in 1808 but it was nine years before the Award

Table 2 Bedfordshire enclosures, 1802–1820

Place	Year Act Passed	Date of Award	Time Taken (years)
Shillingford & Holwell	1802	1817	15
Clophill	1808	1826	18
Flitton(-cum-Silsoe) & Pulloxhill	1809	1826	17
Roxton and Chawson & Colesden	1810	1819	9
Biddenham	1812	1828	16
Stagsden	1812	1828	16
Potton	1814	1832	18
Upper and Lower Gravenhurst and Upper Stondon	1820	1851	31

[Source: Tate, W.E., *A Domesday of English Enclosure Acts and Awards*, M.E. Turner (ed.) (Reading 1978), pp.56–7.]

appeared.[10] In the same county, Engelfield (1809)[11] took 20 years during which time there was an amending Act, Hungerford (1811)[12] took nine years, and a very late Private Act for just over 1,000 acres at Frilford in 1846 took 15 years.[13] Elsewhere, in Breconshire, a Public General Act of 1808 was concerned with 40,000 acres of common and waste in Brecknock Forest. The Award did not appear for 11 years.[14] Such drawn-out enclosure processes are not so common in other counties such as Gloucestershire, but even here there are exceptional cases. Horton (1798) appears to have taken 18 years[15] and Haresfield (1812) 19 years.[16] In short, within the pages of W.E. Tate's *A Domesday of English Enclosure Acts and Awards* and John Chapman's *A Guide to Parliamentary Enclosures in Wales* can be found many examples—sometimes singly, other times in groups—of enclosures which apparently took many years to complete. Even then, the time taken to complete an enclosure cannot be assumed to have expired with the reading of the Award. In many enclosures, there was a further delay before the Award was enrolled. The 1801 Act for Barkway and Reed in Hertfordshire, for example, did not result in an Award for seven years. It was, however, another 21 years before it was enrolled.[17]

Although it is very rarely done, it is often possible to investigate these schemes to establish the reasons for the delay in completing the Award. One such enclosure which got, quite literally, bogged down was that of Irthlingborough in Northamptonshire. This enclosure has been investigated using the largely uncatalogued collection handed in to the county record office by a Wellingborough solicitors' practice whose predecessors were clerks to the Irthlingborough enclosure. The Irthlingborough Act was passed in 1808 and the Award was produced five years later in 1813. The precise date for the enrolment is not known but work continued for another three years at least after the reading of the Award because the accounts record a payment of £42 14s. 5d. being made on 19 June 1816.[18] Although the enclosure was conducted by experienced commissioners, errors were made, particularly in the estimates of the cost of the scheme which ran over budget by nearly a third. There were serious underestimates of both the clerks' and the commissioners' fees and several fundamental items of expenditure were completely overlooked including, amazingly, the cost of public fencing. The commissioners also seem to have failed to recognise the significance of the local geography. Much of the land to be enclosed was low-lying meadow land in the Nene valley. This required many bridges and culverts to allow proprietors access to their allotments. There were also many examples of accounts being settled by the enclosure clerks without any entry in the minute book, which suggests that they may not have been presented to the commissioners.

The effect on the Irthlingborough enclosure was that it took more time than antici-pated and consequently cost more than estimated. The scheme was financed by the levying of a rate on the proprietors but, when this ran out, a second rate was imposed on them. It is clear from the accounts that many of the proprietors were resentful of this and were very reluctant to pay. As a result, several Warrants of Distress were drawn up before the last of the second rates were begrudgingly paid.[19]

The Irthlingborough example is an interesting one to investigate but where com-missioners' working papers, sometimes called extra-award material, exist, other enclosures can be researched in the same way.

THE FIRST MEETING OF THE COMMISSIONERS

To understand the relevance of the commissioners' working papers, it is necessary to return to that point in the enclosure process when someone, perhaps the local solicitor who was to become clerk to the enclosure, arrived on a sweating horse from London with the news that the Bill had been passed into an Act. (It is difficult to imagine that any of the later enclosures conducted under a General Act would have generated the excitement and verve of the 18th-century enclosures where, often, the outcome was far from certain.)

Where the enclosure involved arable land, the immediate effect of the receipt of this news was that the commissioners assumed the power to conduct the course of husbandry. This meant making the transition from the open fields to enclosed fields as smooth as possible and might involve the commissioners arranging for land to be ploughed or new pastures sown with grass or clover. Typical were the commissioners at Podington in Bedfordshire. There were two commissioners, William Pywell and Havey Sparke, a third, John Paine, having resigned through ill health. Meeting at Sparke's house on 6 April 1765, they dealt with a number of matters concerning the agriculture of the manor. First, they agreed with two of the tenant farmers, Richard Turland and Thomas Clarke, that they could sow Hinwick fallow field with oats, barley or beans. They were to pay a total of £12, pro rata to their proportion of the area of land. The crops had to be removed by the following Michaelmas (29 September). The two commissioners also issued an order that all the other fields were to be sown with red clover at the rate of 16 lbs per acre. They directed that Stephen Kemshead of nearby Wymington obtain the seed and arrange the sowing.[20] Although the documents generated as a result of this sort of work are not always extant, occasionally a 'Ploughing Book' or other evidence survives and tells something of the pattern of arable agriculture at the time.

Whereas the course of husbandry became an immediate responsibility of the commissioners enclosing open arable land, this did not necessarily demand decisions until the appropriate time of year. There were other matters which did require urgent attention, though, usually at the first meeting of enclosure commissions. The first and most contentious of these was the issuing of notices for claims to land and common rights. The second task was the making of arrangements for a perambulation of the bounds. A perambulation was not always necessary but in mountainous areas or on large wastes and commons the boundaries, as we have already seen, were not necessarily marked, nor universally accepted. Claims, though, were the basis of all enclosures and the allotting of land in the new enclosures depended upon them. An Act passed in 1796 authorised the enclosure of approximately 15,000 acres of common and wastes west of Montgomery including the manor of Kerry.[21] In total, the Act was concerned with land dispersed across more than 10 manors and parishes. The two commissioners (both of whom were later replaced by others) issued the public notice in Figure 20 on 1 August 1797.[22]

The first half of the Kerry notice is concerned with giving notice of the intended perambulation of the bounds. This was a recognition of the terrain and the intercommoning between the villages which could lead to misunderstandings and disputes later in the process. Precise times and places for the expedition were given in the notice and it was in the commissioners' interests to encourage everyone concerned to attend.

Lastly, notice was given that claims from interested persons would be received by the commissioners the following week at the *Sign Inn* in Kerry. The second half of the notice appears to have been added almost as an afterthought. It stressed the importance of the claims procedure and pointed out that anyone not submitting a claim would not receive land in the new allotments.

The Kerry notice was clearly intended to be fixed to the local church doors and perhaps displayed elsewhere. Another method of giving notice was via the local press. Richard Yates, the valuer appointed under the General Acts to enclose Ruthin in Denbighshire in 1852, made extensive use of the local newspapers, giving notice in the *Caernavan & Denbigh Herald* of several meetings at the local inn to receive claims in writing. Most of these advertisements are extant in the working papers held at the county record office.[23]

Setting aside the commutation of the rector's tithes for the moment, at enclosure land could be allotted to proprietors on two main counts. First, new allotments could be awarded in lieu of land previously held in open arable fields. Second, an area of land could be awarded in lieu of grazing or other rights held in the open pastures, commons or wastes. In the case of Kerry, there was no arable land to be divided; all the land was rough pasture and wastes which had been grazed according to local custom. This land was to be divided up and shared amongst the landowners, large and small, in proportion to the amount of use each had been previously allowed. Where new arable land was being awarded in lieu of old arable land, the transaction was relatively, but not completely, trouble free. Where land was being given in lieu of *rights*, there was a greater propensity for dispute. The important principle at stake, however, was that whatever a proprietor owned in the pre-enclosure landscape had to be established and recorded so that he received a fair share of land in the new enclosures.

Figure 20 Kerry enclosure, 1797

Kerry Enclofure.

[Source: D/LE/691, Flintshire Record Office, notice of perambulation of bounds, Kerry Enclosure, 1 August 1797. Reproduced by permission of the County Archivist.]

AUGUST 1ft, 1797.

NOTICE is hereby given, That purfuant to an Act of Parliament for dividing and enclofing the Wafte Lands in the MANOR of *KERRY*, in the County of *Montgomery*, a Perambulation of the Boundaries thereof, and of the Townfhips and other intercommoning Diftricts therein, will be commenced on *Tuefday* the 5th Day of *September* next, at Ten o'Clock in the Morning, at the North-Weft Corner of the Farm Sheepwalk, near to, and on the Eaft Side of the Camp Bank, on the Hill, called *Cefn-y-coed*, where the three Manors of *Kerry*, *Kedewen* and *Hopton* adjoin each other, and the faid Perambulation will be proceeded in from thence wefterly, along the adjoining Townfhips of *Rhandir* and *Bronywood*, in the Parifh of *Llandyffil*, and fo onward. And that on *Monday* the 11th Day of *September* next, at Ten o'Clock in the Forenoon of the fame Day, at the Sign Inn, in the Village of *Kerry*, in the faid County, Claims from the feveral Perfons interefted in the faid Enclofure, and alfo fuch Maps and Admeafurements as may be then produced will be received.

VAL. VICKERS, Junr.
THOMAS COLLEY.

The Act requires every Perfon claiming any Common or other Right upon the Wafte Lands in the faid Manor, to caufe a written Account thereof to be delivered at fuch Time and Place as fhall be appointed for that Purpofe, defcribing the Nature and Extent thereof, and the Meffuages, Lands and Tenements in refpect whereof fuch Claim fhall be made, with the Names of the Occupiers and computed Quantities, and in Cafe of non-compliance therewith, every Perfon making Default, will be barred and excluded from all Right and Title, in or upon the faid Wafte Lands.

The claims procedure was open to all sorts of shenanigans but, where there were accepted levels of grazing, a formula for sharing out the land could be worked out. In the enclosure of Shap Rough Intake in the Lake District, under the General Act of 1836, there was an established pattern of grazing.[24] This was a small enclosure of a single area of common of only 37 acres. The two commissioners, Thomas Bland and William Smith, were yeomen themselves and held a meeting with the proprietors to establish the claims to cattle gates, dales and other rights. (Cattle gates represented the right to graze cattle, dales were shares of any common rights.) At the meeting, the commissioners found that the common was divided into 18 cattle gates, the proprietors providing them with the schedule which appears in Table 3 although, during the process of the enclosure, some of the cattle gates changed hands.

Table 3 Shap Rough Intake: Schedule of cattle gates, *c.*1836

Name	Cattle gates
Mary Ann Salmond and James Salmond	1½
James Lancaster	2
Thomas Walter Packer	2
Thomas Wilkinson	2
Matthew Betham	2
Sarah Weymss	4
Adam Potts	1½
William Garnett Johnston and William Garnett	1⅔
Joseph Purness	1⅓
TOTAL	18

[Source: WD/HH/137, Cumbria (Kendal) Record Office, miscellaneous working papers. Reproduced by permission of the County Archivist.]

The commissioners then used data from the Poor Rate to calculate values and produced a new schedule of the amount of land to which each proprietor was entitled in the new enclosures. Of course, the Shap Rough Intake enclosure seems to have proceeded smoothly because all the proprietors were in agreement with each other's entitlements which was not necessarily always the case. Also, this enclosure was a relatively small one and occurred in what appears to have been a well-regulated community.

Whereas the Shap proprietors seem to have organised the original schedule of cattle gates, it was usual for the commissioners to do this; in order to receive each proprietor's claim, they asked for it in writing. The form in which each claim appeared varied over time and place. In the 18th century, it was common for the proprietors to make their claim by hand on small slips of paper. Later, pre-printed forms were issued by the commissioners for the proprietors to complete. In some isolated cases, large estates which became involved in regular enclosure processes produced their own printed forms. The Kirk Ireton and Callow enclosure of 1803 attracted written claims of the first type, four of which appear in Figure 21.[25]

Part of another handwritten claim appears in Figure 22. This was for land held in open arable fields at Mickleton by an absentee landowner, John Smith of Sunderland.[26] Smith's claim lists each parcel of land by name and its area in acres, roods and perches. Working from notes like this, the commissioners were able to establish exactly what the proprietors of land had held in the open fields and wastes. There are 26 parcels covered by this particular document which amount to less than 14 acres. This is an indication of the frustration that

Figure 21   Four claims from Kirk Ireton, with transcriptions.

[Source: D 4459/1/2, Derbyshire Record Office, Kirk Ireton Claims, 1803. Reproduced by permission of the County and Diocesan Archivist.]

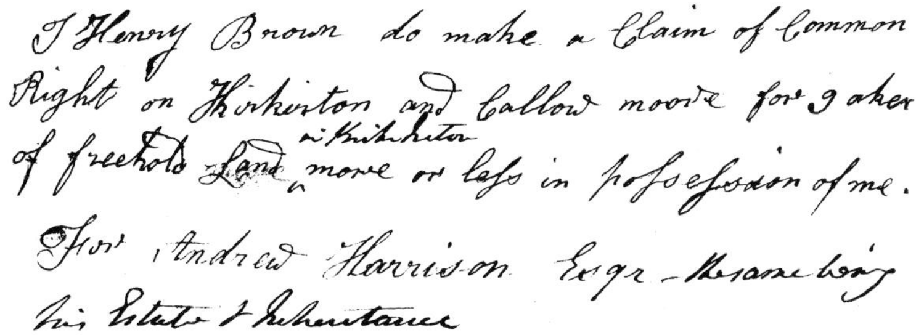

I Henry Brown do make a Claim of Common Right on Kirkirton and Callow Moore for 9 akers of freehold land in Kirkirton more or less in possession of me. For, Andrew Harrison Esq[ui]re - the same being his Estate of Inheritance.

I Hannah Buxton Do make a Claim of Common right for one Messuage House and Garden, Freehold, situate at Kirk Ireton and in possession of the aforesaid Hannah Buxton.
10th. Oct. 1803

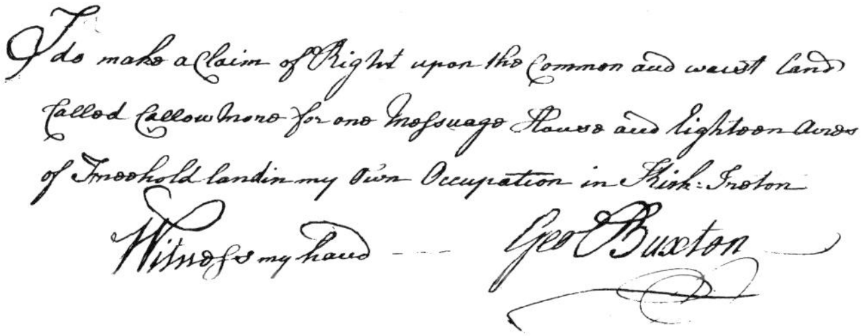

I do make a Claim of Right upon the Common and waste land called Callow More for one Messuage House and eighteen acres of freehold land in my own occupation in Kirk Ireton
Witness my hand   Geo Buxton

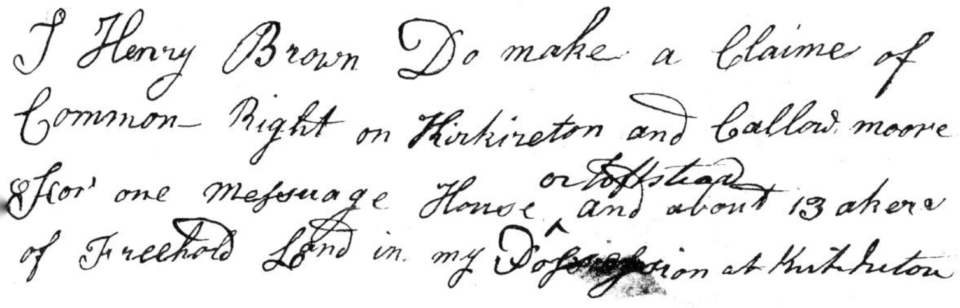

I Henry Brown Do make a Claim of Common Right on Kirkireton and callow moore for one messuage House or toftstead and about 13 akers of Freehold land in my possession at KirkIreton

Figure 22 John Smith of Sunderland's claim.

[Source: D/St/E3/19/19 (7), Durham Record Office, Mickleton enclosure, John Smith of Sunderland's Claim. Reproduced by permission of Lord Strathmore.]

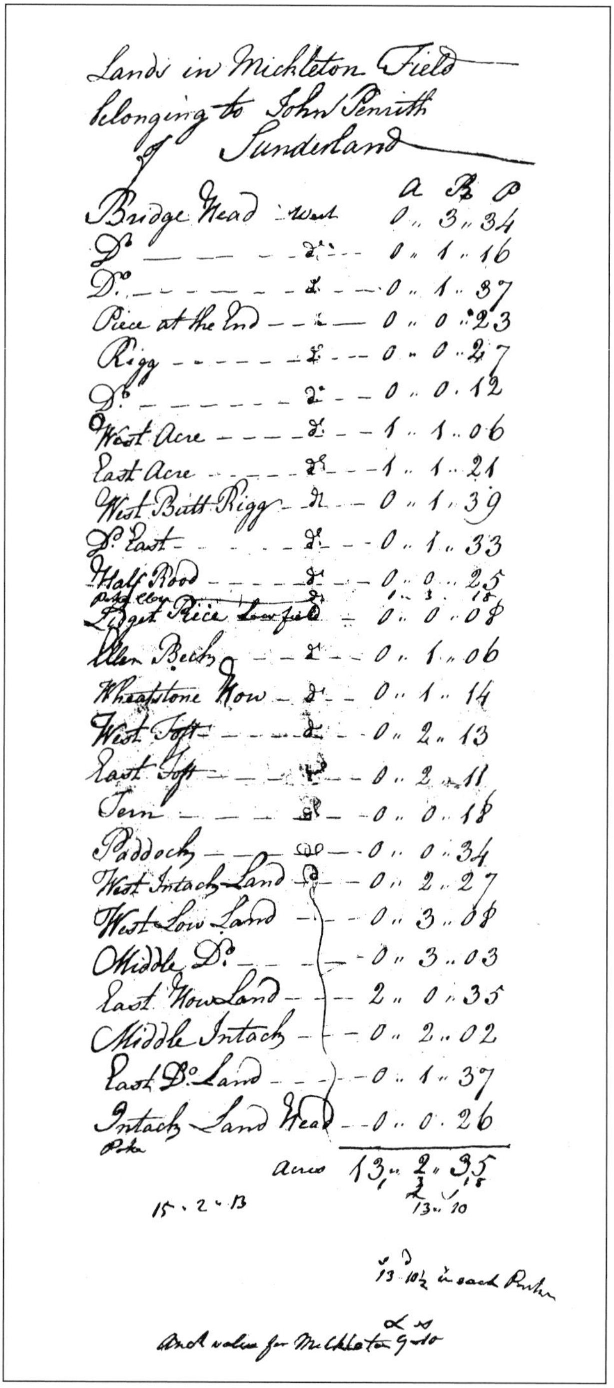

Lands in Mickleton Field belonging to John Smith of Sunderland

		a	R	P
Bridge Head	West	0	3	34
Do	do	0	1	16
Do	do	0	1	37
Piece at the End	do	0	0	23
Rigg	do	0	0	27
Do	do	0	0	12
West Acre	do	1	1	06
East Acre	do	1	1	21
West Butt Rigg	do	0	1	39
Do East	do	0	1	33
Half Rood	do	0	0	25
Longet Piece Low field		0	0	08
Ellen Beck	do	0	1	06
Wheatstone How	do	0	1	14
West Toft	do	0	2	13
East Toft	do	0	2	11
Tern	do	0	0	18
Paddock	do	0	0	34
West Intack Land	do	0	2	27
West Low Land		0	3	08
Middle Do		0	3	03
East How Land		2	0	35
Middle Intack		0	2	02
East Do Land		0	1	37
Intack Land Head		0	0	26
	acres	13	2	35

15 . 2 . 13

13 . 10

13 10½ in each Perch

And value for Mickleton 9 . 10

landowners must have felt arising from the uneconomic dispersal of their land in the pre-enclosure landscape. Absentee proprietors like Smith benefited through the consolidation of their land into one or a few allotments because these were much easier to rent out than a myriad of small plots. In addition, there was a sudden increase in average rent following most enclosures.

Pre-printed forms tended to follow the same pattern as the earlier handwritten ones; the standard text was in print with spaces left for names, quantities and dates. However, when George Colpitts, steward to the Rt. Hon. John Bowes, Earl of Strathmore, lodged a claim to the commissioners of the Mickleton enclosure in 1803, he did so on his own pre-printed form produced just for that enclosure.[27] The original form, shown in Figure 23, was printed on paper approximately the size of modern A3. The first paragraph was printed and in formal language addressed the claim to the Mickleton commissioners. Colpitts then entered his name and position as agent to the Earl of Strathmore by hand in the space below before claiming possession or entitlement to the cattle gates in the stinted pastures which were then detailed in hand. The cattle gates in the East Pasture were given first, then those in the West Pasture. In each case, Colpitt gave the name of the tenant, how many gates he rented from the lord and how much per gate he paid. The final column describes the nature of the Earl's title to the land, in this case, freehold. In the final paragraph, Colpitts undertook that the claim was just and true and signed and dated the document in front of two witnesses.

The arithmetic in Colpitts' claim is interesting but complicated. However, an understanding of it is necessary to appreciate fully the nature of the Earl of Strathmore's claim and any study of the economic history of such enclosures would have to take account of this. In particular there is the money amount entered in the 'Number of Gates' column, which appears to have been levied on some people but not others. Conversely, others seem only to have such an amount next to their name but no gates. To illustrate this more clearly, Table 4 is a summary of the entries for the East Pasture. At first, the second payment appears to have been something like a quit rent, a manorial payment in recognition of the lord of the manor's rights and title. This was not the case. Even more puzzling at first are what we would like to presume are totals at the bottom of the table. The gates column, for example, only amounts to 24, not 28, and the amount at the base of the money columns bears no resemblance whatsoever to a total. The answer to this conundrum appears to the left of the original document in Figure 23 where an original calculation was carelessly entered, either by Colpitts himself or by one of the enclosure commission officers, checking his claim.

The answer is based on the principle that the tenants were paying six shillings per gate. This then was the value of a complete gate. Some people, such as William Addison, also owned fractions of a gate. He, for example, rented four complete gates plus half a gate

---

Figure 23 *(overleaf)*   George Colpitts' Claim to the Mickleton Commissioners for the Earl of Strathmore, 1803

[Source: D/St/E3/19/22(1), Durham Record Office, Mickleton enclosure, Earl of Strathmore's claim, 20 April 1803. Reproduced by permission of Lord Strathmore.]

To the **COMMISSIONERS** named in an Act of Parliament passed in the forty Second year of the Reign of his Majesty King George the third intitled "An Act for dividing allotting and inclosing the Moor or Common Open Fields, Stinted Pastures and other Commonable Lands within the Township of Mickleton and Parish of Romaldkirk in the North Riding of the County of York."

I, *George Colpitts as Agent for and on behalf of the Right Honorable John Bowes Earl of Strathmore* do claim to be seized or possessed of or entitled to the several Beast or Cattle or Pasture Gates in over or upon the stinted Pastures called Mickleton East and West Pastures in and by the said Act directed to be divided and inclosed herein after particularly mentioned and setforth (viz)

Names of persons enjoying same — Number of Gates		Freehold or Leasehold.
William Addison	4 Gates & 3. ² at 6.ª a Gate	
William Parkin	3 D. and 1ˢ at do	
Thomas Raine	4 D. & 2. 11 at do	
Mary Lancaster	3. at do	
Ann Raine	3. 6 at do	
William Wright	4 D. & 2. 11 at do	Freehold
John Raine	2 D. & 2. . at do	
Robert Addison	1 D. 5. 10 at do	
George Prudah	3 D.	
George Heron	1 D.	
James Langerwood	2 D. 5. 4½	
Gates	28 . 2. 7½	
William Addison	4 Gates & 3. ² at 6.ª a Gate	
William Parkin	3 D. . & 1ˢ at do	
Thomas Raine	4 D. & 2. 11 at do	
Mary Lancaster	3 .. at do	
Ann Raine	3. 6 at do	
William Wright	4 D. . 2. 11 at do	Freehold
John Raine	2 D. . 2. . at do	
Robert Addison	1 D. . 5. 10 at do	
George Prudah	3 D. ..... at do	
George Heron	1 D. ..... at do	
James Langerwood	2 D. . 4½ at do	
	27 . 5. 7½	

And I the above named *George Colpitts* do hereby undertake that the Account by me herein setforh of and Concerning the Premises is just and true according to the best of my knowledge and belief As witness my Hand this *20th* day of *April 1803.*

Joseph Granger

George Colpitts

Wm Allithorne

Table 4 Mickleton enclosure: the Earl of Strathmore's Claim in the East Pasture, 1803

Tenant	Number of Gates			
	gates	s	d	rate
William Addison	4 &	3	-	at 6s a gate
William Parkin	3 &	-	1	at "
Thomas Raine	4 &	2	11	at "
Mary Lancaster	-	3	-	at "
Ann Raine	-	3	6	at "
William Wright	4 &	2	11	at "
John Raine	2 &	2	-	at "
Robert Addison	1 &	5	10	at "
George Prudah	3			
George Heron	1			
James Langerwood	2 &	3	4½	
Gates	28	2	7½	

[Source: D/St/E3/19/22(1), Durham Record Office, Mickleton enclosure, Earl of Strathmore's claim, 20 April 1803. Reproduced by permission of Lord Strathmore.]

or three shillings' worth of a six-shilling gate. Other tenants rented more awkward fractions of a gate. William Wright, for example, rented four complete gates and 2s. 11d. worth of a gate. Some tenants rented less than a complete gate, such as George Heron who only rented one shilling's worth or one-sixth of a gate. So, in completing the earl's claim to freehold rights in the East Pasture, Colpitts first added up the fractions of gates in the money columns. Altogether, this amounted to £1 6s. 7½d. He then divided that by six shillings to give a total number of six complete gates with 2s. 7d. left over which was entered in the money or fractions column. The six complete gates were carried into the gates column which, when totalled, came to twenty-eight. This, then, represented the value of the Earl of Strathmore's holding in the East Pasture. By multiplying the number of complete gates by six shillings and adding the left-over fraction, a total of £8 10s. 7½d. is obtained, this being the rental value of his pasture rights.

Many enclosures were concerned with claims for much smaller areas of land but a more complex range of assets. E. and R. Russell found that, during the claims stage of the 1813 North Kelsey enclosure in Lincolnshire, Thomas Draton claimed for a cottage and common right with 2 roods of garden and yard, 6 acres of carr ground and 5¼ acres in the open fields.[28] All such claims though had to be reduced to a form which would enable them to be compared and then compensated for in the subsequent Award.

OBJECTIONS TO CLAIMS

The nature of claims was generally known beforehand and the claims process produced very few surprises. However, before awarding land in the new enclosures on the basis of claims, there was one more important process—the receiving of objections to claims. In inviting claims from the landowners and commoners, the commissioners hoped for a level of honesty and precision that was not always forthcoming. In a previous chapter, we heard about one Devon farmer who claimed more land than the common held; because commissioners rarely came from the parish that they were enclosing, they were not always aware of who held what. By inviting objections to claims, all the proprietors were able to examine and verify each other's attempts to gain the best possible deal from the enclosure. They acted as the jury but the commissioners were the judges.

While some enclosures proceeded through this stage with little or no upset, others experienced more than their share of difficulty. The process might start with a public notice either fixed to the church door or appearing in the local press inviting objections to claims. Objections were usually as a result of someone thought to be claiming more than their legal entitlement. The most contentious area was that of common rights. It has been seen how common rights were essential to the cottage economy and redress for their loss was often sought during the claims stage of an enclosure. Rights of grazing and turbary were often mentioned. At the 1845 Fowlmere enclosure in Cambridgeshire, reference was made to the commoners' right to gather dried manure on the common for use as fuel. There was also a right of mowing sedge in the fens and marshes. As early as the Bill stage at Shapwick in Somerset (enclosed in 1777), there was a debate regarding rights to the common (which included parts of several other parishes including Street, Glastonbury, Ashcott and Walton). The dispute included rights of turbary, common of vicinage or wrangle rights.[29] Turbary was simply the right to dig turf on the common for fuel. It was reported that each village recognised its own turbary boundaries on the heath. The more vexing problem was that of wrangle rights—the right of local people to herd cattle on the common. In this case, the commoners relied heavily on the evidence of an elderly witness who claimed to remember having driven the cattle belonging to one of the Shapwick farmers on to the common.

Elderly residents often testified about ancient practices and common rights during the claims stage of an enclosure, particularly where objections to claims were made. Professor Mingay found that, during the 1802 Westbury enclosure in Wiltshire, the commissioners had recourse to an elderly gentleman of 80 years.[30] As with the Shapwick dispute, the problem at Westbury was based on the claims on the common by non-Westbury residents, in this case, commoners from the nearby settlement of Bratten. The old man recalled that he had worked on a local farm many years ago and that the farmer and Bratton commoners had all used the Westbury common for cattle grazing without any obstruction. The Commissioners dealing with such disputes were anxious to establish whether claimants could actually show long-term usage without let or hindrance. By so doing, it could be shown that their *rights* had been accepted as local custom or were, as E.P. Thompson put it, *lex loci*.[31]

Some enclosures were subject to extensive disputes over claims. J.F. Broadbent has suggested that 70 principal objections to claims were received by the enclosure commissioners of the West Riding settlement of Dewsbury (1803).[32] This was a small enclosure of only 298 acres which included the interests of two lords of the manor, one being the Duke of Leeds, and a common with many encroachments on it—cottages erected without permission. It was normal to allow such encroachments of 20 years or more but some of the more recently erected dwellings were bound to cause a dispute. The 66 cottages owned by Mr. Carr, the other manorial lord, were claimed as freehold but, following objections that they were erected on the wastes, all were disallowed. Broadbent has found that, of 260 messuages claimed for, 230 were objected to. The claimants who were subject to objections were written to and invited to a meeting at the *George and Dragon* inn to prove their claims. Of the 260 claims, only half were allowed. Other reasons for objecting included claims for land said to be copyhold but later disputed; claims for common right in respect of shops (which did not possess common rights, only cottages or other dwellings); an objection to the vicar's claim in respect of his lesser (vicarial) tithes; and claims for common right in respect of cottages which were less than 100 years old.[33] In this case, 100 years seems to have been chosen as the cut-off point for establishing antiquity and cottage commons. Elsewhere, different ages seem to have been arbitrarily chosen. In another example of oral evidence from elderly villagers being used to settle disputes, Henry Ford Senior, aged 85 years and a Derbyshire pack-saddle maker, testified to the commissioners of Kirk Ireton and Callow regarding the histories of 41 houses said to be more than 30 years old.[34] These were termed 'ancient' and Ford described houses, messuages and toftsteads in his evidence.

From another of the study enclosures, Mickleton, we find one of the more bizarre objections to claims. Despite the apparent ordered nature of this enclosure, there were 16 objections to claims. Of these, 12 were concerned with encroachments on the common. In particular, Lord Strathmore counter-claimed that 12 of the properties claimed for were encroachments and should be considered as part of the common.[35] Other objections were concerned with the nature of the title to the land, whether it was really freehold as claimed or leasehold. But the strangest objections were those lodged by various members of the Raine family—against each other. There was clearly a family feud, the details of which we can only guess. That the sores ran deep can be seen from the objection lodged by William Raine (Figure 24) for which a transcription is provided. It would seem that there had been some sort of internal power struggle between the father and his sons, and the father was refusing to lie down. Although the circumstances are not entirely obvious from the surviving documents, they show how the upheaval of a local enclosure could trigger all manner of disputes and grievances.

On rare occasions, objections at this stage of an enclosure achieved a higher dimension. In 1793, a conflict erupted between two Flintshire enclosure commissions, that of Hope (Act 1791) and Mold (Act 1792). The first laid claim to part of a large common by constructing a road across it. When the Mold commissioners discovered this, they issued the notice reproduced in Figure 25, summoning the Mold freeholders and their lord of the manor to a meeting to discuss the matter.[36] A year later, it was still unresolved because the Hope commissioners issued a similar notice.[37]

Once all the claims and objections had been received, depending on their volume, some commissioners felt the need to enter them into a table or schedule. This was certainly the case with Washington in Sussex. Washington Common, comprising 284 acres, was enclosed under the General Acts of 1845 and 1847. Levi Bushby, the valuer (valuers having replaced local commissioners under the General Acts), drew up a schedule of all claims and

Figure 24   William Raine's Objection to Claims, 1803

[Source: D/St/E3/19/24(5), Durham Record Office, William Raine's Objection to Claims, Mickleton enclosure, 29 August 1803. Reproduced by permission of Lord Strathmore.]

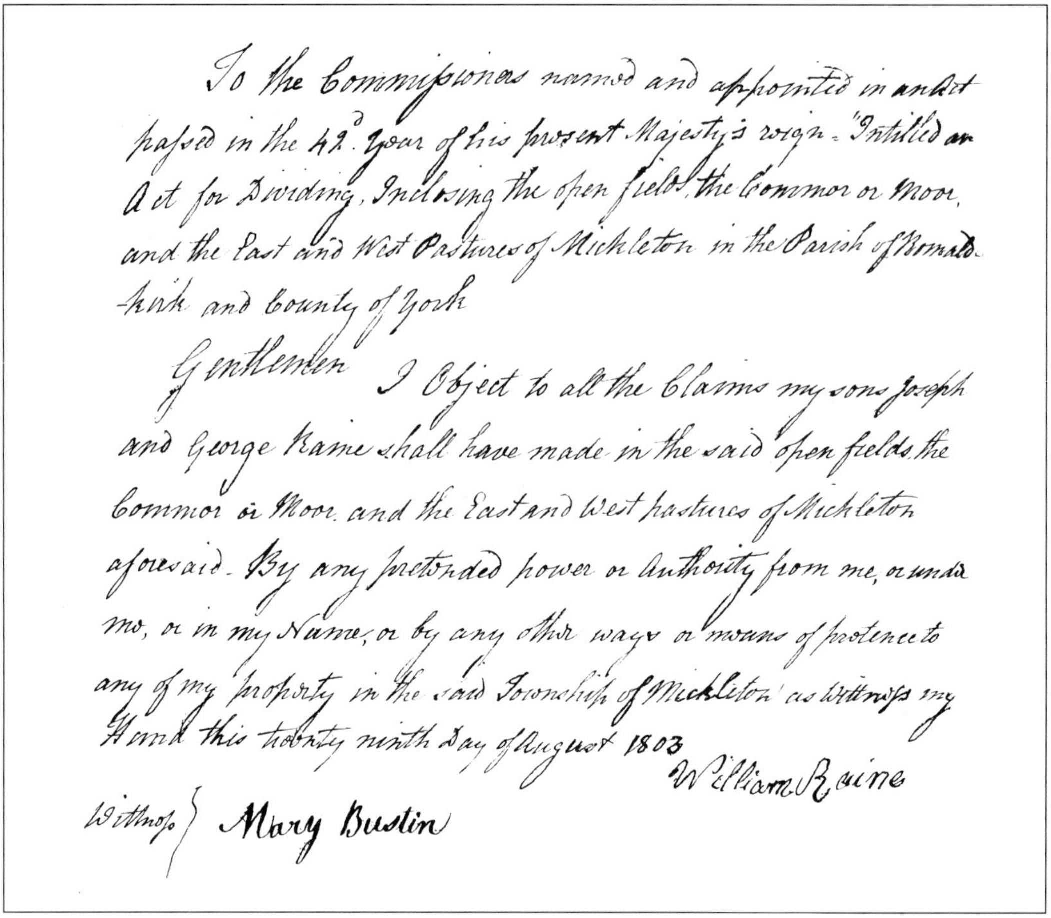

Transcription

To the Commissioners named and appointed in an Act passed in the 42[n]d Year of his present Majesty's reign Intitled an Act for Dividing, Inclosing the open fields, the Common or Moor, and the East and West Pastures of Mickleton in the Parish of Romaldkirk and County of York.

Gentlemen

I Object to all the Claims my sons Joseph and George Raine shall have made in the said open fields, the Common or Moor and the East and West pastures of Mickleton aforesaid – By any pretended power or Authority from me, or under me, or in my Name, or by any other ways or means of pretence to any of my property in the said Township of Mickleton as wittness my Hand this twenty ninth day of August 1803

William Raine

Wittness   Mary Bustin

Figure 25 Mold commissioners' notice of meeting to discuss Hope enclosure

[Source: D/LE/685, Flintshire Record Office, 1 November 1793. Reproduced by permission of the County Archivist.]

Sir

THE COMMISSIONERS for dividing the Commons within the Manor of *HOPE* having form'd a Road over Part of the Common in TRYTHIN within the Manor of *MOLD*, and thereby mean to include within the said Manor of *HOPE*, about one hundred and seventy-three Acres of the said Common which has always been perambulated and considered as Part of the Commons appurtenant to the said Manor of *MOLD*.

I am defired by the Commiffioners of the *Mold* Inclofure, to inform you, that a Meeting of the Lord of the Manor and Freeholders will be held at the GRIFFIN, in *Mold*, on Monday the 9th Day of *December*, to take into Confideration, and to give Inftructions to the Commiffioners in what Manner they are to proceed in the Bufinefs, at which Meeting you are requefted to attend.

And it being the Wifh of feveral of the Freeholders, that a fufficient Part of the Commons fhould be fold to defray the whole Expence of the Inclofure, which cannot be done unlefs Application be made to Parliament, to to enlarge the Powers of the prefent Act; the Senfe of the Freeholders, as to the Propriety of fuch Application will then be taken.

I am, Sir

Your moft obedient Servant,

Will. Wynne

Clerk to the Commiffioners.

MOLD, *November* 1, 1793.

Mr Eyton

objections in a document measuring approximately 13 inches by 16 inches.[38] The five columns are headed: Claimants, Property in respect of which Claim was made, Tenure of Property, Objections, and Determination of the Valuer. As an example, the schedule shows that the Vicar of Washington, the Rev. Thomas Nixson of Blagden, claimed to have pasturage for six beasts (cattle) over and above that of the lord of the manor's pasturage. Further, he claimed common of pasture for all manner of animals on the commons and wastes of Washington and Ashington. Not surprisingly, perhaps, this wide-sweeping claim was challenged, the objection being lodged by the agent of Charles Goring, Esquire. No reason is given for the objection but, after consideration by the valuer, who no doubt spoke to both parties, the objection was withdrawn but the vicar agreed to an amended claim which amounted to a restricted annual value of £12.[39]

The benefit to the commissioners of entering the claims on to a schedule was that this would form the basis of the Award schedule. There was much to do before then, however, and once objections to claims had been resolved the commissioners or, later, the valuer had to consider their quality. The phrase from many Acts may be remembered, '... consideration to be given to quality as well as quantity ...'. And so it was that the commissioners had to agree on the quality and hence value of all the claims in order to ensure that their final Award was fair and just. There were a number of tools at their disposal for achieving this state of affairs. First, we have seen how the commissioners of the Shap Rough Intake were asked to use information from the Poor Rate to establish a valuation. Similarly, the Mickleton commissioners were to use both the Poor Rate and the Land Tax.[40] Both of these documentary sources contain, at least in principle, assessments and valuations. Of the two, Land Tax Assessments (LTAs) have been the most commonly used in enclosure studies. This use, as we shall see in a later chapter, has been controversial but they can tell us much about the turnover of land tenure before and after an enclosure. LTAs or duplicates of them can usually be found in local record offices within their Quarter Sessions records. Only occasionally is a copy found amongst enclosure commissioner's working papers.

Equally rare amongst commissioners' working papers are Poor Rate assessments. These are a little used documentary source and can sometimes be found in parish records at local record offices. That their survival is poor compared with the LTAs goes only a little way towards explaining their lack of use in enclosure studies. There is no doubt that, where they exist, much more valuable information could be extracted from them. Southease in Sussex was enclosed under the 1836 General Act with 758 acres being awarded in 1844.[41] Amongst the working papers for this enclosure is the copy of the assessment for the relief of the poor of the parish dated 7 January 1845 which appears in Figure 26.[42] Was this assessment used to value land and other claims which had been submitted?

First, it seems curious that this particular assessment appears to be pre-dated by the Award. It is possible that it was retained, after the valuation process, in order to provide corroboration if required, but this hardly seems likely. Surely the actual assessment used would be retained? There is another possibility—that the Southease poor relief assessment was used for another purpose later in the enclosure process. In the bottom left-hand corner is a table showing the rate levied over the seven-year period prior to the enclosure, fluctuating from 5s. 8d. in the pound in 1838 to 5s. in the pound in 1844—the year of the enclosure Award. Each annual rate has then been added together and the total divided by seven to give the arithmetic mean, over the period, of 6s. 6¼d. in the pound. This contrasts with the 1845 rate given in the heading of only 14d. in the pound. The main schedule across the middle of the assessment contains seven entries ranging from houses and yards to tithes and glebe. On the far right, the three columns contain, respectively, an estimated rateable value, the actual rateable value and the rate due, calculated at 14d. in the pound. The total due from the parish is £36 17s. 11d. This suggests that this was no ordinary rate assessment, being much lower than normal. Perhaps there was a second rate levied in 1845 and this

Figure 26   Assessment of Poor Rate, Southease, 1845

[Source: SAS/ACC/1100/1/9, East Sussex Record Office. Reproduced with permission of the Sussex Archaeological Society, copyright reserved.]

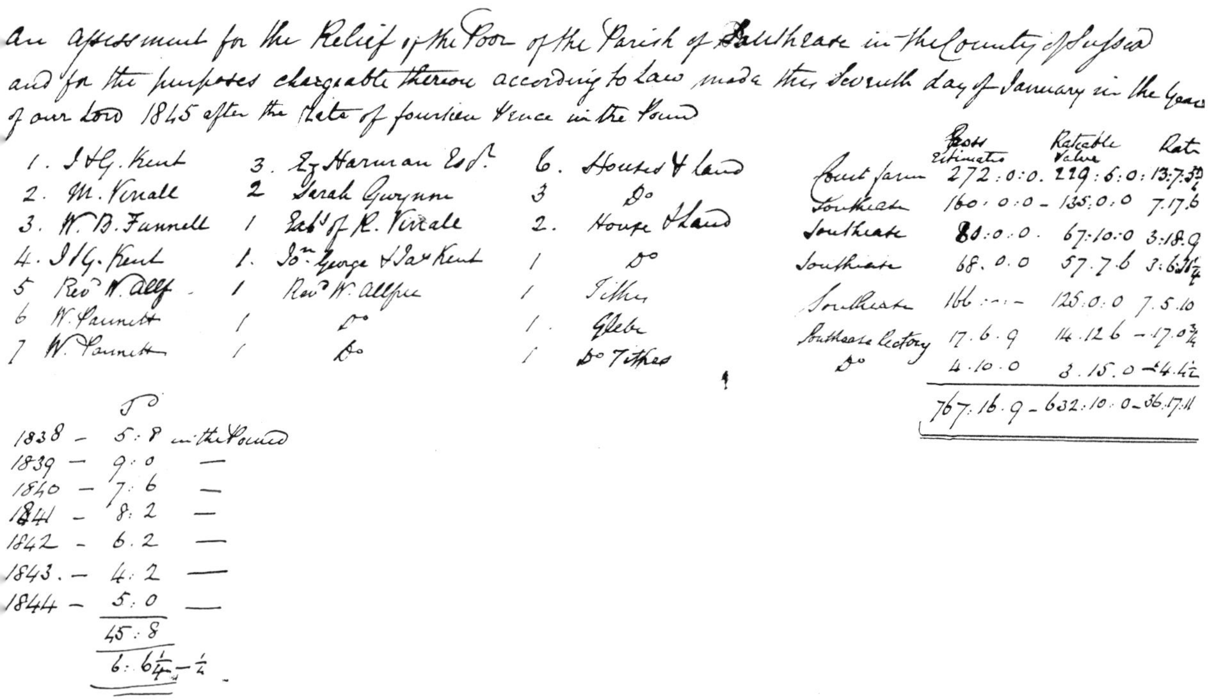

An assessment for the Relief of the Poor of the Parish of Southease in the County of Sussex and for the purposes chargeable thereon according to Law, made this Seventh day of January in the Year of our Lord 1845 after the Rate of fourteen Pence in the Pound

				Gross Estimate	Rateable Value	Rate
1. J & G. Kent	3. Ez Harman Esq.r	6. Houses & land	Kent farm	272.0.0	229.6.0	13.7.3½
2. M. Verrall	2 Sarah Gwynne	3 Do	Southease	160.0.0	135.0.0	7.17.6
3. W. B. Funnell	1 Ext of R. Verrall	2. House & land	Southease	80.0.0	67.10.0	3.18.9
4. J & G. Kent	1. Jos. George & Jas Kent	1 Do	Southease	68.0.0	57.7.6	3.6.3½
5 Rev.d W. Allpy	1 Rev.d W. Allpee	1 Tithe	Southease	166.-.-	125.0.0	7.5.10
6 W. Funnett	1 Do	1. Glebe	Southease Rectory	17.6.9	14.12.6	—.17.0¾
7 W. Funnett	1 Do	1 Do Tithes	Do	4.10.0	3.15.0	—.4.4½
				767.16.9	632.10.0	36.7.11

1838 –	5.8	in the Pound
1839 –	9.0	—
1840 –	7.6	—
1841 –	8.2	—
1842 –	6.2	—
1843 –	4.2	—
1844 –	5.0	—
	45.8	
	6.6¼ – ½	

first one was used for other purposes. That it was filed with the enclosure working papers suggests that the £36 17s. 11d. was levied specifically to meet the costs, or some of the costs, of the enclosure. Only a detailed investigation of the Southease enclosure and parish records could uncover the entire story but it is a good example of the usefulness to the local historian of the Poor Rate assessments.

Finally, in placing a value on the claims submitted to an enclosure commission, the help of the surveyor and sometimes the qualitymen could be sought. These local and expert practitioners could place a price tag on land, grazing, property and common rights. Their work was essential to the smooth passage of an enclosure—whether of open arable fields, meadows and pasture or moorland and wastes. So much depended upon their skill and integrity that many of the consequences of their work can be seen in the countryside today. Because of the importance of their contribution to the enclosure process, much of the following chapter is devoted to them and their work.

Chapter 5
Surveyors, Surveying and Awards

THE SURVEYORS

The commissioners were undoubtedly the most powerful figures in parliamentary enclosure, but very little could have been done without the surveyors and, in practice, much of the actual work of the enclosure commission was done by them. In the 18th century, land surveying was one of the emerging professions and, perhaps because of this, the duties of the surveyor varied greatly from one enclosure to another.

Just as there was an attempt to control the commissioners' fees, so there was also a desire to curtail excessive costs incurred in the hiring of surveyors. In the latter part of the enclosure period, surveyors' fees were specified by the Act. Some imposed a rate based on acreage, others a maximum daily fee. In Northamptonshire, at Corby in 1829 and at Little Addington the following year, the Acts specified 1s. 6d. per acre or a maximum of two guineas per day. Ten years later at Ringstead 3s. per acre was allowed.

Like the commissioners, some surveyors were from outside the county in which they were working, although many more were comparatively local. Looking at Buckinghamshire enclosure, Professor Turner discovered an unusual phenomenon in the form of a pocket of professional enclosure commissioners and surveyors from the Brackley area (on the Buckinghamshire-Northamptonshire boundary).[1] To his original list of six, more can now be added, as shown in Table 5. Robert Russell, from the small market town of Brackley itself, was the surveyor to two Northamptonshire enclosures and may have been related to William Russell or to Michael Russell, who also served twice as surveyor in his own county and at least seven more times in Buckinghamshire.[2]

All the people in Table 5 came from either Brackley itself or one of its immediately neighbouring villages. This suggests that Brackley was a major centre of enclosing activity based on two or three professional families and professional practices.

Family connections can also be found in other counties. In Oxfordshire, William Hurd Chamberlin and John Chamberlin were both from Cropredy. The former served as a surveyor as well as a commissioner on at least five enclosures across at least as many counties. John Chamberlin also served as a commissioner on several Midlands enclosures.

J. Crowther, looking at enclosure personnel in the East Riding of Yorkshire, found that many surveyors were Quakers.[3] Membership of the Society of Friends precluded them from political life and so they turned towards the professions, being particularly encouraged towards surveying and agriculture. She found two families in the East Riding who specialised in surveying—the Dickinson and the Stickney families. The occupation spanned several generations, the skills being passed down within the family.

In the East Riding, as elsewhere, some surveyors also acted as commissioners. We have already seen that the Beer Hackett enclosure in Hampshire was to be performed

Table 5   Commissioners, surveyors and clerks from the Brackley Area

Commissioners	Surveyors	Clerks
Francis Burton	James Collingridge	A. Hayward
William Collison	Richard Collison	Robert Weston
John Farebrother	John Mitchell	
William Goodwin	Michael Russell	
Barnett John Hopcraft	Robert Russell	
Richard Shortland	William Russell	
Robert Weston	Richard Shortland	
	Robert Weston	
	John Weston	

[Source: Northamptonshire Inclosure Awards, Bound Volumes, NRO; Turner, M.E., 'Enclosure Commissioners and Buckinghamshire Parliamentary Enclosure', *Ag.HR*, 25 (1977).]

under the guidance of a commissioner who was a surveyor by profession and, when the project was halted by his untimely death, he was replaced by his partner—another surveyor. Crowther found that some of these surveyor-cum-commissioners, as she termed them, were also land agents and valuers. In fact, under the later General Enclosure Acts of the mid-19th century, the local man in charge of the enclosure was called a valuer rather than a commissioner.

Some surveyors worked alone and others in pairs—not simply as permanent partners as in the modern way of professional partnerships but often with different partners on different enclosures. The Rev. Henry Homer suggested the possible reason for these pairings.[4] Writing from Warwickshire in 1766, he explained that there were two surveys to be carried out: the general survey was of the entire parish or manor to be enclosed and the particular survey was the survey of each individual proprietor's land. If the two surveys were performed by different surveyors, it was possible to check one set of results against the other (the sum of all the particular survey areas should equal the general survey area). A small difference between the two was usual, due to the increased surface area caused by the ridge and furrows not allowed for in the general survey. If, however, a more substantial difference was found, Homer recommended that both the surveyors went out into the fields together to establish the cause. It is difficult to discover from the documentary records the extent to which this ideal of two surveys was actually realised in practice.

As with the commissioners, the work of the surveyors varied from enclosure to enclosure. It was not simply confined to what we would today consider as measuring, marking out and drawing the landscape. A survey and admeasurement was certainly required by most of the Enclosure Acts[5] but often much more was demanded of the surveyor. Some of his official duties were prescribed by the Acts, but others seem to have evolved as the enclosure process got under way and the only main sources of reference to them are in clerks' minute books and accounts. We must, however, be grateful to Thomas Cowper who kept a daily journal for the year 1765–6 which records his activities in connection with the Wellingborough enclosure.[6] Personal notes also give us a valuable insight into Cowper who was, to say the least, eccentric by the standards of his day and possibly an alcoholic by the standards of ours! He enjoyed an active interest in astrology and astronomy, corresponding with seafaring captains on the subject of stars as well as working out complex family horoscopes.

Two surveyors were appointed for the Wellingborough enclosure in 1765, William Freeman being the other. Of the two, Cowper seems to have been the senior partner, being involved in several other enclosures at the same time. A typical working day for Cowper was Tuesday, 28 June 1765, when the Wellingborough enclosure was well under way. It was a wet day but Cowper began by meeting his cousin, William Cowper, at the *Chequers Inn* at Wellingborough. Next, as he put it, he rectified his partner's (Freeman) chain. This is a reference to the Gunters' chain which surveyors used to measure land. Next, Cowper moved on for a drink with John Page at the *Hind Inn* and then left for the open fields of Wellingborough where he surveyed 82 lands before joining William Cooper at the *Dog and Partridge*. Later, he managed to fit in another glass with Thomas Packwood at the *White Hart* before returning home to receive Cod Brown for yet another beverage.

This is not to say that Cowper was lazy. He often worked long hours either surveying in the fields or casting up his measurements in the evening. On Saturday, 1 June he surveyed 150 lands, not returning home until sunset—a 14-hour day. His problem was that, because of the nature of enclosure, he had to liaise with many people and the obvious meeting places were local inns. Thus, on Tuesday, 21 June, he recorded that he was 'Very much out of order this morning through my intemperance the last four days'. However, he still managed to survey 100 lands and hades (small parcels of land on a slope) before 7 or 8 o'clock in the evening when he found himself in distress because of lack of money and was forced to borrow 7s. 6d. from his sister Martha.

Apart from surveying land on behalf of the Wellingborough Enclosure Commission, Cowper also acted privately for some of the farmers. This would have been a first step for the proprietors of land who would then have formulated a claim for new allotments in the enclosed township. As we have seen, claims for allotments were based on the amount of land held prior to enclosure together with any rights of pasture in the common fields or wastes. Thus it was that Cowper spent several days in the open fields surveying land for Thomas Robinson.

Cowper usually treated Sunday as a rest day which he spent with his children, hearing the younger ones read and checking their spelling, but on Sunday, 6 January 1765, a manuscript version of the proposed Bill for the Wellingborough enclosure was delivered to him. He set about copying it out in neat form—a total of 17 pages—and finished checking it at about 11pm. On the following Wednesday, he witnessed many signatures from the Bill's supporters (this naturally necessitated a great deal of to-ing and fro-ing between the inns of Wellingborough). This continued for several days. By the middle of February, the Bill was ready for presentation to the Commons and Cowper set off, initially at least, in a chair for London. On the 15th, he was cross-examined by a Commons Committee about the proposed enclosure. On his return to Wellingborough, there were more signatures to witness and, at the end of the month, he returned to London once more for the Bill's hearing before the Lords. During the first two days of March, Cowper, travelling in snow, returned to Wellingborough via six inns.

It is clear from his journal that Cowper was concerned with much more than merely surveying, although this was an important part of his work. Later in the enclosure period, some surveyors, for example, were charged with organising the funding for the enclosure.

THE SURVEYOR'S WORK IN THE FIELDS

Notwithstanding what might be called the surveyor's non-surveying duties, the core of his work lay in mapping out the open fields, moors and commons and then drawing up a plan for their re-allotment to the interested landowners in a fair and equitable manner. This was no mean feat and demanded skill and diligence. Figure 27 shows a sketch which J.G. Maxwell, the surveyor of Henlow in Bedfordshire, drew along the bottom of his award map. This sketch, drawn in a naïve style, is now famous and rightly so for it is the best representation we have of enclosure surveyors at work. Although the scale and perspective are undeveloped, it shows a number of important features of the work.

Being watched by one of the locals, perhaps a shepherd, the surveyor is standing second from the right and is surveying in the open arable fields. The direction of the ridge and furrow is indicated by the groups of parallel lines. In his left hand, he holds a long

Figure 27 Maxwell's sketch of enclosure surveyors at work

[Source: Henlow Award, PU.1 10/1966, reproduced by permission of Bedfordshire and Luton Archives and Records Service.]

sighting pole and his two assistants on either side have bundles of shorter canes or hazel sticks. These have a small square of paper or parchment fixed in a narrow split at the top; the bottoms are pointed to allow them to be pushed into the ground. The surveyor sights these through with his pole and indicates to his assistants where their other markers should be placed. The picture is partly framed by Maxwell's land chain, upon which, in the middle, he has signed his work.

The land chain used by the enclosure surveyors was devised much earlier by the British mathematician Edmund Gunter (1581–1626), who was also the first to use the trigonometrical terms, cosine and cotangent.[7] Being 22 yards long, it is often associated with the length of a cricket pitch and is assumed to be part of the imperial system of measurement which also includes inches and feet. Although equivalents can be given, in the measuring of large areas such as agricultural land, feet and inches were not used and the surveyor's system was quite separate. Each chain consisted of 100 links and the link was the smallest unit. In practice, to help fold the chain away, each link did not consist of a single piece but one long piece of steel wire with one or two smaller rings at either end. As can be seen in Figure 28, this made the chain more flexible. Each complete link, however it was made up, was 7.92 inches (approximately 201 mm) long. At either end of the chain was a brass handle, usually mounted on a swivel so that twists were automatically pulled out of the chain when it was drawn tight. Each chain was marked every 10 links, usually by a small brass plate. The plates began at both ends and worked towards the middle. The first plate at either end was marked as *one*, the second as *two* and so on. The centre plate, being the fifth from both ends, was usually marked as such by being larger.

The link, then, was the smallest unit of length in the surveyor's system and there were 100 links in a complete chain. The final unit of measurement in the system was the change. This was equivalent to 10 chains laid end to end. Thus, it can be seen from Table 6

Figure 28   Section of a surveyor's land chain

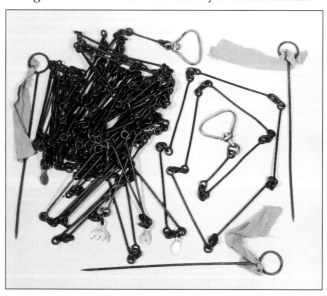

Table 6   Units of length used by enclosure surveyors

Surveyor's units	*Imperial lengths*
100 links = 1 chain	22 yards
10 chains = 1 change	220 yards (1 furlong)

that 17th- and 18th-century British surveyors were using a decimal system of length, well before the metric system was adopted. The change equalled 220 yards or a furlong (a furrow long) indicating perhaps the origin of the two modern meanings of the word furlong. Today, a furlong is a unit of length of 220 yards or an eighth of a mile; it is also the name given to the usually rectilinear shape of a group of strips in the open fields. It may be that, at some point, the ideal length of a strip was thought to be 220 yards. By enclosure, strips appeared in all sizes, usually less than a furlong.

How did the surveyors use the land chain? To measure a long length such as a strip in the open arable fields, the surveyor took his chain, an assistant and 11 wire pegs each with a red flag or piece of rag attached. The first peg was set down at the beginning of the strip and the assistant marched down the strip with the other end of the chain and five pegs. At the end of the chain, he placed one of his pegs into the ground and stood still while the surveyor picked up the remaining five pegs and, armed with his end of the chain, proceeded to leap-frog past him until the chain was once more taut further down the field where he placed the next peg. The process was repeated, the surveyor and assistant taking it in turn to leap-frog each other until all the pegs had been used. The eleventh peg indicated that 10 spaces had been measured and this was the first change. The pegs were collected in and the process repeated until the last complete change had been measured. Then the remaining complete chains were counted and, finally, the remaining links. The entire length was then recorded in the surveyor's casting up book. The width of a strip was much easier to measure, being often less than a chain and so measured in links only. If the strip being measured was tapered, then the widths at top and bottom were both measured and the mean average found by adding them and dividing the answer by two.

Surveyors' casting up books like the one in Figure 29 only occasionally survive. Often they were made up in the evening by surveyors using off-cuts of paper sewn together with thread. Casting up was the method of using the linear measurements of a parcel of land to calculate its area in acres, roods and perches. Sometimes, as in Figure 29, the calculations are accompanied by a sketch plan of the strip.

From the example in Figure 29, which was probably drawn up by a member of the Aplin family at Banbury in Oxfordshire, it can be seen that the calculations refer to a land or strip in a furlong called Six Lays. The strip is 38 links wide at one end tapering to 34 at the other, giving a mean average of 36 links. The strip is only 7 chains, 40 links long and, although this is a small plot of land today, it was typical of the size of parcel encountered at enclosure. In the first part of the process shown, the length is shown in a decimal form and is multiplied by the width as follows. (Note, for ease of explanation, Mr Aplin's final answer—the area of the land—is given at the end of the calculation rather than at the beginning as in his book.)

Figure 29   Surveyor's casting up book

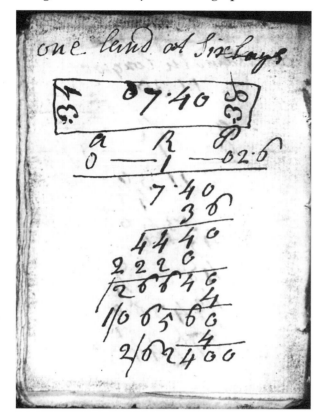

[Source: Surveyor's casting up book, A plan of Banbury (in X 4577), Northamptonshire Record Office. Reproduced by permission of the County Archivist.]

7.40	
36	Length times width by long multiplication
4440	
22200	
/26640	The slash is inserted into the answer to leave 5 digits after it. As there are no digits before the slash, the quantity of acres in the final answer is zero.
× 4	The answer to the first part is then multiplied by 4—the number of roods in an acre.
1/06560	As before, a slash is inserted to leave five digits. This time, there is a 1 in front; this represents 1 rood and is moved out to the final answer.
× 4	The remaining digits are apparently multiplied by 4 again but the inclusion of an extra nought at the end of the answer shows that the surveyor is actually multiplying by 40—the number of perches in a rood.
2/62400	A slash is inserted exactly as before but this time, the 2/6 at the beginning becomes 2.6 perches and is moved out to the final answer.

Acres	Roods	Perches
0	1	2.6

Of course, not all parcels of land were in strip form. Some fields were triangular and so the formula, Base × Height divided by two, replaced the first long multiplication sum above. The slash was then inserted into the answer so as to give five digits following it as before. If the field, meadow or common was of a more complex and irregular shape it was first divided into rectangles and triangles and the area of each worked out separately to be added together to give the total.

QUALITYMEN OR QUALITEERS

Once the surveyor had established who had what in the open fields, moors and commons and was armed with the claims submitted by the proprietors, the next part of the process was the setting out of the new allotments. Apart from considerations of quantity, Enclosure Acts usually required the surveyor to have regard for the quality of the land—both in the open fields as well as in the new enclosures. This was achieved in different ways at different times. In 1766, the Kingsthorpe enclosure in Northamptonshire appointed three of the five commissioners to act also in the capacity of qualitymen (or qualiteers). It was their specific duty to advise on the quality of mainly arable land which was to be enclosed. This pattern of commissioners who were also required to act as qualitymen continued for some years. Sometimes they were individually named as such in the Act but on other occasions the entire commission was also appointed to act as qualitymen as a body.

During a 30-year period beginning in the mid-1760s, it was common in enclosures of arable land to appoint specific qualitymen; some were commissioners as well but others were independent men. The typical independent (non-commissioner) qualityman was relatively local and quite often described himself as a grazier. They were, in other words, good local practitioners—farmers with sound practical experience of soils and farming methods. Details of their findings were sometimes recorded in Quality Books, such as those produced for the Northamptonshire enclosures of Long Buckby in 1765[8] and Badby in 1779[9] and the East Riding enclosure at Burton Pidsea in 1761.[10] Quality Books often appear similar to code books, with each surveyor or qualityman using his own system of abbreviations and calculations. Perhaps, as a result, they are a very much under-used source. It is to be hoped that future local historians will make a greater effort to extract the detailed information held within them and discover much more about enclosure, land values and farming methods from the late 18th century.

Qualitymen could not expect such high wages as the surveyor or clerk but, at Farthingstone (Northamptonshire) in 1751, the expenditure for the surveyor was £77 7s. 0d. and for the qualiteers and labourers it was £53 17s. 4d.[11] Some of the qualitymen were experienced enclosers, of whom some were appointed by virtue of also being commissioners. Others served as qualitymen in their own right such as William Collingridge of Mixbury in Oxfordshire, who was no doubt related to James Collingridge, the Brackley surveyor. John Sultzer of Burton Overy in Leicestershire was a qualityman but, apart from enclosure work in his own county, he was also a commissioner on at least 14 enclosures in neighbouring counties.

CONSTITUTING ENCLOSURE MAPS AND PLANS

When the issue of who was to receive what in the new enclosures was settled, the surveyor's next task was to draw up this information into a document. At first, this meant providing accurate descriptions of each allotment in the subsequent Award. Without a plan or map, each allotment was described in terms of its position in the obsolete open fields, its size and its location with respect to all of its neighbouring allotments or other features. As an example, a typical Award from the late 1770s might include an entry such as the one below, which in this case had been allotted to the rector, Rev. Thomas Smith, in lieu of his tithes:

> All that plot or parcel of land or ground situate in the said Upper Field and containing nine acres two roods and thirteen perches. Bounded on the north-west by the said public carriage road herein set out from Ashton aforesaid towards Wick aforesaid, on the east and on the south-east by the said wood called Ashton Wood aforesaid, on the south-west by an allotment to the said Thomas Smith for his glebe lands, and on the north and north-east by an allotment to Elizabeth Betts.

There has been much interest in recent years in re-constituting enclosure maps from this period (or more properly, *drawing* maps from this period, for many were never constituted or drawn in the first place). The accepted method is to base them on an early edition of the Ordnance Survey 6 inches to the mile series, the principle being that the first and second series maps were drawn before modern farming methods led to the destruction of much of the enclosure hedging.[12] Indeed, in the case of a few very late enclosures in the closing years of the 19th century, the O.S. maps actually include the pre-enclosure landscape. But this is incidental to the problems of drawing a map of a mid-18th-century enclosure. Although many such enclosure plans have been drawn using the 6-inch maps, it remains a very difficult and imprecise method; a better one is suggested below.

First, the information given in the award for each allotment is transferred to a card index. A sample of a blank card is shown in Figure 30(a) and a completed card for the Rev. Thomas Smith's allotment described earlier is shown in Figure 30(b). Today, all fields and parcels of land have an Ordnance Survey parcel number and the space at the top is for this number to be entered when the field has been identified. The second line is for the name of the new owner of the allotment and whether it is to be rented out; the occupier's name follows on the third line. Next is the field name, if there is one. Old enclosures, especially, already had names and some even survive to the present. The fifth line on the index card is for the location. Information was sometimes given in which of the old open fields or commons the new allotment was to be situated in and perhaps even (although less frequently) the name of the furlong.

Sixth is the area as given in the Award in acres, roods and perches followed on the next line by the decimal acreage. There are a number of formulae and methods for converting the acreage into a decimal; a computer-based spreadsheet or a database can be used; so can a simple shopping calculator. The number of complete acres is written down first, followed by the decimal point. The number of roods is multiplied by 40 and the answer added to the number of perches. This total is then divided by 160. This final answer is the decimal figure which follows the point and should be given to two places only. A worked example shows how to convert 2 acres 3 roods and 20 perches into decimal acres.

Figure 30 (a) Blank index card　　　**Figure 30 (b)** Completed example

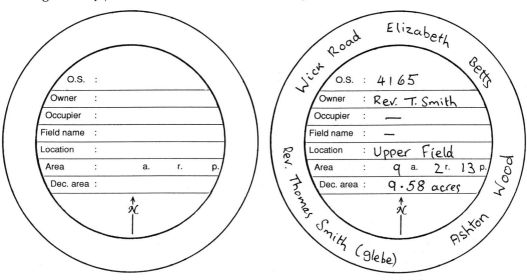

Place the 2 complete acres at the beginning, followed by a decimal point.

$$\begin{array}{r} 3 \\ \underline{40} \\ 120 \end{array}$$ × Multiply the number of roods by 40

$$\begin{array}{r} \underline{20} \\ 140 \end{array}$$ + Add the number of perches

160 ÷ Divide by 160

= 0.875 Correct this to 2 decimal places, i.e. 0.88 and add it on to the complete acres at the bottom.

2.88 acres

The reverse of the card can be used for miscellaneous notes. In the Rev. Smith's case, for example, this could include information showing why he received the land (i.e. in lieu of his tithes). Other entries might show that the awardee had received land in exchange for glebe or impropriate tithes. The lord of the manor might receive land in lieu of his rights to the soil or other proprietors might receive their share with respect to their freehold or copyhold land in the open fields. There are many snippets of information given in the Award which might help the modern historian to identify the allotments.

The outer ring of the card represents the points of a compass, north being towards the top. Into this ring, an abstract of the abuttal information can be entered. In Figure 31(b), for example, Wick Road, being to the north west, has been entered in the top left of the outer ring. Ashton Wood, being on the south east, is entered in the bottom right. The rector's allotment for glebe being on the south west, all the outer ring from the bottom left-hand corner to the left-hand side is designated accordingly and, similarly, with Elizabeth Betts' allotment in the north and north east. Eventually, a pack of index cards will result, each of which represents a parcel of land at the time of enclosure.

The next step in constituting the enclosure plan is to obtain a set of 1:2,500 scale (formerly 25 inches to the mile) Ordnance Survey maps. Many such maps will be needed to cover a large enclosure and, once again, an early edition is to be favoured. They can sometimes be found in county libraries and record offices but local planning offices or parish councils may also be able to help. Apart from the obvious one of scale, the main advantage of the 25-inch maps over the 6-inch maps is that they carry extra information— principally, the decimal acreage for each field. The next step is to lay out as many of the maps as possible on a large floor. If it is possible to obtain large sheets of acetate or cellophane to lay over the top of the maps, OHP felt-tip pens can be used to mark out each enclosure allotment. These are identified by sliding the index cards around the maps, initially by matching the decimal acreages and then by checking the abuttal information in the outer ring of each card. In the example used earlier, a check would be made to see if Ashton Wood really was where it should have been and so on. At the end of this stage, a very loose jigsaw puzzle should emerge.

Problems may arise where hedges have either been removed or were not planted in the first place. It is possible that, in some isolated cases, one of the first proprietors may have become the owner of two adjacent parcels of land. For whatever reason, he may have decided against hedging or fencing them separately but, instead, farmed them as one field. When all the allotments have been identified on the 25-inch map, it is then comparatively easy to transfer this information to a 6-inch map or a modern 1:10,000 map.

The Surveyors' Maps and Plans

By the end of the 18th century it was becoming normal for surveyors to draw up an enclosure plan or map. The Awards became shorter as there was less need for all the abuttal information. The methods used to draw such maps were still in an embryonic state. Modern surveying methods depend upon dividing the landscape into a series of triangles. The features within each are measured in detail and transferred to a scale plan. The early enclosure surveyors seem not to have used this system but their methods can sometimes be discovered from their draft maps. Construction lines show that many used large landscape features such as streams, rivers and parish boundaries. On top of these, the surveyor superimposed a straightened, more regular construction line. When surveying and recording important features on either side of this main construction line, he simply drew a perpendicular to the feature and measured its length. This method, although crude by today's standards, enabled the enclosure surveyors to produce remarkably accurate maps.

By the first half of the 19th century the quality of maps had developed still further. The aesthetic qualities of the early maps had given way to precision, accuracy and detail.

Figure 31 *(opposite)*   Linton draft enclosure map, 1837

[Source: Linton Draft Enclosure Plan, 152/P13, Record Office. Reproduced by permission of Cambridgeshire Archives Service.]

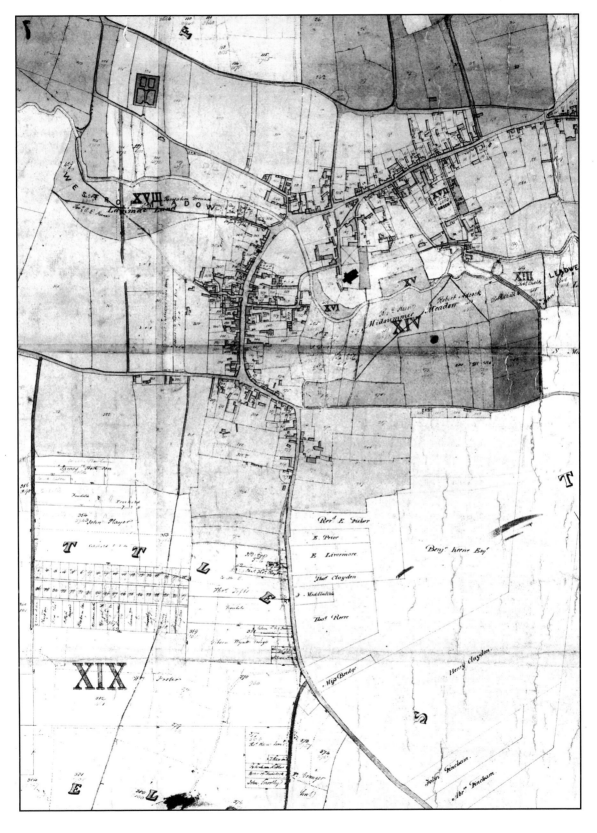

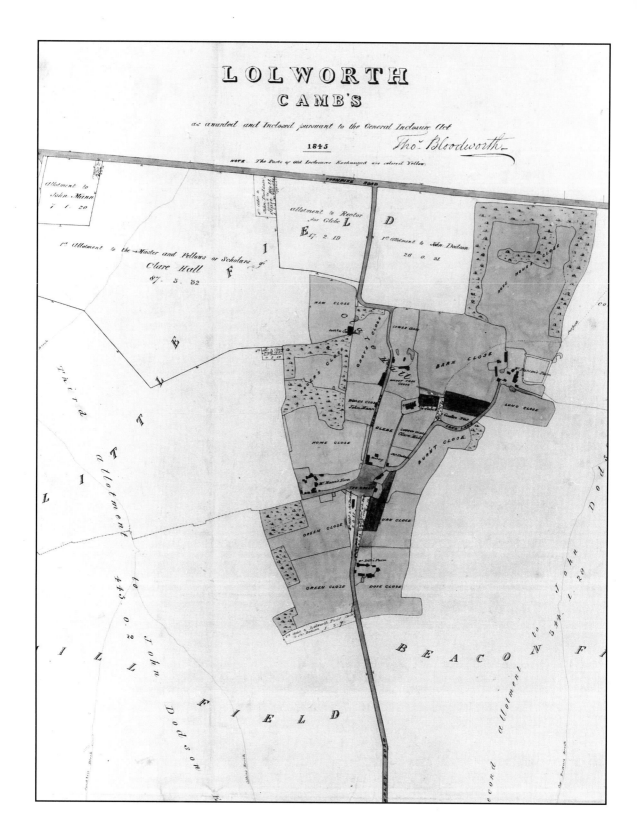

Even the draft enclosure maps were of a far higher standard than in previous times. By 1837 when the draft enclosure map of Linton in Cambridgeshire (part of which is shown in Figure 31) was produced, it had become common for such drafts to be drawn twice their finished size. This resulted in large and unwieldy maps which often received a lot of punishment, as they were rolled up tightly and taken out to the fields to resolve problems with new owners. The final version of the Lolworth enclosure from the same county, drawn by Thomas Bloodworth, no doubt a relation of Charles Bloodworth of Kimbolton, another enclosure surveyor, is shown in part in Figure 32. Drawn in 1845, it is drawn to a scale of six chains to an inch or 1:4,752. The names in large upper case are the former open fields of the parish. The smaller text gives the acreage, the name of the allottee and, sometimes, his claim to it, for example, 'for glebe'.

Not all the surveyor's work was concerned with surveying and, of that which was, not all was in the drawing of the main enclosure plan. Small plans of allotments and groups of allotments were also drawn from time to time. Figure 33 shows some sketch maps and calculations from East Sussex, probably drawn by local surveyor, William Figg. These were small draft plans of enclosed fields and were the equivalent of the earlier surveyor's casting up books. The methods for calculating the area for enclosed fields were the same as for strips or lands. In contrast, Figure 34 is a map drawn for the enclosure of land at Soughton in Flintshire (Northop, 1826). This was a final or fair copy of three parcels of land which were referred to as encroachments and had been made by Griffith Jones some 18 years earlier. The map also shows an allotment that had been sold to W. J. Bankes Esq. Such small maps or plans could be used to accompany correspondence where land at enclosure was subject to a dispute. In other cases, some enclosures were sold to help finance the project. Again, small plans were produced for the sale both to advertise it and to accompany the deeds thereafter. In this way, both extracts from enclosure Awards and small plans like the Soughton example became attached to deeds where they remain to this day.

By the mid-19th century, the process of enclosure under the General Acts had become steadily easier. By the time of the Washington enclosure (1845–7) in Sussex the local commissioners had been replaced by valuers who acted on behalf of the central Inclosure Commission. The documents consisted mainly of a summary sheet, a reference book and a map. The summary sheets were pre-printed with detailed instructions taking a little over half of each sheet; there was a blank schedule at the bottom. The instructions reflect a highly standardised approach to the process. Areas of land, for example, were not to be entered on the map. Only reference numbers were to be used to identify each plot and these were to be entered in numerical order in the reference book. Letters were not to be used on any account! To reinforce the instructions, a small example sketch map was included to show the surveyor how to draw his map. Finally, the surveyor was instructed to ensure that his maps, when sent to the Inclosure Office, were to be securely packed in cases or on strong wooden rollers. The Inclosure Commissioners disclaimed any responsibility for delay or annoyance caused by neglect of their rules.[13]

Figure 32 *(opposite)*　Lolworth enclosure map, 1845

[Source: Lolworth Enclosure Plan, Q/RDc 68, Cambridgeshire Record Office. Reproduced by permission of Cambridgeshire Archives Service.]

Figure 33 Draft sketches and calculations

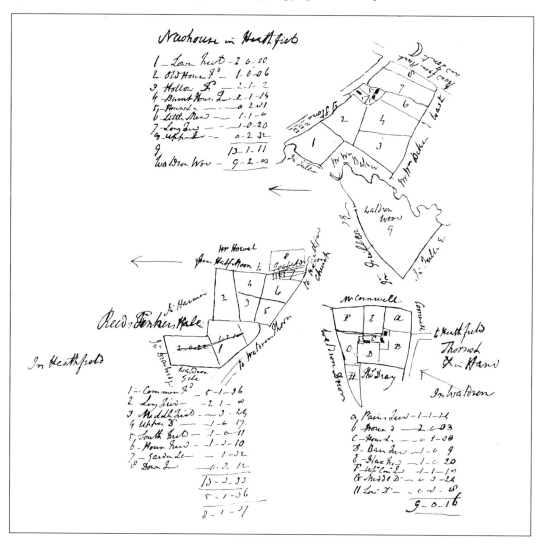

PREPARING FOR THE AWARD

Before drawing up the Award, the surveyor could have had a number of other duties to attend to. As we saw in Chapter Three, the Acts contained a broad range of requirements. All of these, including roads, hedges, drains and the like, had to be attended to by the commissioners and the surveyor. In some enclosures, the surveyor's role was greater than others. Sometimes, all the practical work in the field was undertaken by the surveyor. Where the working papers for an enclosure have survived, they often include bills and accounts for work undertaken on behalf of the surveyor. These are often unprepossessing little scraps of paper but they give an insight into the practical demands and expenses of

Figure 34 Soughton enclosure: extract of plan, 1826

[Source: Soughton enclosure drawings, D/GW/484, Flintshire Record Office. Reproduced by permission of the County Archivist.]

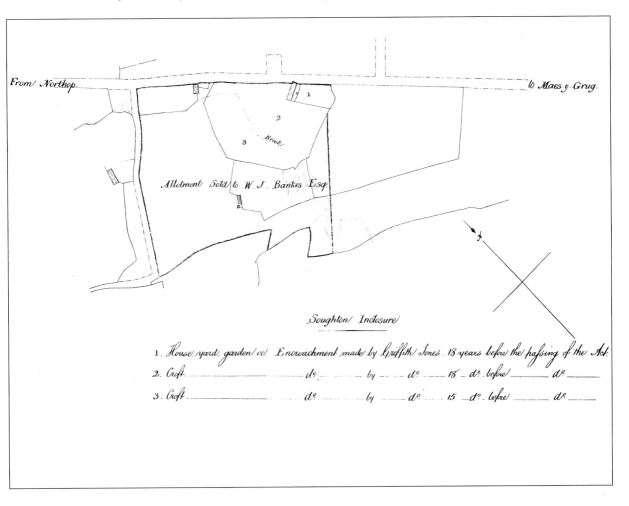

enclosure. The 1813 account for hedging in Figure 35 is a typical example. This was for work completed during the Caerwys enclosure (Act passed in 1809 but the Award was not produced until 1850). This was an enclosure of 1,200 acres of waste known as Brickhill Common. Banking, quicksetting and hedging usually consisted of the digging of a ditch, and the spoil would be thrown up on the owner's side to form a bank. On this bank was planted the young hawthorn or quicksets. Very often, a post and rail fence was erected as well, in order to make the boundary stockproof for the first 15 years or so while the quicksets became established. Hawthorn was usually used for enclosure hedging because it took only a short time to become established—hence its common name, quicksets or quickthorn.

Similar accounts can be found for walling, road-building and drainage work. Other surviving documents from the later stages of an enclosure are the road certificates. Many enclosures, whether by a Private Act or under a General Act, included the construction of new roads. We saw in an earlier chapter how the later Acts, especially, laid down detailed technical specifications—widths and so on. Following the staking out of four private carriage roads and one public footpath at Southease in Sussex, the commissioner, John Smith of Lewes, issued a public notice on 24 April 1844, to announce that a map of the proposed routes had been drawn and was available for public inspection at the office of the surveyor, Mr. William Figg.[14]

Figure 35   Hedging account, 1813

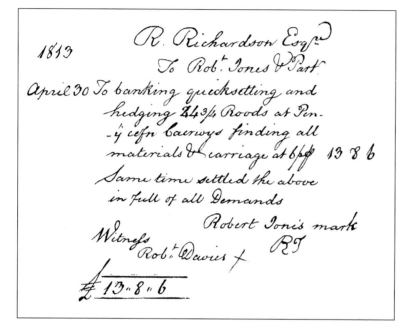

[Source: Account for hedging, Caerwys Enclosure, D/KK/457 (7), Flintshire Record Office. Reproduced by permission of the County Archivist.]

Transcription

	R. Richardson Esq[ui]re
1813	
	To Rob[er]t Jones & Part[n][er]
April 30	To banking quicksetting and
	hedging 44³/₄ Rood at Pen-
	y-cefn Caerwys finding all
	materials & carriage at 6[d per] d[a]y 13 8 6
	Same time settled the above
	in full of all Demands
	Rob[er]t Jone's mark
Witness	R J
	Robert Davis
	£13·8·6

When the work on new roads was completed, it had to be inspected by two Justices of the Peace. If they were satisfied with the work, they held a special session to award Road Certificates. Thus, for example, a special session was held on 18 November 1819 to discuss, amongst other things, the new roads which had been constructed as part of the enclosure of Llanarmon an Llandegla (Llanarmon-yn-Ial, 1811). A detailed description of the roads is given, the same description that would be given in the Award. The Certificate describes the direction and route taken by each road and its width. Finally, the Justices declared in their Certificate that the roads were 'fully and effectually formed and completed' and that they were in a good state of repair.[15] Road Certificates can often be found in Quarter Sessions records at the local record office.

THE AWARD

The Award represented the fruit of everyone's labour, but especially the surveyor's. The format of the Awards changed over the years. As we saw earlier, before the inclusion of a map, they were comparatively long documents and, especially if written in what today is called 'landscape' format, i.e. with the length of the parchment horizontal, they are sometimes very difficult to work with. After the inclusion of maps, the later Awards became shorter and were more commonly bound in book form. These are easier to use and the legal language is also a little less incomprehensible.

There were usually at least two copies of the Award. One was held in the parish chest and the second was enrolled at Quarter Sessions. In most cases, both copies are now with the county record office—one in the parish collections and the other in the Quarter Sessions records. The latter have often been bound together in large volumes covering the entire county. As well as these copies, which would have been signed, sealed and dated by the commissioners, other copies may have been drawn up for the principal landowner or land-owners. If such copies are extant, they may be found in estate papers at the county record office.

The contents of an Award follow the headings in the Act very closely since the Act dictated the scope of the matters to be dealt with by the Award. A typical parish copy of an Award from the first half of the 19th century begins with written copies of the signed oaths taken by the commissioners and perhaps the surveyor as well. The rest of the document, often written in a broad nib, Gothic style, begins with a preamble describing the background to the enclosure, taking much of its wording from the Act. Something will be said in these early pages about the process that had been employed regarding such things as the commissioners' oaths, public notices, whether an umpire or referee had been appointed and whether a map accompanied the Award. Valuations, the dealing with disputes, and whether a perambulation of the parish had taken place will conclude this section.

The parish boundaries may next be described in detail before moving on to the roads and footpaths. The public roads are usually dealt with first, followed by the private roads and then the footways. Widths as well as a description of the route were set out in the Awards and most of these legal details have remained the same ever since. Arrangements for drainage or public water courses may be dealt with next. Where drainage was a major motive of the enclosers, this was an important section and each public drain was described in detail. Positions and dimensions were given, including the width at the top and the bottom of the channel. The main section of the Award, of course, dealt with the allocation of land in the new enclosures. The order in which the allotments are described follows that given in the Act, starting with the lord of the manor (if there was one), followed by the incumbent and any other major landowners. The yeomen follow, with the cottagers and their odd, quarter-acre plots bringing up the rear. Any land set aside for special purposes will also be mentioned. Examples include land set aside for public quarries, watering places or a village pound for stray animals. Where a map accompanies the Award, less information about its position will be given in the text. The Award may give extra information on the background to some of the allotments. So, for example, if the local rector agreed to commute his great tithes for land, the Award will mention this alongside the entry for his new allotment. This was also the case for land he received in lieu of his glebe farm in the open fields. Some yeomen might have two allotments, one in their own right and one in their wife's, being land inherited from her side of the family but which the law did not allow her to hold in her own name.

Some of the allotments might have been granted to organisations rather than to individuals. Much land was owned by charities and colleges, especially in the Oxford and Cambridge regions. It was also a custom to award two small pieces of land, the income from one to be used towards the upkeep of the parish church and from the other to subsidise the parish Poor Rate. The first was vested in the churchwardens, the second in the overseers of the poor of the parish.

General instructions to the new proprietors, concerning their obligations to fence and the way in which exchanges of land should be made, concluded the main part of the Award. It is at this point that most Awards were signed and sealed by the commissioners in the presence of an attorney. A detailed summary of the allotments sometimes appeared in schedules at the end. The entries were numbered and can be correlated with the map which was either bound with the Award or rolled separately. The parish copy may include a postscript to the effect that it had been enrolled in the Office of the Clerk of the Peace of the county in which the enclosure had taken place, with a date and the location of the other copy. As well as other delays, there was sometimes a significant time lapse between the completion of the Award and its enrolment. The public reading of the Award before the major parties signalled the end of the official work of the surveyor and commissioners, although, as we saw in an earlier chapter, in practice the enclosure was not always complete and some of the work may not have been finished for several more years.

Chapter 6
Enclosure: The Issues

So far, the methods by which enclosure changed the landscape of much of Britain have been explained, and the main documentary records generated by all the parties at the time have been described. Many local historians are primarily interested in their own parish and so look, quite naturally, to this direction as a possible case study. Several problems may arise. First, the unlikely possibility that somebody has got there first. This does occur, especially where a once small town or village in the 18th century is now a major population centre containing many local historians. More common problems are that the parish under examination is not the result of a known enclosure or that the documentary evidence is no longer extant. This is particularly the case where enclosures pre-dated parliamentary intervention. Actual agreements, Chancery Decrees or Awards from this period are not always readily available and correspondence and other documents associated with them even less so.

Although many interesting single parish studies have been published over the years, on their own they tell us very little about enclosure *per se*. Some of these studies enter into the most detailed minutiae of the parish being studied, but are completely unable to discuss trends or the general effects of enclosure across the region or country. To be able to do this, a broad knowledge of the issues and debates regarding the nature and effects of enclosure is essential. There are many such issues which have been, and continue to be, addressed by agricultural historians. They include: the costs of enclosure; the area of land mass affected by both parliamentary and non-parliamentary enclosure; the effect of enclosure on agricultural improvement; the fortunes of small landowners; the experiences of commoners and common rights; and the relationship between non-agricultural occupations and enclosure. Some of these issues and the debates that surround them are looked at below with particular reference to the documentary records that might be used in their study.

THE EXTENT OF PARLIAMENTARY ENCLOSURE

The vast majority of the English and Welsh countryside is now enclosed. It is self-evident that it has been subject to either parliamentary enclosure or non-parliamentary enclosure. The question that has intrigued many historians is how much of the land surface was enclosed by Parliament?

Professor Turner has offered a reasonable estimation that approximately 6.8 million acres was enclosed by this method, about half of which occurred in the Midlands counties.[1] However, Turner's claim has initiated a debate on the extent of Parliamentary enclosure. In particular, his source material in arriving at this figure has been discussed by a number of writers including Professor J. Chapman[2] and Dr. J.R. Wordie.[3] Chapman claimed that

Turner's use of data from Tate's *Domesday of English Parliamentary Enclosure Acts and Awards* included entries where the quantities of land were not known and that others used were based on the quantities supplied by the Act, which can be, as we have already seen, wildly inaccurate.

Wordie noted that many of the Parliamentary enclosures used by Turner in his calculation of the total area of land so enclosed included ancient enclosures—land which was already enclosed—or in some cases were simply rubber stamps for land more recently enclosed by private agreement. Wordie was concerned to show that, in fact, Parliament accounted for far less an area of land than had previously been acknowledged and that, in contrast, the private agreements and other methods had been responsible for the enclosure of much larger areas of land in the 17th century than earlier writers had accepted. Using the available data from the Leicestershire *Victoria County History* (representing a sample of approximately 65 per cent of the Leicestershire parishes), Wordie arrived at the results shown in Table 7, showing the extent, nature and timing of enclosure in that county. From this, he concluded that the period of so-called agricultural improvement lay embedded in the 17th and not the 18th century. R.A. Butlin,[4] J.V. Beckett[5] and, more particularly, J. Chapman[6] have questioned such results—particularly the large number of 17th-century enclosures when compared with the sixteenth. Chapman also questioned whether Wordie had adequately distinguished between the enclosure of open fields and that of commons and wastes.

Table 7 Leicestershire enclosure, pre-1844

Period	Number of Enclosures	Percentage of the County
pre-1500	28	9.06
1500–1599	26	8.41
1600–1699	104	33.66
1700–1759	7	6.69
" " of which parliamentary =		4.42
" " non-parliamentary =		2.27
1760–1799	-	35.47
1800–1844	-	6.71

[Source: Wordie, J.R., 'The Chronology of English Enclosure, 1500–1914', *Ec.HR*, 2nd ser. 36 (1983), pp.483–505.]

Wordie subsequently accepted that he may have over-stated the volume of 17th-century enclosure by using data from the Tudor commissions of inquiry which had been mainly concerned with conversion to pasture.[7] He felt that the over-statement was relatively small and refuted the claim that he had ignored the wastes in his calculations. There is now a general acceptance that, regardless of detail, enclosure was already firmly established before the intervention of Parliament in the 18th century.

Any attempt to contribute to this particular topic would require the study of more than a few parishes. Indeed, it is difficult to see how meaningful results could be obtained from anything less than a complete county. Apart from Award acreages (which in most cases are easily accessible from W.E. Tate's *Domesday ...*[8] for English enclosures or from J. Chapman's *Guide ...*[9] for Welsh enclosures) other data can be extracted from the 1831 Census returns which include the total area of parishes. Problems arise when Awards do not give acreages. A possible alternative is to use information from the Acts but, as we have seen, these are notoriously inaccurate.

There is a need for a similar examination and estimation of the extent of non-parliamentary enclosure. The total area of land so enclosed can be calculated if the area enclosed by Parliament is known. However, this could be taken further to establish how much was enclosed by formal or informal agreement. This would require a diligent search through local record office catalogues and then those at the Public Record Office to trace enclosures enrolled by the Court of Chancery or the other courts of record. For those researchers based a long distance from London, this represents a considerable commitment. It is to be hoped that, before this new century is too much older, the PRO catalogues and indexes will be available on the internet!

COMPARISON OF ENCLOSURE ACROSS DIFFERENT SOIL TYPES

Arising out of the debate on the extent of land enclosed by Parliament, Professor Chapman[10] looked for correlations between enclosure and soil type. He looked at four classes of land: open field arable, meadow, common waste and pasture, and old enclosed land. He found that Parliamentary enclosures were predominantly concerned with open arable and open pasture land. In his study sample, he found that 33 per cent of the land enclosed was open field arable and approximately 60 per cent was open pasture.

Chapman claimed that the use of enclosure as a means of reclaiming wastes and re-organising arable land into more efficient and compact units was of only secondary importance. However, this pattern changed over time. In the early part of the period of Parliamentary enclosure, for example, arable land seemed to be the main target. Later, from the start of the Napoleonic Wars onwards, the wastes became the principal objectives of the enclosers. Geographically, Chapman claimed to find different patterns for the enclosure of arable and waste. He found regional differences in both but, generally, the enclosure of arable land peaked at roughly the same time throughout the country. At the time of the wastes enclosures, some, which were furthest from a central point identified by Chapman, seemed to lag behind the rest. This work shows the importance of considering enclosure patterns both spatially and temporally.

Chapman's article was the first of five written during the 1980s by himself and J.R. Walton, who together have conducted a lively debate through the pages of *Agricultural History Review*.[11] Walton, in reply to Chapman's original article, questioned his statistical techniques. The final article by Chapman[12] in this debate defended his own use of statistics but counter-criticised Walton's. This exchange of views through the 1980s and early 1990s illustrates the difficulty of research in this area and the lack of universally accepted results which have emerged from it. Again, large samples of enclosures are needed to produce useful data. The enclosure Awards, where they exist, are the principal documentary source.

The Cost of Parliamentary Enclosure

Professor Turner has pointed out the importance of costs as economic determinants when looking at the extent and timing of Parliamentary enclosure.[13] In particular, costs were the most important facet of enclosure that affected both the rich and the poor—but not necessarily to the same degree. So it may be that this aspect, above all others, should be examined.

Cost may well have been one of the deciding factors which influenced the timing of an enclosure or group of enclosures. The landed gentry and the church were concerned with a broad range of economic factors which might encourage or discourage them from starting an enclosure process. The squire, the church and the often absentee proprietors of larger farms within a township invariably began the first moves towards obtaining an Act, and were aware of their capacity to pay for the enclosure. The small landowners were more particularly concerned with the immediate cost to them of the process of an enclosure, over which they had little control. The owners of small parcels of land either acquiesced or opposed the plans laid before them but they rarely initiated them (some exceptions were identified, for example, in Cumbria by C.E. Searle who found that the customary tenants, who held a third of the land at enclosure, played an important role in the movement[14]). Nevertheless, the small landowners would have had to pay their share of the costs and there is little dispute that this financial burden could have been considerable. Generally, the fewer the number of landowners, the easier an enclosure was and vice versa.

In some counties, there was a temporal and spatial pattern to enclosure by Private Act of Parliament. In Northamptonshire, it had its origins in the west of the county in the mid-18th century and then moved eastwards into the lowland valleys in the early 19th century. This is generally accepted as being related to soil types (the heavier clays being enclosed before the lighter soils), but were costs another factor? Was there a higher cost per acreage in some parts of the country than others? If so, it is reasonable to assume that costs were lower in the areas where enclosures occurred first.

Much of the previous work on enclosure costs by J.M. Martin,[15] W.E. Tate[16] and T.H. Swales[17] was based on the 18th rather than the 19th century. Information on costs is more readily available from early enclosure awards, where it was often included in schedules until approximately the period of peak enclosure activity in the late 1770s. There are, as Turner has pointed out, many problems associated with Awards as a source of data[18] but some trends can be identified. An example of this type of source is the costs for the Northamptonshire enclosure of Upper and Lower Boddington in 1758, shown in Table 8.[19] This award is typical, in terms of both content and problems when used as a data source.

William Caldecott of Rugby in Warwickshire was clerk to the enclosure but his fee also included the costs incurred with counsel and Parliament in procuring the Act. The victualler's account was for food and drink, mainly consumed in the fields. This was not usually for labourers engaged in fencing but for the surveyor, the commissioners and their helpers in measuring and marking out the new enclosures. There were two surveyors for this enclosure—hence the large proportion of the total cost which they claimed along with the relatively small amount paid to the qualiteers. The commissioners' expenses at this time were modest, accounting for only 12.7 per cent. Unfortunately, the costs given in the

Table 8   Administrative Costs (to the nearest £) of the Upper and Lower Boddington enclosure, 1758

Victualler	£109
Surveyors	£242
Qualiteer	£30
Labourers and Parish Clerk	£33
W. Weston (mason)	£30
Commissioners	£126
W. Caldecott (Clerk) for procuring Act, etc.	£425
TOTAL	£995

[Source: Upper and Lower Boddington Enclosure, Northamptonshire Inclosures, bound volumes, Northamptonshire Record Office.]

Award do not include the cost of fencing and hedging materials. This is an example of the incompleteness of such accounts and it is not an isolated case.

Whereas the data from individual awards is incomplete, there is nevertheless a large enough body of information from many enclosures to allow some trends to be examined. For example, there was an upward trend in the cost of enclosure which was addressed to some extent by the Acts in the latter half of the enclosure period. During the boom years of enclosure in the late 1770s, the average cost per acre of enclosure in many parts of the country rose rapidly. This may have been because of the increase in returns which encouraged the enclosure of parishes which had earlier missed out owing to comparatively high costs or other complications. It was against a background of rising enclosure costs, though, that attempts were made to control expenditure. As we have seen, the idea of sliding scales for professional fees to encourage early completions, the definition of the working day and annual audits were all introduced to this end. This and other trends can be investigated in any enclosure where the data is extant.

In some rare cases, the complete working papers for an enclosure have survived. We saw, for example, in the previous chapter how many of the surveyors' records can be found and the same is also true for the clerks' papers, which often include financial data. This is contained in a range of minor documents such as fencing and hedging accounts, accounts for roads, walls or other public works, ploughing accounts, tavern bills, bills for seed (usually grass or clover) or a host of other small vouchers, receipts and accounts.

By far the most important documents are the clerks' expense accounts. They might include only the administrative charges, as in the Kirk Ireton account in Figure 36.[20] Dated 1803, this represents the expenditure incurred in the early stages of the enclosure whilst procuring the Act. Totalling £216 16s. 1d., it includes charges for drawing up the petition, perusing and settling the Bill, making a brief and copy for the Speaker, printing the Bill and Act and so on. Other clerks' accounts might also cover the other stages of the enclosure including servicing the meetings of the commission. If there are commissioners' minute books as well as good sets of accounts, it becomes possible to reconstruct balance sheets for the larger enclosures, which can then be audited against the minutes. By this means it

Account of Expences in passing the Kirk Ireton Inclosure Act. —

	£ s d
Drawing Petition and Copy ———	1. 11. 6
Making Copies of Committee on Petition ———	0. 10. 0
——— Order for Notices ———	0. 10. 0
——— Copy of Notice and Petition signifying Notices were given &c and Order ———}	1. 6. 0
Making Copies of Committee ———	0. 10. 0
Settling Report and drawing Orders &c	0. 10. 0
Perusing and Settling the Bill ———	6. 6. 0
Making Copy of Bill for the House ———	5. 0. 0
Do press in part ———	0. 18. 0
——— Brief and Copy for the Speaker ———	1. 6. 0
——— Committee on the Bill ———	0. 10. 0
Preparing Amendments for the Committee	1. 11. 6
Filling up and altering Bills ———	1. 16. 0
Making Copies of Clauses ———	1. 10. 0
——— Special Reports for Speaker and others and Attendances thereon ———}	2. 2. 0
Paid House Fees on Petition and Bill ———	17. 10. 8
——— Committee Clerks Do ———	20. 4. 2
——— Housekeeper and Messengers Do ———	1. 10. 0
——— Doorkeepers for delivering Bills ———	1. 1. 0
Making 2 Bills complete for Ingrossers & Press	0. 0. 0
Paid Ingrossing Fees ———	27. 18. 9
Examining House Bill Ingrosm.t & Proofs ———	2. 8. 0
Paid Gratuities to Housekeeper & Messengers &c	2. 7. 0
Printing Bill and act ———	23. 12. 0
Lord in the Chair & attending him ———	2. 2. 0
Paid House Fees at Lords ———	27. 0. 0
——— for Order for Committee ———	1. 1. 0
——— Committee Clerks fee & Gratuity ———	4. 4. 0
——— Yoman Usher and Doorkeepers Do ———	5. 5. 0
——— for swearing Witnesses ———	0. 6. 0
Porters Postage & other small Expences ———	3. 13. 6
Solicitation fee ———	21. 0. 0
	£187. 16. 1
Public act Clause ———	13. 5. 0
Fees at the Duchy Office ———	15. 15. 0
	£216. 16. 1

is possible not only to establish the cost of the enclosure, but also to provide a breakdown of the costs and to discover how closely the clerks were following the instructions of the commissioners. For example, were all items of expenditure authorised by the commissioners? These and other questions can be addressed in such studies.

The other side of the financial equation is income, information about which is also necessary if the accounts of an enclosure are to be reconstructed. Income was received by the enclosure commissioners principally via the sale of land or the levying of a rate on the freehold proprietors, or by a combination of them both. Figure 37 is almost self-explanatory. The enclosure of Braunton Marsh in Devon (Act passed 1811, Award dated 1824) was one which received an income when 'divers parts of the said Marsh' were offered for sale on 11 September 1813.[21] Figure 37 shows the printed notice of the sale with 36 plots described in relation to a plan.

Where an enclosure rate had been raised, a breakdown of the different proprietors' shares might survive, as in the East Riding enclosure of Etton (Figure 38).[22] More rarely, there might be a hint of the basis upon which the rate was calculated. As we have already seen, Poor Rates or Land Tax Assessments could have been used, but a simple system based pro rata on the amount of land held could also have been devised. In establishing the cost of an enclosure, it is helpful to know how fair the allocation of it was. For example, Figure 38 shows the range of contributions for the Etton enclosure. Robert Belt, the principal landowner in the scheme, paid £2,222 15s. 9d.; Mary Grasby paid only £17 1s. 1d. which, nevertheless, might have still been a considerable sum to her. Collecting the enclosure rate or tax was sometimes arduous. The Etton commissioners included the following postscript which can be seen at the bottom of the schedule:

> Any money not paid on the[x] day
> to pay Interest
> 13th February

Particularly when a second enclosure rate had to be levied, it was necessary for the clerks to maintain a record of who owed what. The Dufton enclosure of 1827 required the levying of two rates.[23] Inevitably, by the time the second rate was due, some proprietors still owed the first. The accounts sheet in Figure 39 is undated but was drawn up some time after the second rate was due. It shows the names of the proprietors, how much, if any, of the first assessment they had paid and, if none, what they owed and the consequent interest that the debt accrued. In the fifth column, the second rate or assessment is given and the final column shows the amount that each proprietor now owed in total. The incorrect answer at the bottom reminds us of the difficulties of computation in an age before electronic calculators.

Figure 36 *(opposite)*   Kirk Ireton account of expenses, 1803

[Source: D4459/1/5/19, Derbyshire Record Office, 'Account of Expenses in Passing the Kirk Ireton Enclosure Act', 1803. Reproduced by permission of the County and Diocesan Archivist.]

Figure 37 *(overleaf)*   Braunton Marsh, 'To be Sold', c.1811-24

[Source: 3704 M/SS/I/5, North Devon (Barnstaple) Record Office, Braunton Marsh Enclosure, 'To Be Sold', (1813). Reproduced by permission of the County Archivist.]

Braunton Marsh
INCLOSURE.

TO BE SOLD,
By Public Survey,

At the Assembly Rooms, in *Barnstaple*, on Saturday the 11th day of September next,
at 4 o'Clock in the Afternoon;

*By Order of the Commissioners named in an Act, passed in the 51st year of the reign of his present
Majesty, entituled " An Act for inclosing, draining, and embanking Land in Braunton in the County
of Devon,"*

Divers Parts of the said Marsh,

Lying on the Western Side thereof,

As the same are marked out on the Map or Plan thereof, deposited with Mr. John Williams,
of *Barnstaple*, Solicitor, and also on the said Marsh by stakes and other marks.

LOT		MEASURE. A.	R.	P.
1	A Piece of Ground marked A adjoining to Swanny Pool,	5	1	8
2	Ditto marked B lying on the west of lot 1st.	5	1	4
3	Ditto marked C lying on the west of lot 2d.	6	3	2
4	Ditto marked D lying on the west of lot 3d.	8	1	26
5	Ditto marked L lying on the south of lots 1st, 2d, and 3d.	4	0	0
6	Ditto marked M lying on the south of lot 5th.	4	2	7
7	Ditto marked N lying on the south of lot 6th.	4	3	0
8	Ditto marked O lying partly on the south of lot 7th, and partly on the south of divers closes belonging to Joseph Davie Bassett, Esq. and others,	9	3	4
9	Ditto marked P lying on the south of lot 8th.	9	0	11
10	Ditto marked Q lying on the south of lot 9th.	8	3	11
11	Ditto marked R lying on the south of lot 10th.	9	2	32
12	Ditto marked S lying on the south of lot 11th.	10	0	4
13	Ditto marked T lying on the south of lot 12th.	10	2	2
14	Ditto marked E lying on the west of lots 5th, 6th, 7th, 8th, and 9th.	6	0	12
15	Ditto marked F lying on the south of lot 14th.	6	2	22
16	Ditto marked G lying on the south of lot 15th.	6	3	8
17	Ditto marked H lying on the south of lot 16th.	7	1	13
18	Ditto marked I lying on the south of lot 17th.	8	0	4
19	Ditto marked K lying on the south of lot 1st.	6	3	39
20	Ditto marked U lying on the south of lot 13th, and bounded on the east by a drain or water course, lately cut on the said marsh,	4	0	12
21	Ditto marked V lying on the west of lot 20th.	4	2	4
22	Ditto marked W lying on the west of lot 21st.	5	1	1
23	Ditto marked X lying on the west of lot 22d.	6	0	7
24	Ditto marked Y lying on the south-west of lot 23d.	6	0	24
25	Ditto marked Z lying on the south of lot 24th.	5	1	7
26	Ditto marked A A lying on the south of lot 25th.	4	1	4
27	Ditto marked B B lying on the south of lot 26th.	5	1	0
28	Ditto marked C C lying on the south of lot 27th.	4	3	23
29	Ditto marked D D lying on the south of lot 28th.	5	2	8
30	Ditto marked E E lying on the south of lot 29th.	6	1	28
31	Ditto marked F F lying on the south of lot 30th.	6	1	23
32	Ditto marked G G lying on the south of lot 31st.	7	0	32
33	Ditto marked H H lying on the south of lot 32d.	6	2	18
34	Ditto marked I I lying on the south of lot 33d.	10	1	0
35	Ditto marked K K lying on the south of lot 24th.	12	2	28
36	Ditto marked L L lying on the south of lots 26th, and 35th, and particularly well calculated for a Rabbit Warren	88	0	0
	Also, all that Piece of Land called VELLATOR, lying on the north-east side of Braunton Marsh, and separated from the same by Braunton Pill,	23	3	12

To look at the Map and for particulars, apply to Mr. Williams, and to view the several
allotments, apply to Samuel Hammond, of *Braunton*, Shoemaker.

Dated July 26th, 1813.

AVERY, PRINTER, BARNSTAPLE.

Figure 38 Etton Enclosure Tax, 1818

[Source: DDX 309, East Riding Record Office, Etton Inclosure Tax (1818). Reproduced by permission of the County Archivist.]

Etton Inclosure Tax

Names of Proprietors

	£	s	d
Belt Robert Esq.	2222	15	9
Brigham John	54	2	10
Byass John	17	2	10
Clark Thomas	143	2	3
Drury William	17	3	4
Fox Revd. John	17	9	"
Gilby Revd. John	1344	14	9
Gouldborough Richard	30	19	7
Grassby Mary	17	1	1
Grimston Henry Esq.	119	4	11
Heward Richard	17	9	7
Hodgson Thomas	19	4	2
Hotham Rt. Hon. Lord	504	2	9
Legard Sir Thomas Bart	811	11	3
Roantree Thomas	49	3	"
Roantree George	19	13	9
Schoolcroft William	90	9	3
Stephenson Ralph	19	19	3
Thompson Sarah	19	19	9
Turner George	20	15	1
Vickers John	171	11	11
Walkden Geo. & Frith Thos.	227	19	11
Watson Elizabeth	112	15	6
Wauldby John	18	3	"
Wilson Thomas	17	1	5
	6103	11	11

Any Money not paid on the day £
to pay Interest. 24th Decr. 1818

15th Feby. 1819

Wm Ware
John Hall
P. Jackson

Figure 39 Dufton enclosure: accounts

[Source: WD/HH/53, Cumbria Record Office (Kendal), Dufton Enclosure (c.1828). Reproduced by permission of Lord Hothfield.]

Dufton Inclosure

Proprietors Names	1st Assessmt Paid £ s d	Not paid £ s d	Interest upon the unpaid £ s d	2nd Assessment £ s d	Amount of 2nd Assessmt with Interest upon £ s d
Allan William	9 „ 17 „ ~			14 „ 10 „ ~	14 „ 10 „ ~
Atkinson Thomas		6 „ 6 „ ~	3 „ 9 „ 2	9 „ ~ „ ~	10 „ 15 „ 2
Ellwood John Knock	26 „ 14 „ ~			36 „ 16 „ ~	36 „ 16 „ ~
Blenkarn Thos. & Robt.	30 „ 0 „ ~			50 „ 1 „ 7	50 „ 1 „ 7
Blenkarn Robt. senr.		10 „ 0 „ ~	5 „ 14 „ 4	13 „ 10 „ ~	29 „ 12 „ 4
Bland Thomas	3 „ 4 „ ~			5 „ 12 „ 6	5 „ 12 „ 6
Dixon Jnr. or Mr. Ferguson		7 „ 0 „ ~	4 „ 1 „ 4	11 „ 5 „ ~	22 „ 14 „ 4
Ellwood Thomas late forth.		17 „ 12 „ ~	6 „ 3 „ 1	18 „ 5 „ 7	42 „ ~ „ 0
Do. his own Allot.		1 „ 6 „ ~	~ „ 14 „ 2	1 „ 13 „ 9	3 „ 13 „ 11
Do. Bulpot		17 „ ~ „ ~	6 „ 9 „ 0		20 „ 9 „ 0
Ellwood William		3 „ 10 „ ~	2 „ 2 „ 10	5 „ 1 „ 1	11 „ 1 „ 11
Nixon Jonathan		6 „ ~ „ ~	1 „ 10 „ ~	3 „ ~ „ ~	10 „ 10 „ ~
Ellwood John Dufton	23 „ 0 „ ~			32 „ 15 „ ~	32 „ 15 „ ~
Furnas John		21 „ ~ „ ~	11 „ 11 „ ~	29 „ 16 „ 6	62 „ 7 „ 6
Miss Fearns her own	1 „ 12 „ ~			3 „ ~ „ ~	3 „ ~ „ ~
Do. Ellwoods	7 „ 0 „ ~			0 „ 6 „ 4	0 „ 6 „ 4
Do. Pearsons	6 „ ~ „ ~			6 „ 15 „ ~	6 „ 15 „ ~
Do. Tons		10 „ 16 „ ~	5 „ 10 „ 0	15 „ 15 „ ~	32 „ 9 „ 0
Graham Richard	11 „ 14 „ ~			15 „ 5 „ ~	15 „ 5 „ ~
Gowling John		1 „ 19 „ ~	~ „ 19 „ 4	2 „ 13 „ 7	5 „ 11 „ 11
Coats Jane	6 „ ~ „ ~			0 „ ~ „ ~	
Harrison Christopher	9 „ 2 „ ~			11 „ 16 „ ~	11 „ 16 „ ~
Revd. Edwd. Neelis	26 „ 4 „ ~			40 „ 10 „ 1	40 „ 10 „ 1
Revd. Dr. Kilner	6 „ 2 „ ~			11 „ 1 „ 11	11 „ 1 „ 11
Lowas Richard Closehouse		2 „ 2 „ ~	1 „ 2 „ 11	3 „ 2 „ ~	6 „ 6 „ 11
Milward Thomas Esqr.	33 „ 10 „ ~			40 „ 10 „ 9	40 „ 10 „ 9
Horn William	34 „ 10 „ ~			45 „ 16 „ 0	45 „ 16 „ 0
Do. Ann Parkers	3 „ 14 „ ~			5 „ 12 „ 6	5 „ 12 „ 6
Parker Thomas Junr.		3 „ 10 „ ~	2 „ 2 „ 10	5 „ 1 „ 3	11 „ 2 „ 1
Robinson Matthew Hill	51 „ ~ „ ~	0 „ ~ „ ~	3 „ 6 „ 5	70 „ 6 „ 4	79 „ 6 „ 4
Rector	7 „ 3 „ ~			10 „ ~ „ ~	10 „ ~ „ 5
Spedding William own		~ „ 16 „ ~	~ „ 17 „ 5	~ „ 10 „ ~	2 „ 11 „ 5
Do. Brothers	3 „ 10 „ ~			5 „ 0 „ 6	5 „ 0 „ 6
Tuer Richard	1 „ 12 „ ~			2 „ 10 „ ~	2 „ 10 „ ~
Tuer Thomas	3 „ 10 „ ~			5 „ 1 „ ~	5 „ 1 „ ~
Watson Thomas	34 „ 12 „ ~			40 „ 10 „ ~	40 „ 10 „ ~
Wilson Jonathan	~ „ 7 „ ~			0 „ ~ „ ~	0 „ ~ „ ~
Pattinson John	1 „ 0 „ ~			1 „ 16 „ ~	1 „ 16 „ ~
Earl of Thanet	272 „ 19 „ ~			306 „ 10 „ 1	306 „ 10 „ 1
					£1161 „ 6 „ 1

Finally, there are the small documents which together, supply information about income and the way in which bills were paid. Figure 40 shows a Flintshire Bank receipt for £13 7s. 6d. received of Ralph Richardson Esq. and made out to the Caerwys Enclosure (Act, 1809).[24] On its own, the receipt gives very little information but, with the data gained from other documents, its purpose may relate to the hedging account.

Figure 40   Flintshire Bank—receipt for Caerwys enclosure, 1809

[Source: D/KK/457/6, Flintshire Record Office, receipt for Ralph Richardson for Caerwys Enclosure, 8 October 1812. Reproduced by permission of the County Archivist.]

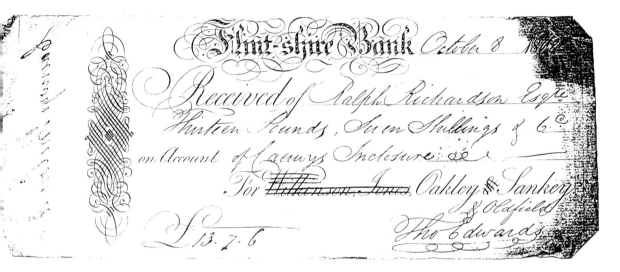

THE FATE OF THE SMALL LANDOWNER AND LAND TAX

We now turn to the complex issue of changes in the pattern of land ownership following an enclosure. After an enclosure, inevitably there were winners and losers. The former group included the principal landowning families and the church but the identity of the losers is more difficult to analyse. The central question is: following an enclosure, did land tend to pass out of the hands of small proprietors and become absorbed into the large estates? If this was the case, this represented a considerable socio-economic shift as the displaced small farmers would have been forced to give up their self-employed status and join the waged labour force working on the larger farms or, worse still, in the mines or burgeoning industrial centres.

Why should such a shift in fortunes take place? There are two broad arguments. The first concerns those with only a small amount of freehold land and the second, those with none at all (and, because the two groups overlap, there is inevitably confusion between them). The small landowner might have found that, following enclosure, his land would have increased in value by as much as 100 per cent. This was no help, though, if he could not raise his share of the enclosure rate—least of all the cost of new buildings or internal hedges. This might persuade him to sell out to another, perhaps larger, landowner. If the small landowner was an owner-occupier and perhaps elderly, the prospect of early retirement in contrast to the topsy-turvy world of post-enclosure agriculture might have suddenly seemed very attractive. The second group—those with no land of their own—relied on the commons to supplement their wages, using it as a source of free, seasonal food and fuel. At enclosure, the common rights were extinguished and the commons, heaths and moorland were taken in with the new farms. As a result, despite sometimes receiving compensation, the cottagers were deprived of a valuable portion of their income, forcing some of them, like the other group, towards the new industrial centres to gain employment.

In the 19th century, parliamentary enclosure attracted as much criticism as earlier conversions to pasture. Foremost among these critics were the early left-wing writers, of whom one of the first and most influential was Karl Marx. In *Capital*,[25] he made the following claim:

> About 1750, the yeomanry had disappeared, and so had, in the last decade of the 18th century, the last trace of the common land of the agricultural labourer.

Marx was also considering two groups. On the one hand were the yeomanry whom he seems to have considered to be the small, independent farmers and owner-occupiers. On the other were the labourers or cottager class. Marx linked the two events—the disappearance of the English yeomanry class and the impoverishment of the labourers following the loss of their common land after enclosure.

Through the writings of Marx, the idea of the 'Yeomen of England' being disfranchised from the land became widely accepted and this was reflected in the historical accounts of the late 19th and early 20th centuries by such writers as Gray,[26] Tawney[27] and Ernle.[28] Perhaps the most influential opinions were expressed by historians such as John and Barbara Hammond, who published *The Village Labourer 1760–1832* in 1911.[29] Their general theme of the widening social gap between the ruling aristocracy and the working class proletariat closely followed Marx's and was developed further in two more books in the same series, *The Town Labourer 1760–1832* (1917)[30] and *The Skilled Labourer 1760–1832* (1920).[31] The Hammonds saw enclosure as an instrument whereby this shift in power and self-determination between the classes became possible, claiming that this was how the poor were finally deprived of land ownership and common rights. This idea was supported by what appeared to have been a marked reduction in owner-occupation of land by the late 19th century. Generally, the view of the Hammonds and many of their contemporaries was pessimistic, regarding enclosure as the hammer used against the once great English class of yeomen and small farmers.

By the 1940s there was renewed interest in the study of the loss of the open fields. A number of workers re-examined the earlier investigations of the Hammonds and others, and found that a less than complete picture had been described by them. W.E. Tate,[32] for example, defended the role of Parliament in enclosure projects and the supposed degree of collusion between MPs and the local landowning aristocracy. V.M. Lavrovsky[33] found that, in the case of the earlier Parliamentary enclosures, the smaller proprietors did indeed suffer initially, although, as the 18th century came to a close, their lot seemed much improved. He found that they came to hold a greater proportion of land than before. Nevertheless, Lavrovsky concluded that, generally, enclosure eroded the social and economic welfare of the poorer classes. This was due in part to the land which was gained by the church or impropriate rectors in commutation for tithes.

Professor J.D. Chambers, also writing mainly in the period after 1940[34] and in a more optimistic vein than the Hammonds, claimed that, at the turn of the 18th century, there was a general increase in the number of owner-occupiers in the East Midlands. This up-turn in the fortunes of the cottager class, especially in the years immediately following the Napoleonic Wars, directly contradicted the claims of the Hammonds. After the Battle of Waterloo in 1815, and the end of the wars, a deep agricultural depression set in and it may be that, initially, the small owner-occupiers were best able to adapt to the fall in demand. However, as the depression deepened still further, money that during the war years had been available for investment in such schemes as enclosure, became scarce. H.G. Hunt[35] found that, in Leicestershire during this period, there was a decline in the number of small owner-occupiers which was quite irrespective of enclosure. This evidence contrasted once more with the claims of the Hammonds that enclosure dispossessed the small farmers of the land, forcing them to move towards the expanding towns and industrial centres.

Throughout the 20th century, the argument moved back and forth as new studies were carried out. By the late 1960s, Professor G.E. Mingay supported the more optimistic view of enclosure.[36] He investigated the fortunes of *small farmers*—who included tenant-farmers as well as owner-occupiers. The earlier wave of research had concluded that, in the period of industrial change, parliamentary enclosure had been the principal factor which mitigated against the economic viability of this particular group. It was Mingay's view that this position was false and he set out to investigate three aspects of the decline of the small farmer. First, he wanted to discover the extent of the decline in numbers of the small farmers and the acreage of land thus affected. Second, he needed to know more about the timing of such a decline; was it, for example, during the period of parliamentary enclosure or was it earlier? Third, he wanted to find out what had caused the decline. He wanted to know the ways in which enclosure could have affected the small farmer and whether this could have caused their numbers to decline. Alternatively, were there other, more important factors which might have brought this about?

With regard to the supposed decline in the numbers of small farmers, Mingay compared figures provided by Gregory King in the late 17th century with the census returns of 1891.[37] He concluded that, because of insufficient data, it was not possible to arrive at a definite result but that, although there may have been a significant reduction in the numbers of small farmers by the end of the 19th century, there were still large numbers of them remaining in parts of the country where they had traditionally thrived. Despite economic and technological developments which favoured larger units then, there survived a significant body of small operators. Regarding the proportion of land acreage farmed by them, however, Mingay claimed that this had already been reduced to a probable 11 to 14 per cent by the end of the 18th century and that this declined to only a slightly lower proportion during the next 100 years.

Interest in the fortunes of small operators has continued in a number of studies produced in the 1970s and 1980s. Working in Buckinghamshire, M.E. Turner claimed that the turnover of small landowners every two or three years was as much as 50–60 per cent.[38] Of the new owners, it seems that many were cottager class and so, although much of what Marx and the Hammonds had claimed now appeared to be true in that cottagers were giving up their land, equally, it seemed that many others from the lower class benefited from the new arrangements in the same way that the landowning aristocracy did.

In Warwickshire, J.M. Martin also found a turnover in small landowners following enclosure but, unlike Turner, he also identified a steady, overall reduction in their total numbers by as much as 39 per cent.[39] Martin found that, within the group of small landowners, those that fared worst were the absentee landowners who lived in another part of the country as opposed to the owner-occupiers who worked their own land.

J.M. Neeson examined the turnover of original Northamptonshire landholders following enclosures in an attempt to discover what happened to the group she called the '18th-century peasantry'. She maintained that villages at enclosure endured higher rates of turnover of small landholders, a reduction in the sizes of holdings and an overall decline in the numbers of smallholders. Neeson claimed that, at enclosure, two-thirds of the peasantry lost 20 per cent of their land within five years of the Act. In comparison, only one-third of the same class in the open field villages suffered the same fate. The difference between the two types of settlement was even greater if land sales caused by deaths were included. Further, Neeson also discovered that enclosure was coincident with a widening of the gap between large and small operators. After the demise of the open fields, there were fewer small owner-occupiers and tenants but more large tenants and landowners.

Patterns of land ownership amongst small landowners during the later period of enclosure (late 17th to mid-19th centuries) have been investigated by Professor J.V. Beckett,[40] who found that the accumulation of land by large estates was a long-term process which did not seem tied to any particular period. In some areas, landowning magnates obtained land to the exclusion of small-scale owners, but elsewhere it was newcomers who caused the skewed results which left small landowners at a disadvantage. Conversely, in other areas, local circumstances favoured the survival of small estates and landholdings. Beckett found that the period which saw the most growth in large estates was the 19th rather than the 18th century. More recently, he has concluded that there is little or no evidence to support the idea of a decline in the numbers of owners of 300 acres or less during the period 1690–1790. In some parts of the country, there may even have been a small increase in the numbers of such small landowners during the period of the wars with France. After 1815, though, he found a significant reduction in their numbers.[41]

While it is now accepted that the Marxist view of enclosure being used against the interests of the small farmer and the poor is far too simplistic, we have to ask why so many studies appear to display results which are often slightly at variance with each other. The reasons for these apparent differences fall into two groups. The first is concerned with terminology. Who do we mean by yeomen? Were they freeholders or large tenant farmers? Who were the small farmers? Were they tenant farmers or owner-occupiers? Then there were the labourers, cottagers, commoners and poor. Were they all the same people? Some writers have used the term 'peasants' but were there really such people in England in the 18th and 19th centuries? Any study which seeks to determine the effects of enclosure on the less-well-off must first define its study group. Perhaps they can be described in terms of the amount of land they held; less than an acre, for example, or less than five acres or less than 20 acres. Whether they held the land as freeholders, copyholders or leaseholders is also important in identifying the study group.

The second group of reasons for differences in results arises from the documentary evidence and the way in which it is used. In order to find out if any particular group suffered or gained at enclosure, it is clearly necessary to be able to say who owned or rented what, before and after the process. An enclosure Award is an excellent documentary source for establishing who the landowners were at that particular time. The claims submitted by owners of land or common rights in the open fields before an enclosure might also provide an accurate picture of the state of affairs in the weeks or months immediately beforehand. Unfortunately, these documents do not show whether there was already a trend in changes of landownership patterns before the project was initiated, nor what happened in the years after the reading of the Award. In order that trends in land ownership both before and after an enclosure can be traced, it is necessary to find appropriate documentary records of land tenure that span the entire period under study. Figure 41 is a copy of a Land Tax Assessment— in this case for Mickleton, in the North Riding—for the year 1801 and it is this documentary source which has been used by a number of historians to map the fortunes of large and small landowners. Neeson's study mentioned above, for example, was based on the Land Tax Assessments for 1,598 Northamptonshire proprietors, three-quarters of whom lived in parishes which were enclosed between 1778 and 1814, the remainder being open field at that time.

LAND TAX ASSESSMENTS AS DOCUMENTARY SOURCES

How did Land Tax work and how useful are its records in the study of land tenure before and after an enclosure? Land Tax was introduced in the latter years of the 17th century. By the 1700s, it was nominally a tax on land but, to avoid evasion, it became not a personal tax but one in which county, hundred and parish quotas were set. The quotas became fixed and this was confirmed by law in 1798. This remained the case until the Land Tax was eventually abolished in 1963.[42] By the 18th century, then, there was no direct relationship between the quantity of land and the amount of tax paid on it, as it was not charged on an acreage rate. The tax assessments for any particular parcel of land were arrived at in the early years and remained at that level. The parish assessment was drawn up locally, often by several of the farmers who acted as assessors. In 1780, central government directed that duplicates of the assessments were to be kept by clerks of the peace so that they could be used in lieu of an electoral register to establish which members of the parish were entitled to vote. As a result, the Quarter Sessions records in many county record offices include good runs of the duplicate Land Tax Assessments (LTAs) from that date until 1832 when, with the passing of the Reform Act, the Land Tax was no longer useful for electoral purposes.

The LTA duplicates appear in a tabular form, usually similar to that in Figure 41. Each entry consists of the owner's or proprietor's name, the occupier's name and the amount of tax which has been assessed. Sometimes, the entry shows that a particular parcel of land has been exonerated from the annual payments. This would have followed a single, large payment by the proprietor in lieu of all subsequent payments. The entries for the larger landowners might show the nature of their title to the land or its source. For example, the entry might show that the land had been purchased or inherited from a previous owner.

Figure 41 Mickleton Land Tax Assessment, 1801

[Source: D/St/E3/19/13, Durham Record Office, Mickleton LTA (1801). Reproduced by permission of Lord Strathmore.]

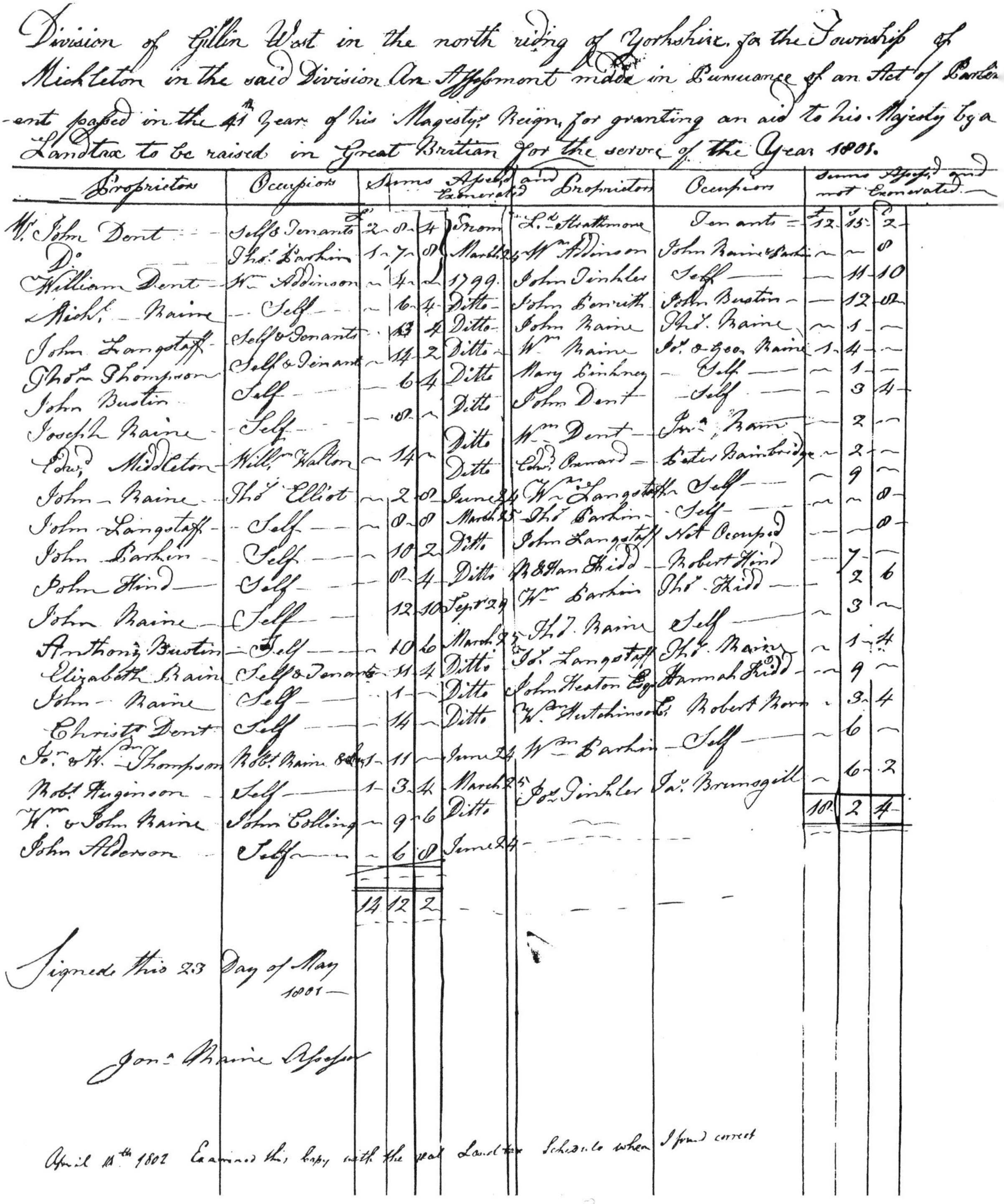

The appearance of LTAs and their duplicates is attractive to the economic historian who is immediately drawn to their neat columns of figures and names which cry out for conversion to a computer database or spreadsheet. There are, however, many traps for the unwary who hope to use them to identify the small landowners and thence to chart their survival following an enclosure. The first has already been mentioned—because the amount of tax on each piece of land was settled early, by the end of the 18th century it bore little relationship to the actual area of land. In one Northamptonshire parish, in 1810, land was taxed variously at the equivalent of 5p per acre through to £1.21 per acre with a mean average of 5.2p.[43] Because of this range and the basis for the calculation of the tax, it is not possible to work back to deduce the area of land on which it was levied. Were this possible, the LTAs could be used to find out the size of each proprietor's landholding and hence identify precisely who the small landowners were before and after enclosure.

Second, the assessments often do not identify the land to which each entry relates, nor even if it is land or a cottage or farmhouse. When land changed hands, quite often the only way to identify the new owner in the following year's assessment is to match the amount of tax which had been assessed because, as we have seen, the tax was usually the same.

There is a third trap. While the LTAs for a single parish might suggest the identity of a small landowner of, say, 50 acres, he may easily have owned 500 acres in another parish or be a substantial tenant farmer elsewhere. There is also the duplication of family names such as John Smith or Daniel Smith. The LTAs are far from being trouble-free, but this is not to say that they have no use at all. In a study of land turnover in Buckinghamshire, Turner recognised many of the problems of Land Tax Assessments.[44] He only used the returns to map the names of the proprietors over time. By this means, he was able to establish when the greatest changes in names occurred. He investigated 60 Buckingham-shire villages, each over a 10-year period. This included the three to four years before an enclosure, the three to four years during the process of the enclosure and the three to four years after the enclosure had been completed. Three types of village were studied: those with old enclosures; those which had comparatively recent enclosures (within the past 20 years), and those which were in the process of being enclosed.

Turner listed all the names which appeared on the assessments at the beginning of the study period and then again at the end. In the old enclosed and the recently enclosed parishes, he found that the turnover was no higher than one would expect in a time of healthy land markets. Similarly, the total number of small landowners declined only very slightly. More pronounced changes in names were found in the villages undergoing enclosure but the total number of small landowners appeared to increase. This was because former common right owners received land in lieu and so were recognised for the first time following enclosure and included in the Land Tax Assessments. Where a noticeable decline in the numbers of small landowners did occur, this was due, claims Turner, to their leaving the land to avoid perceived enclosure costs rather than their being bought out, for example, as opponents of enclosure by other landowners.

While Turner examined a large number of enclosures in this way, there is no reason why a study should not be confined to one village. In such a case, it might be valuable to include a wider period on either side of the enclosure, perhaps 10 years before and 10 years after and compare the annual turnover in names. Alternative sources to LTAs include property deeds but these are not always comprehensive for a particular parish. They remain, though, one of the most numerous of extant documentary sources. Most county record offices hold hundreds, in some cases thousands, of them, very few of which are used by local historians. Where they are extant, they show transfers of freehold land and may indicate trends of land transactions before and after an enclosure. For more information on property deeds, researchers are recommended to consult *Old Title Deeds: A Guide for Local and Family Historians* by N.W. Alcock.[45]

Another little used documentary source is manorial surrenders which can be used instead of, or as well as, Land Tax records in studies of land tenure before and after enclosure. The system varied from manor to manor and the surrenders themselves can be found in various forms, sometimes as small individual sheets of paper but, in other cases, in ledger form. They relate only to copyhold land and not all manors seem to have used them. The principle behind surrenders was that the land, being copyhold, did not belong to the copyhold tenant but to the lord of the manor. By the late 18th and early 19th centuries, this basic fact was easily overlooked. The lord of the manor received only a nominal rent, sometimes known as a quit rent, and had little to do with the land and property so held. Many manorial lords gave up any serious interest in the land but the annual quit rent prevented the complete loss of title.

Because the land did not belong to the copyhold or customary tenant, it was not theirs to sell or bequeath to someone else. Despite this, by the 19th century there was an established market in copyhold land. The way in which the land transactions were conducted was quite different from that for freehold land. Because the lord of the manor was still the recognised owner, all the transactions were conducted through him or his steward. Someone relinquishing his title to the land would *surrender* it to the manor court. Often, this was done by surrendering it *by the rod* to the court, whereby a wooden rod, which symbolised the land under consideration, was handed to the steward or one of the other court officials. This process was called an Absolute Surrender. The new tenant accepted the land by the rod from the steward in a reverse of the process which was recorded in the court minutes and entered on the court roll. This system protected the rights to the title of the land because of the copy of the minutes preserved on the roll—hence it was called copyhold. The fee that the new tenant paid the old tenant was also recorded. Mortgages could also be raised in a similar way and the mortgage lender's name would be recorded and perhaps also the terms of the mortgage including the rate of interest. Such mortgages could be raised to pay an individual proprietor's enclosure rate. This process was called a Conditional Surrender.

Dating from April 1770, Figure 42 shows an example of a conditional surrender used to raise a short-term loan.[46] Hannah Pettit, a widow, and her son Laurence, surrendered an acre of arable land in Fittledine Field (usually called Fettledine Field), two acres in Knightland Field and three doles of meadow in Marsh Meadow to the use of William

---

Figure 42 *(opposite)*   Conditional Surrender, Manor of Irthlingborough, 1770

[Source: Irthlingborough Conditional Surrender (1770), Dean and Chapter, Pet. Cath. (in X5143), Northamptonshire Record Office. Reproduced by permission of Peterborough Cathedral, Dean and Chapter.]

Manor of Irthlingborough

Be it Remembered that on the tenth day of April in the year of our Lord One thousand seven hundred and Seventy Hannah Pettit Widow and Laurence Pettit customary Tenants of the said Manor Did out of Court by the Rod according to the Custom of the said Manor Surrender into the Hands of the Lords of the said Manor by the Hands and acceptance of Thomas Croxton and William Lilley two like customary Tenants there All that One acre of arable Land lying in a certain ffield called ffittleditto ffield And all those two Acres of Arable Land lying in Knightsland ffield And also three Doles of meadow lying in a certain place called marsh meadow All which said premises are lying and being in Irthlingborough aforesaid and holden of the said Manor and were late the estate of Elizabeth Smith Widow together with all and singular the Rights members Hereditaments and appurtenances whatsoever to the said premises every or any part thereof belonging or appertaining To the Use and Behoof of William Wallis the Elder of Irthlingborough aforesaid yeoman his Heirs and assignes forever according to the Custom of the said Manor.

Provided always and upon this condition that if the said Hannah Pettit and Laurence Pettit or either of them their or either of their Heirs Executors or Administrators do and shall well and truly pay or cause to be paid unto the said William Wallis his Executors Administrators or assignes the full Sum of Twenty five pounds with lawful Interest for the same on the tenth day of October next ensuing the date hereof And that without any Deduction or abatement thereof or thereout to be made for Taxes or otherwise Then the said Surrender to be void or else to be and remain in full force.

Taken the Day and Year
abovewritten by us
Thomas Scroxon
William Lilley

Hannah Pettit
the mark X of
Laurence Pettit

The Original Surrender whereof the abovewritten
is a Copy is in my Hands

Thomas Scroxson

Wallis. They were to repay £25 plus interest by the following October to Wallis in order to cancel the surrender.

Where the original tenant wished to leave the land to his son or other heirs, it was again performed via the lord of the manor's court. Here, the original tenant was said to be *surrendering his land to his will*. After his death, his heir would approach the court and accept the land by the rod and his name would be entered into the minutes and onto the roll. In both cases, the surrenders, however they were recorded, provide an excellent record of copyhold land transactions before and after an enclosure. In some parts of the country, by the mid-19th century the copyhold land market was almost as extensive as its freehold counterpart. Not all manors operated such systems, though, and so survival of manorial surrenders is patchy; where they can be found, they can be used to examine the fortunes of all the customary tenants—both large and small, before and after an enclosure. Where significant differences in the patterns are found, they might reasonably be attributed—at least in part—to the introduction of enclosure.

ENCLOSURE AS A MEANS OF IMPROVEMENT

> And whereas the said several Lands and Grounds lie intermixed, and for the Most part inconveniently situate, and in their present State capable of but little Improvement, and it would be advantageous to the several Proprietors to have the same divided and enclosed, but such Division and Inclosure cannot be effected without the Aid of Parliament …

These words taken from the preamble to many Enclosure Acts contain the important implication of a connection between enclosure and the need for agricultural improvement. Although such phrases became stylised, originally there had doubtless been a more substantive motive for their inclusion in so many Bills and Acts. Few writers today claim that enclosure was the sole means whereby the agricultural improvements of the 18th and 19th centuries became possible. G.E. Mingay,[47] for example, took the view that enclosure did not carry the economic advantages that had formerly been attributed to it; other writers have adopted more optimistic views of the open fields as efficient agricultural units. D. McCloskey has drawn attention to the open-field system as a means whereby individual operators enjoyed a fair and equal distribution of good and bad land across the manor. This insured them against extreme losses in bad years.[48] E. Kerridge, also writing in defence of the open-field system, claimed that the individual farmer enjoyed considerable freedom in his choice of crops within the confines of his own strips.[49] J.V. Beckett, in particular, refutes any notion of a dramatic improvement in agricultural techniques after enclosure. As he points out, immediately following the demise of the open fields, the principal operators were the same people as before and they had the same outlook. It would have been surprising, therefore, if agricultural methods on most of the holdings underwent a sudden programme of innovation.[50] After investigating enclosure in England and Wales, M.E. Turner concluded that, 'the inefficiency of the open fields is by no means as plain and obvious as it once seemed'.[51]

Why then did the enclosers of the 18th and 19th centuries imply that the open fields were barriers to agricultural improvement? The argument was re-examined in the 1980s by

Turner who once more highlighted enclosure as an important factor in the adoption of new agricultural techniques.[52] Accepting that enclosure alone had not brought about a rapid revolution in agricultural methods, he believed, nevertheless, that it could allow agriculture to become more efficient. Many of the new techniques developed during the 18th century, for example, were better suited to enclosed land than open-field farming.

There are two interpretations of the notion of improvement, each distinct from the other but inter-related. The first was concerned with the rental value of the land and was explained by the Warwickshire enclosure commissioner, Rev. Henry Homer. The 'General Improvement of the Field' which was a result of enclosure was the increase in the monetary value of land. It was calculated following the completion of the general survey and was explained by Homer as follows:

> Supposing that the rents of an open field before enclosure, are seven hundred and fifty pounds, and the whole of what are set out for the proprietors, amounts according to the valuation and survey, to fifteen hundred; then the field is said to improve from seven hundred and fifty to fifteen hundred or to double its value.[53]

It can be seen that this calculation depends on the rents being received before enclosure and the surveyor's opinion of what rent it could attract after (following subtraction of the value of land used for new roads or other works). If, as part of this calculation, the surveyor took into consideration the rents being received from other, already enclosed villages, there was a likelihood of an inflationary cycle with high rents in the first enclosed parish causing higher rents in the next and so on. Homer, however, recognised that the General Improvement need not be as high as in his example. If existing rents were already high, this would have an adverse affect. This could occur in at least two ways. First, if a substantial proportion of the open field to be enclosed was meadow, let annually on a rack rent, little improvement was possible. Secondly, if the field to be enclosed was made up of small parcels or tenancies, these too, because of a demand for such plots, would already attract higher than average rents. Therefore, little extra revenue was to be gained following enclosure.

The other interpretation of 'improvement' is the purely agricultural one, which itself has two aspects. It can be expressed in terms of either the process or the product: that is to say, we can look at the agricultural processes before, during and after the period of parliamentary enclosure, or we can look at the results in terms of total agricultural output. The latter is the more direct, since this was the ultimate aim of all improvements. Successful improvements in total agricultural output could take several forms: increased yields, increased areas being farmed, or improved balances between arable and animal husbandry. The benefits of General Improvement as expressed by Homer were virtually immediate. Enclosure was accompanied by new leases and rental agreements. The benefits of agricultural improvement were much more long-term as they arose out of more efficient practices and the availability of improved implements and livestock.

There are a number of problems for those researching agricultural output because the process of improvement did not automatically achieve the required ends. First, there were many improving ideas which may not have worked but which were nevertheless innovative and may have led to other ideas and developments. Even the successful ideas may not have yielded immediate results in terms of improved productivity. Improvements to drainage and crop fertilisation may have taken several seasons before the benefits began to appear. The results of improvements in the production of fodder crops which were consumed by livestock on the same farm would have been masked for several years and even then distorted by the prevailing market prices of meat. For example, Leicester sheep, a popular breed in the mid-19th century, could be sent to market as fat lambs at only 18 months old, having been fattened on the fodder from only one or two seasons.[54] Beef cattle, however, might wait as long as three years before being sold to the butcher. Thus improvements to fodder crops could be slow in producing increases in revenue. When the vagaries of market prices are added to the equation (the average price of meat could be unusually low at the time of slaughter owing to unforeseen circumstances), it can be seen that calculating the effects of changes on fodder production is an imprecise art.

Apart from the aspects of agricultural improvement outlined above, two central questions can be addressed when examining the effects of enclosure. First, is there evidence of improvements being made in agriculture during the enclosure period? Second, to what extent did these improvements depend on the enclosure itself?

Enclosure and the subsequent farming in severalty would have led to a greater personal autonomy in farmers' crop planning and other decision making. This, for example, would be evident in the decision to concentrate production on either cereals or beef or mutton. If it could be shown that more farmers in enclosed villages were actively taking such a decision and changing their cropping patterns (and presumably improving the total agricultural product of their farm), it would be fair to attribute at least some of this change to enclosure.

What, then, are the documentary sources that make studies of agricultural improvement possible? First come the county reports drawn up in the late 18th and early 19th centuries for the Board of Agriculture. These reports were very detailed accounts of the state of agriculture, researched and written by experienced practitioners of the art. They describe soils, crops, implements, animals, manure and other aspects of husbandry. Few counties had more than one such report and so it is difficult to use them in a comparative way. In any case, their timing with the enclosure of the study parish is purely coincidental. Similarly, in the later 19th century there were the Prize Essays submitted to the *Journal of the Royal Agricultural Society*. These too provide accurate information about the state of agriculture in many counties. Copies of both of these sources can be found in some county record offices, local studies libraries or university libraries.

THE CROP RETURNS

In any study of agricultural improvement over an enclosure period, another very important documentary source is the Home Office crop returns or grain surveys. From 1793 until 1815, Britain was at war with France. In 1794 a dry summer led to a poor harvest and by the following year wheat had risen in price from 52s. 3d. per quarter to 75s. 2d.—an increase of 44 per cent. This was followed by two more poor harvests and by 1796 the average price had reached 78s. 7d. per quarter—an overall increase of 51 per cent. Thereafter, prices began to fall back to their original levels but in 1800, following an extremely wet summer the previous year, the price rocketed to 113s. 10d. per quarter and then to 119s. 6d. the following year.[55]

The Home Office responded to the food shortages by conducting a number of grain surveys. Of these surveys, the one carried out in 1801 is the most comprehensive and the most statistically reliable source of information on the state of agriculture.[56] In practice, information is given on a range of arable crops, not just cereals. They are relatively accessible since, apart from the original returns which are kept at the Public Record Office, the List and Index Society have produced county-by-county abstracts which are typewritten.[57] Copies of them can be found in local studies libraries and university libraries.

Depending on the timing of the enclosures, the crop returns offer detailed information about the acreages of crops being grown in each parish. Typical studies using this source compare the agriculture of two groups of parishes, one group enclosed before 1801 and the other group enclosed after 1801, the differences being assumed to be, partly at least, due to the enclosure.

Although an apparently objective source of information, the validity of the returns has to be considered. The main problem lies in the way that the original data was collected. Responsibility for this was delegated by the Home Secretary to the Anglican dioceses and by them to the parish incumbents. Many of this latter group were tithe-holders and, when they tried to question the farmers about their crops, some were understandably met with suspicion and sometimes outright hostility. The reporters for the Northamptonshire parishes of Boughton, Brigstock, Byfield, Long Buckby, Middleton Cheney and Watford all recorded in their analysis that they believed the totals supplied to them to be under estimates. At three other villages[58] the farmers refused point blank to co-operate and would have nothing to do with the incumbents' questions. One indignant reporter noted that the task of collecting the required data ought not to be carried out by the tithe-holder. 'Besides,' he went on, 'the clergy need not be degraded by such employment at a time when every ill-disposed person can open a conventicle for schism and sedition at the easy price of sixpence!'

TITHE FILES

This leads to the final, major source of data for studies of agricultural improvement at the time of enclosure, particularly during the first half of the 19th century. In the early years of that period, tithes were still being paid in much of England and Wales although, by this time, payment in kind was no longer the sole method of doing so. Despite the introduction in many districts of a modus—a cash payment in lieu of tithes—there was a growing dissatisfaction with the system. It was even suggested that tithes were a disincentive to agricultural improvement because a tenth of any increased output was lost to the tithe-holder.[59] The 1836 Tithe Commutation Act was designed to resolve this problem by replacing tithes in kind with corn rents or tithe rent charges.

The Tithe Commission sent assistants to each tithe district to assess the situation and to arrive at what was, ultimately, a compulsory agreement between the tithe-holder and the tithe-payers. They found that many parishes in the counties with the highest levels of parliamentary enclosure had converted the tithes into a one-off payment—land. Where this was not the case, a long and detailed questionnaire was completed which described the tithe district, its pattern of agriculture and what action the tithe commissioners had decided upon. These questionnaires or *Reports on Agreement*, together with any correspondence, statements or other information, were entered into files[60] and have been the basis of much work carried out in recent years by R. Kain.[61]

Whereas the crop returns offered a parish breakdown of crops, the tithe files give parish breakdowns of land. It amounts almost to the same thing, except that the tithe files are less precise, especially regarding minority crops. Usually, they give the total area of the titheable land (not all land in the parish was subject to tithes—the glebe farm, for example). There is a brief description of the parish which usually indicates whether it is open or enclosed. There is then a breakdown of the titheable land to show how many acres are set down as arable, how many as grass, how many as woods and so on. There is sometimes information about the glebe farm, and the area of common land may also be given. The arable land is further broken down to show how much is given over to fallow, turnips and other roots, barley, wheat, oats, peas and beans or other important crops. The files sometimes offer other miscellaneous information about the parish as well as data concerning crop rotation. Tithe files are a valuable source of information but, despite the work of Kain, remain very much under used. This may be because most are only available at the Public Record Office in Kew and none but the keenest historian seems willing to make the journey. For those that do, they are rewarded with an interesting and easy to use documentary source.

OPPORTUNITY COST OF ENCLOSURE

The issues surrounding the cost of introducing an enclosure have been discussed. Another facet that has not been explored is the opportunity cost of enclosure and its worth as a form of investment. The opportunity cost of enclosure was that incurred by not spending the money on alternative investments. By the 19th century, it was known that land could very soon double in value following an enclosure. This was not always the case, and other forms of investment beckoned. The returns on Consols and Navy Stock, for example, offered attractive alternatives. The way in which opportunity cost may have affected the timing of enclosures can be investigated to improve our understanding of the mechanisms involved. We can ask, for example, if there is any connection, as C. Clay suggests,[62] between enclosure and the price of land or other contrasting forms of investment? If so, does this coincide with the economic returns and pattern of incidence of parliamentary enclosure? Arising from the question of costs and opportunity costs is that of where the money came from to finance enclosures? Prices of agricultural produce as well as government stocks were published in provincial newspapers, which are now readily available on microfilm in local studies libraries. The interrelated issues of investment, land price and opportunity costs can all be examined in studies of enclosure.

RURAL OCCUPATIONS AND OPPOSITION TO ENCLOSURE

It is possible to investigate the nature and extent of non-agricultural occupations and their relationship, if any, with enclosure. It is easy to imagine 18th-century Britain as being based purely on an agricultural economy but there were a large number of other established trades and occupations in the extractive industries, textiles, ship-building, boot and shoe, building and construction, forestry and craft industries.

Using as wide a range of sources as possible, including parish records such as Baptism Registers, many of the individual personalities from the study villages can be identified. Their occupations and the period of their active presence in the enclosure village can be mapped to provide an overall picture of the economic life of the community. In identifying the non-agrarians, using their own descriptions of themselves given in wills, parish registers, correspondence and other records, a register of alternative occupations can be compiled.

The aim of such an exercise is to explore a number of issues. First, what were the alternative occupations to land work before and after an enclosure and what was their extent? In particular, how did these other occupations compare with agriculture in terms of the number of employees? Arising out of this area of research is an investigation into the possibility that the presence of alternative occupations cushioned the economic effects of enclosure and that, further, those involved in such occupations benefited from enclosure in the short and medium terms. Early writers assumed[63] that one of the effects of enclosure was to expel agricultural labourers from the land, forcing them into the mines, factories and mills. If it can be shown that there were already plentiful job opportunities in the rural-based, non-agricultural trades and occupations, a reassessment of this view becomes necessary.

Second, opposition to parliamentary enclosure can be considered using the same data. The importance of the relationship between enclosure and the pattern of occupation, particularly the apparently non-agrarian occupations, has been accepted by a number of writers. It was J.M. Neeson's view, for example, that the non-agrarians formed the core of opposition to parliamentary enclosure. She suggests that villages which resisted enclosure were 'usually mixed agricultural and manufacturing rather than solely agricultural in economy'.[64] The relationship between opposition and non-agrarian workers can be examined and, in particular, comparisons between known riots and disturbances on the one hand and employment opportunities on the other can be drawn.

Other approaches to opposition movements can be looked at. E.P. Thompson pointed to the often subtle difference between opposition to enclosure and opposition to loss of common right[65] and noted that urban protests concerning loss of common rights following enclosure were more formidable, more visible and more successful than rural protests. This difference may have been partly accounted for by the increased numbers of protesters (and the resultant anonymity). Equally, though, the nature of opposition in the towns and larger villages may have resulted from differences in the nature of dependency on common rights of non-agricultural workers. It would be valuable to compare enclosures with known disturbances and opposition movements and to consider whether commons and common rights were indeed a determining factor.

Another facet to the opposition movements and enclosure riots were their similarity to the mainly later disturbances that followed the end of the agricultural boom in the early years of the 19th century. A sustained agricultural depression, coupled with a lack of confidence in the political and the poor law systems, led to a series of demonstrations and riots. The Swing Riots of 1830–1 were described by Mingay as a combination of peaceful demands for higher wages, machine breaking and armed menaces.[66] The depression which set in immediately after the end of the Napoleonic Wars in 1815 had led to a fall in agricultural wages, increases in the price of bread and the collapse of easy credit for farmers. By the late 1820s, the situation was no better, with droughts and poor harvests in the middle of the decade followed by wet harvests and sheep rot in 1828, 1829 and 1830.[67] With the exception of the winter of 1879–80, 1830 was claimed to be the worst year in either the 18th or 19th centuries for sheep rot—approximately two million animals were lost, leading to inflationary prices for wool.[68] Faced with low wages and expensive food, many agricultural labourers blamed new technology such as threshing machines for their plight. During the winter months, when there was little work on the land, labourers were employed to hand thrash the previous year's harvest. The new machines threatened to take over much of this work.

Protest was usually anonymous and took three forms: incendiary attacks on farmsteads, machinery breaking and animal maiming. In July 1830, John Pebody was acquitted of burning a straw stack at Little Bowden (then in Northamptonshire, now in Leicestershire) earlier in the year.[69] The acquittal was in spite of considerable circumstantial evidence. By October of the same year, news of unrest in other counties began to spread. A threshing machine and a large quantity of straw had been destroyed by fire at North Fen near Deeping in Lincolnshire. There was no doubt that it had been caused by arsonists.[70] By the end of the month, it was known that there had been outbreaks of trouble across a wide swathe of the country. In Kent, seat of many of the troubles, outsiders were blamed for burning a stack of wheat.[71] Suspicion rested on a respectably dressed stranger who had appeared some time before and predicted the blaze. Mingay classifies some of the rioters as educated or skilled craftsmen such as wheelwrights, carpenters, joiners, smiths, bricklayers and shoemakers.[72] The unrest was not confined to agricultural workers—in Cumberland, troops were summoned to deal with expected disturbances caused by the colliers.[73]

Back in Kent, at the scene of one fire at Otford, men smoking pipes stood around the blaze, hindering others who were attempting to quell the flames.[74] In neighbouring Surrey, a spate of fires broke out, including one at a farm which had survived seven or eight earlier attacks.[75] By the end of November 1830, the situation had worsened. Many Members of Parliament were reported absent from the House, having returned to their constituencies because of the disturbances there. Sir Robert Peel blamed the local magistrates for being too lenient.[76] At Banbury in Oxfordshire, a large mob assembled to burn effigies of political leaders and extended the fray to include the destruction of several threshing machines. In Northamptonshire, five men were committed to gaol for breaking a threshing machine at Warmington and a sixth man was arrested for trying to secure the escape of two of the others.[77] At Thrapston, a meeting was held on 30 November to organise a protection committee to guard 20 of the villages in that area.[78] Not all the labourers were protesters. When a large fire broke out at Higham Park, Higham Ferrers, the local fire engine turned out and was accompanied by a large body of labourers and shoemakers who assisted in the fire-fighting.[79] But, in December, a threshing machine was sawn up at Overstone Park[80] and five men were arrested at Watford (Northamptonshire) for being in the company of 'a great number of other persons' who had riotously met in the village and smashed a number of windows.

Giving evidence to a select committee some years later, one of William Cobbett's followers, John Houghton who, amongst other occupations, was a farmer, claimed that in

1830 farmers had paid inflated wages to their workers through fear.[81] Another witness, John Cooper, expanded on this: 'The men were paid by the farmer, more money for the same work performed, in consequence of the intimidation arising out of the fear of fires'.[82] He claimed to have had fires in his district and, as Mingay points out, outbreaks of animal maiming continued throughout the 1830s and arson occurred until the 1850s.

Were the enclosure disturbances of the 18th century connected with the later Swing Riots? Did communities have histories of protest and opposition and did those communities who opposed enclosure later attack the increasing mechanisation of farming? Sources for the local historian are the counter-petitions and correspondence generated at the time of enclosure and the newspaper reports and Quarter Sessions records which recorded the unseemly events of the 1830s.

From these and other topics, it can be seen that the topic of enclosure still has many questions to be answered. The local historian, whether professional or part-time, has much still to investigate. Enclosure, in all its forms and over such a long period of time, had a profound effect on both local and national society. These effects, many of which were complex and often apparently contradictory, were both social and economic. Only in recent years have we begun to understand the subtle way in which they came to bear on the rural way of life. There is still much to be uncovered before we know the complete story.

Epilogue
Enclosure and the Law Today

This book has looked at the history of enclosure, the way it was introduced, the types of documentary record that have survived and suggestions for lines of historical enquiry. What are the legal implications of Parliamentary Enclosure Acts today? Do they have any bearing on or relevance to country issues? In fact, there are at least 14 Public Enclosure Acts still on the statute books as well as others that are concerned primarily with commons. Then there are the many hundreds of Private Enclosure Acts passed in the 18th and 19th centuries. More than this, there are comparatively modern laws, regulations and legal precedents that build on the Enclosure Acts and which together form part of what we might call country law and country lore.

There are areas of legal activity and disputes where the rules and plans laid down by the early Enclosure Acts have either direct relevance today, being admissible evidence, or have been amended or supplemented by new regulations within the past few years. In this section, some aspects of modern law, as it is affected by Enclosure Acts and Awards, are described. Because of the volume of material, we can only scratch the surface here, but it is hoped that the reader will get an idea of the wealth of issues. Some of the legal matters that confront countryside dwellers today are surprisingly complex, but perhaps this should not be unexpected, a little over 200 years since the peak of enclosure activity saw off the remains of the open-field villages. The three broad areas covered here are: hedges, boundaries and public highways.

It should be stressed that anyone who is either considering a legal action or who has become the subject of one should take immediate advice from a lawyer who specialises in the appropriate area. Also, of the types of disputes which are described below, Enclosure Acts and Awards no longer always provide the solution. Indeed, in some areas of the country, enclosure by Act of Parliament was never or only rarely used.

HEDGES AND LEGAL BOUNDARIES

Hedging and fencing were fundamental components of enclosure, whether of open arable, common pasture, meadow, fen, moorland, mountain or heath. The principal aim was to establish farming in severalty—the division of the common land into discrete farms. Integral to this process was the creation of fields as we know them today. In some parts of the country, the fields were enclosed by stone walls and, where timber was more plentiful than stone, quickset hedging (hawthorn) was planted with wooden fences to protect the young plants, for the first seven to ten years. Most Enclosure Acts included several clauses which dealt with different aspects of hedging, fencing and walling. It might be helpful to consider some of them. Generally, there were two types of fencing in the new enclosures. First was the ring-fence which completely circumscribed each new farm, separating each from its neighbour. Each new landowner was required by the Act to erect or pay for his share of fencing. The Acts usually made several allowances for this and where, because of the local geography, one proprietor was forced to take on more than his share (in comparison with the size of his holding in the new enclosures), the Commissioners were usually empowered to compensate him. Some Enclosure Acts specified in detail the design of this public fencing, for example, by demanding post and rail fencing, walling or whatever. It was usual for the Acts to require a gap to be left in the fences between neighbouring farms for perhaps a year. This was to allow the farmers to move their implements and stock from their old open-field lands to their new enclosures.

If, however, a proprietor failed to complete his share of the fencing within a given period, usually a year from the signing of the Award, then the Act usually authorised the commissioners to refer the matter to the local Justices of the Peace. After a hearing, the Justices could order the commissioners or their agents to arrange for the fencing to be carried out. An account of the costs was to be written out and, in the presence of at least one credible witness, a copy was to be attached to some part of the premises in question. If the intransigent landowner failed to pay the fencing bill, the Justices could issue Warrants of Distress, leading to confiscation of personal goods to the same value.

The other type of fencing or hedging was sometimes called the private fencing, in that it included only field boundaries within each farm and so had no direct effect on other proprietors. In practice, the method used for these internal enclosures was no different from that for the ring-fencing. Unlike the public fencing, though, the landowner was under no legal compulsion to erect them within a particular timescale, he could choose his own style of fence, hedge or wall, and could even elect to do nothing (and some did!)

As we have seen, many Enclosure Acts included a clause which required the other proprietors to meet the cost of ring-fencing the incumbent's allotments and perhaps even maintain it for an agreed period, usually seven years. There was usually a clause which prevented the pasturing of lambs in any of the new enclosures for periods ranging from four to seven years. Lambs and sheep were not loathe to add young hawthorn to their daily diet despite the prickly nature of the forage. In some parts of the country, such as Devon and the North Riding of Yorkshire, this ban was extended to asses.

The Acts often prescribed other measures to enable the maintenance of fences during the first years following the signing of the Award. One regulation that appeared in many Enclosure Acts concerned freeboards. Although these remain largely unresearched, they were strips of land alongside a fenceline which were claimed by the owner of the other side. It may be that these were originally associated with parks or forests but by the 18th and 19th centuries, they were equally common for arable and waste land, particularly on parish boundaries. They do not appear to have accounted for much land—many parishes had none at all—but nevertheless they were allowed for in many Enclosure Acts. Some, without recognising their existence at all, included a clause for the benefit of new landowners who might find there was an existing freeboard on their allotment. For this to occur, the allotment had to be bounded on one side by an existing enclosure or parish boundary. The new landowner was allowed by the Act to enter on to the freeboard and fence and hedge it as though it were his own until such time as the neighbour who claimed it erected his own fences and hedges to include it with the rest of his land. As a permanent solution, a very few Enclosure Acts allowed the commissioners to test claims for freeboards and then award other land within the enclosing parish in exchange for the freeboard which was then extinguished.[1]

The first years were critical for the establishment of new quickset hedges. Many Acts recognised this by allowing farmers in the new allotments to enter upon their neighbour's land to carry out maintenance to hedges, mounds, ditches, fences, walls or whatever else marked the boundary. By this time the format and phraseology of Enclosure Acts had become highly stylised, but there were subtle differences between the measures laid down for hedges, ditches and boundaries and exactly what a proprietor could do on his neighbour's land and for how long. The Denford Act (Northamptonshire 1765), for example, allowed the new proprietors to erect a post and rail fence up to two feet from the outside of the ditches bounding their allotments.[2] This was to help preserve the new quicksets for the first 10 years. The Moulton Act (Northamptonshire 1772) allowed only seven years, during which time owners could erect post and rail or other fences and foot trenches within three feet of the opposite side of their ditches.[3] The Bedfordshire enclosure at Shelton (1794) allowed a maximum of four feet on the other side of the ditch for the erection of post and rail fencing and what it described as back-ditching or trenching of the posts, within the four feet.[4] Later it ordered the fence to be removed and the post holes and back-ditch to be filled in. Beyond this initial period, necessary to enable the new quickset hedges to become established, neither Acts nor Awards generally made any specific provision for a farmer to enter his neighbour's land to cut or lay his hedge. This raises two important questions. First, where was the legal boundary between two fields: was it the hedge, the centre of the ditch, the edge of the ditch or some other imaginary line on one side or the other? Second, does a landowner or his tenant have the right to enter his neighbour's property to carry out repairs and maintenance? The answers are vitally important because the boundaries and rights envisaged at the time of enclosure are still extant today and disputes about them regularly cause strife and ill-feeling between neighbours.

Unfortunately, the answers are not straightforward and are rarely, if ever, dealt with in detail by either Acts or Awards. First, the boundaries: by examining a large number of Enclosure Acts, it becomes apparent that, in any one, the necessary information is either incomplete or missing altogether. Only by combining what little information there is, can the intentions of the commissioners and surveyor be determined. There are common trends. Many Enclosure Acts required that a ditch should be constructed outside the hedge. Thus the hedge itself could not be the boundary but was to be planted firmly on the land owned by the proprietor to whom it was awarded and whom the Award declared was to be responsible for it. Some Acts ordered that this ditch was to be four feet wide from the lower table of the quicksets, meaning the roots of the new hedge. In practice, the ditch seems to have been dug first, along the edge of the proprietor's allotment, and the earth from it

---

Figure 43 *(opposite)*   Midlands enclosure hedging dating from 1778

[Source: RAF air photograph CPE/UK 1926, 3050 taken 16 January 1947. © British Crown Copyright, Ministry of Defence, reproduced with the permission of Her Majesty's Stationery Office.]

thrown up into a long mound along his side of the ditch; along the top of the mound were planted the quicksets.

In some less usual cases, the ditch was not specifically required by the Act but a four foot width for one was to be left.[5] It is apparent, from studying a great many such Acts, that the ditch was intended as the boundary, but this was not its main function, which was of course one of drainage. On light, well-drained land, drainage was not a problem and so ditches may not always have been dug; of those that were, some were filled over time with dead vegetation and silt.

Nevertheless, the assumption that the boundary was four feet from the hedge or, more properly in the case of a ditch, at the edge of the ditch farthest from the hedge, has become enshrined in local custom or at least has been believed to be so in many areas. This answers the first question posed earlier regarding the actual line of a boundary. Under this arrangement, there arose a legal concept known as the 'hedge and ditch presumption', which was explained in a boundary dispute in 1810 by Judge Lawrence:

> The rule about ditching is this. No man, making a ditch, can cut into his neighbour's soil, but usually he cuts it to the very extremity of his own land: he is of course bound to throw the soil which he digs out, upon his own land; and often, if he likes it, he plants a hedge on top of it ...[6]

So, today, the hedge and ditch presumption declares that the true boundary is the edge of the ditch furthest from the hedge unless evidence to the contrary can be produced.

This now allows an answer to the second question: is it possible to enter a neighbour's land to carry out repairs, hedgecutting and the like? In fact, it is not legally possible to do this under the Enclosure Acts, nor is it necessary because, as we can see from the hedge and ditch presumption, unless evidence to the contrary can be found, the hedge is not on a neighbour's land and, if the owner of the hedge doesn't mind occasionally working in a ditch, the hedge can be cut and laid without trespassing on either his neighbour's land or his good will. In practice, it is now possible to enter a neighbour's land under specific circumstances to carry out necessary work as new laws have been introduced to fill the legal gap left by the Enclosure Acts.[7]

ENCLOSURE HIGHWAYS

It would not be right to omit at least a brief mention of highways, many of which were first formed or at least confirmed as part of an enclosure by Act of Parliament. Most Awards will include mention of public carriage roads, public bridleways and public footpaths. In the 18th century, there seems to have been a tendency to accept the current layout of rights of way and to design the new enclosures within that framework. By the 19th century, enclosures carried out under the General Acts began by literally re-drawing the landscape and setting out the roads first. As a result, the new roads of the later enclosure period are generally much straighter than those in the older enclosed parishes. Exceptions to this were enclosures of open heathland and wastes in any period where the absence of an existing field system allowed the commissioners and surveyor to start from scratch. In whatever century the enclosure took place, the commissioners were usually forbidden in the Act from tampering with any turnpike roads which were privately managed by trusts. The same also came to apply to canals and canal property.

The Award always gives the width of public roads and the occurrence today of narrow lanes with wide verges is a legacy of this. This may have been because the traffic was less than envisaged but, more commonly, it was a reflection of the state of unmetalled roads in the 18th century when room had to be left for vehicles to move over into a shallower set of ruts. Footways were also comparatively wide, the dimensions being given in the Award. Despite the many legal changes during the 20th century concerning the management of public rights of way, in cases of dispute recourse to the enclosure Award may still provide the answer about the line and width of such routes.

THE ENCLOSURE INHERITANCE

Enclosure Acts were among Parliament's first entry into the arena of rural justice, gradually replacing common law and customary practice with statute law. So effective were the 18th-century politicians that their laws changed for ever the very appearance of the British landscape. The pattern of hedgerows, walls and drainage ditches is a legacy from that period. But that legacy extended beyond mere topographical features—it also encompassed the rights of individuals and groups. Whether it was the loss of common rights or the right to use an ancient forest track, enclosure affected almost everyone in the parish and beyond. As a further measure of the profound changes wrought by enclosure, we can see how the new rules and laws it introduced still influence the rhythm of the countryside. How many miles of public footpath, enjoyed today by an increasing number of walkers, were laid out by enclosure commissioners? And sadly, how many miles of enclosure hedge were lost during the period of mechanised farming following the Second World War?

Finally, the question must be asked, what if one of the Private Enclosure Acts of the 18th century were repealed? Would Laxton in Nottinghamshire no longer be the only open field village in England? In the introduction to her work on commoners, common rights and enclosure, J.M. Neeson described her first visit to Laxton and expressed her view of the old, pre-enclosure, way of life:

> After years of thinking about commoners I went to see Laxton in Nottinghamshire last year. I had not gone before because I did not expect much: I knew most of the fields were no longer held in common. In the end I went because I saw a film about it made in the 1940s. For a few minutes on the screen I saw men sowing seed broadcast together, talking across the furrows. The image stayed with me. When I got to Laxton, it was late afternoon. I was tired because it had taken a long time to get there. But when the road dipped down under the railway bridge on the western side of the parish and came up next to the old common, without doubt it invaded an older world. The description of common fields as open fields is entirely appropriate. Distances are shorter when fields are in strips. You can call from one to the next. You can plough them and talk across the backs of the horses at the same time. You can see at a glance whose bit of the hedges or mounds need fixing, what part of the common ditch is choked with weeds. Standing at the centre of the village feels like standing at the hub of the whole

system: the fields spread out around you, the decision to sow one with wheat, another with barley is written on the landscape. For all that individual men and women work their own bits of land, their economy is public and to a large degree, still shared.[8]

Could villages be returned to the open field agriculture that has survived at Laxton? If an enclosure were reversed today, it is unlikely that the villagers could return to the bucolic paradise envisaged by Dr. Neeson. Whatever the answer, the prospect of a return to a less-pressured lifestyle is attractive to many people and the mechanism that changed rural life forever is still resented by many. As John Clare put it:

> Inclosure came and trampled on the grave
> Of labour's rights and left the poor a slave ...[9]

And there the matter lies. Given the recent uses made of Enclosure Acts by environmental campaigners, consideration of the *anti*-enclosure writing of the poet, John Clare, actually provides a delicious irony. Clare was no friend of enclosure and despised the new enclosure fences. His poem *The Mores* includes the lines:

> ... Fence now meets fence in owners little bounds
> Of field and meadow large as garden grounds
> In little parcels little minds to please
> With men and flocks imprisoned ill at ease ...[10]

Clare was undoubtedly opposed to enclosure and the loss of the commons, moors and heaths on social and environmental grounds. Through his poetry and prose, he was an environmental campaigner before there was such a body of people. Nevertheless, he was defeated by the enclosure laws which had been introduced to improve agricultural efficiency.

Enclosure was not an entirely bad thing though. It created a strong agricultural economy that arguably helped to found an empire. More importantly today, we have inherited a unique landscape and, with all its many imperfections, the right to walk and ride through much of it. As we consider the new Right to Roam measures, we might reflect upon the fact that many of our existing rights in the countryside were enshrined in the Enclosure Acts of the 18th and 19th centuries that caused Clare and others so much anguish.

Notes

Preface

1 Mortimer, I. (ed.), *Record Repositories in England* (1997), ISBN 1 873 162 54 5.

Introduction, pp.1–9

1 Wordie, J.R., 'The Chronology of English Enclosure, 1500–1914', *Ec.HR*, 2nd ser. 36 (1983), p.483.
2 Chapman, J. and Seeliger, S., 'Enclosure by Non-Parliamentary Means: Some Comments on the Records', *Archives*, 22, No. 95 (1996), p.100.
3 Thirsk, J., 'Enclosing and Engrossing' (gen. ed. Finberg, H.P.R.), *The Agrarian History of England and Wales*, 4 (1967), p.201.
4 Watts, K., 'Wiltshire Deer Parks: An Introductory Survey', *The Wiltshire Archaeological and Natural History Magazine*, 89 (1996), pp.88–98. Watts, K., 'Some Wiltshire Deer Parks', *The Wiltshire Archaeological and Natural History Magazine*, 91 (1998), pp.90–102.
5 ibid., pp.92–3 and 95–8.
6 Hoskins, W.G., *The Making of the English Landscape* (1955, reprinted 1986), pp.20–32.
7 Seebohm, F., *The English Village Community* (1915), the argument is carried throughout large sections of the work but see particularly Chapter 10, pp.368–411.
8 Thirsk, J., *Alternative Agriculture* (Oxford, 1997), p.8.
9 Rous, J., *Historia Regum Angliae* (c.1459, 2nd ed. Oxford, 1745).
10 Fryde, E.B. and Fryde, N., 'Peasant Rebellion and Peasant Discontents' (ed. Miller, E.), *The Agrarian History of England and Wales*, 3 (Cambridge, 1991), pp.810–1.
11 Rous, *Historia …*
12 Leadham, I.S., *The Domesday of Inclosures*, 2 (1897), p.521.
13 Thirsk, 'Enclosing and Engrossing', p.204.
14 ibid.
15 More, Sir T., *Utopia* (1516–17).
16 Thirsk, 'Enclosing and Engrossing', p.223.
17 Gay, E.F., 'The Midland Revolt and the Inquisitions of Depopulation', *Trans. RHS*, N.S. 18 (1904).
18 Depopulation Act, 39 Eliz. cap. 2 (1597).
19 Stow, J., *Annals* (1615), p.889, quoted in Tate, W.E., 'Inclosure Movements in Northamptonshire', *NP and P.*,1, No. 2 (1949), p.19.
20 Hall, D.N., *The Open Fields of Northamptonshire* (Northampton, 1995), p.322.
21 Gay, 'The Midland Revolt …', pp.195–244.
22 Bridges, J., *The History and Antiquities of Northamptonshire* (Oxford, 1791), p.206.
23 Gay, 'The Midland Revolt …'.
24 ibid., p.215.
25 Thirsk, 'Enclosing and Engrossing', p.233.
26 Gilbert, K., *Life in a Hampshire Village: The History of Ashley* (Winchester, 1992).
27 Morris, J. and Draper, J., 'The 'Enclosure' of Fordington Fields and the Development of Dorchester, 1874–1903', *Dorset Natural History and Archaeological Society Proceedings*, 117 (1995), pp.5–14.
28 Private Inclosure Agreement, Maidford, 23 August 1585, in Box X 5265 (Grant of Litchborough MSS), uncatalogued as at 6 June 1999. The Agreement does not contain any information regarding its authority. In particular, it does not explain how the Arbitrators were appointed other than that they were to represent the interests of all the parties to the agreement and not just the mesne lord of the manor. There is no indication that the agreement was enrolled in any of the Courts of Record but it appears to have been a mutual agreement arrived at by all the parties and drawn up by someone with legal training such as a local solicitor. The enclosures so created seem to have been accepted as legitimate by the Parliamentary Commissioners in 1778.

Northamptonshire Record Office.

29 Sparsholt, Hampshire, T4/2/6/45, Winchester Cathedral Archives: Note in Chapman and Seeliger, 'Enclosure by Non-Parliamentary Means', p.103.

30 Chapman and Seeliger, 'Enclosure by Non-Parliamentary Means …', p.106.

31 See, for example, the series of agreements for Abington, Northampton, where approximately 280 acres were enclosed by agreement in c.1604 but then ratified in 1640 by an exemplification of a Chancery Decree. The agreement included the exchange of a piece of enclosed glebe with land in the demesne farm. T(a) 1, Thornton MSS, Northamptonshire Record Office.

32 CP43/789 rot 400, PRO, cited by Chapman and Seeliger, 'Enclosure by Non-Parliamentary Means', p.101.

33 Beresford, M.W., 'Commissioners of Enclosure', Ec.HR, 2nd ser. 16 (1946), p.131.

34 Crowther, J., Enclosure Commissioners and Surveyors of the East Riding (Beverley, 1986), pp.11–12.

35 Henlow enclosure map, Bedfordshire Record Office.

36 CRES 28/5, Public Record Office, Reports of the Commissioners of Inquiry into the Woods, Forests and Land Revenues of the Crown: Reports to Parliament (c.1790s).

37 Parton, A.G., 'Parliamentary Enclosure in Nineteenth-Century Surrey – Some Perspectives on the Evaluation of Land Potential', Ag.HR, 33 (1985), p.51.

Chapter 1: Non-Parliamentary Enclosure, pp.10–27

1 Leadham, I.S., The Domesday of Inclosures (1897).

2 Gay, E.F. 'Inquisitions of Depopulation in 1517 and the Domesday of Inclosures', Trans. RHS., N.S. 14 (1900), pp.195–244. Also see 'The Midland Revolt and the Inquisitions of Depopulation', Trans. RHS, N.S. 18 (1904); 'Inclosures in England in the Sixteenth Century', Quarterly Journal of Economics, 17 (1902–3).

3 Tate, W.E., A Domesday of English Enclosure Acts and Awards (ed. Turner, M.E.) (Reading, 1978).

4 Royal Pardon: Danyell Ward of Little Houghton, 20 June 1608. Davidge MSS, Northamptonshire Record Office

5 Jas. 1 (Sta. Cha. 8), Public Record Office.

6 Gifts and deposits, 30/38, Public Record Office.

7 For example see: Thoyts, E.E., How to Read Old Documents (1980), p.134 and pp.138–43; Stuart, D., Manorial Records (Chichester, 1992), pp.114–17.

8 Beresford, M.W., 'Glebe Terriers and open field Yorkshire', Yorkshire Archaeological Journal, 37 (1950), pp.325–68.

9 Watts, S., 'Glebe Terriers and Local History: Shifnal 1612–1853', Shropshire History and Archaeology, 71 (1996), p.136.

10 ibid.

11 Hall, D.N., The Open Fields of Northamptonshire, p.355.

12 Private Inclosure Agreement, Maidford, 23 August 1585, in Box X 5265 (Grant of Litchborough MSS), uncatalogued, Northamptonshire Record Office.

13 Private enclosure agreement by decree of the Court of Chancery, 18 July 1623. Two copies are extant, the first in Grant (Litchborough) MSS (old H5), now in X 5294, the other in the Knightley MSS, K 776. Both Northamptonshire Record Office.

14 D/DE 210 Licence to enclose, 1713, Glamorgan Record Office.

15 TF/576, Lease, 26 February 1728, Cornwall Record Office.

16 Campbell, B.M.S. 'The Extent and Layout of Common Fields in Eastern Norfolk', Norfolk Archaeology, 38 (1981), p.5.

17 Chapman, J. and Seeliger, S., 'Enclosure by Non-Parliamentary Means: Some Comments on the Records', Archives, 22, No. 95 (1996), p.105.

18 CHR 18, rentals and AMS 6106, map of Netherfield Hundred in the Rape of Hastings, East Sussex Record Office.

19 CHR 18/1, Rentals, Earl of Chichester, 1788, East Sussex Record Office.

20 Tyson, B., 'Murton Great Field, near Appleby', Trans. of the Cumberland & Westmorland Antiquarian & Archaeological Society, 92 (1992), pp.161–82.

21 Courtenay MSS, 1508/M/London, Devon (Exeter) Record Office.

Chapter 2: Processes of Parliamentary Enclosure: Stage I, pp.28–51

1 WPR 8/Acc. 630, Cumbria (Kendal) Record Office, Act for Inclosing Lands within the Townships or Divisions of Strickland Roger, Whinfell and Helsington, in the Parish of Kirkby, in the County of Westmorland ... [Royal Assent, 11 June 1838].

2 D. 9410, Dorset Record Office, letter, and Act to enclose Great Canford et al., 1805.

3 *The Poetical Works of William Cowper* (London and Edinburgh, c.1853), p.273.

4 L. 1258 M/SS/L/13, Devon Record Office, Act (1835) and miscellaneous papers.

5 GLY 3162, East Sussex Record Office, copy of the Act for enclosing Ashdown Forest and Broyle Park.

6 Searle, C.E., 'Customary tenants and the enclosure of the Cumbrian commons', *Northern History*, 29 (1993), pp.126–53.

7 See, amongst other titles, Young, A., *The Farmer's Tour through the East of England* (1771). Also the county reports by various authors for the Board of Agriculture in the late 18th and early 19th centuries.

8 KY 16/18, Dorset Record Office, letter, 12 April 1843.

9 KY 16/10, Dorset Record Office, letter, 29 September 1843.

10 D 4459/1/1/1, Derbyshire Record Office, letter, 8 December 1802.

11 DDIN 190, East Riding Record Office, note, 'Proposals for an Inclosure at Kilham', undated.

12 GLY 3163 and 3164, East Sussex Record Office, Agreement and copy, 26 June 1766.

13 ibid. and GLY 3165, East Sussex Record Office, Award, 4 March 1767.

14 DDX 309, East Riding Record Office, Etton Inclosure notebook, 2 August 1817.

15 DFFo/KY/16/40, Dorset Record Office, Beer Hackett enclosure; also, D 4459/1/149, Derbyshire Record Office, Kirk Ireton and Callow enclosure.

16 QSD IDS/2/9 Denbighshire Record Office, *Chester Courant*, Wednesday, 5 June 1850.

17 Stuart, D., *Manorial Records* (Chichester, 1992). See especially, pp.9–11.

18 Boxes X7484 and X7485, Northamptonshire Record Office. Partially uncatalogued Burnham, Son & Lewin MSS.

19 DDX 309, East Riding Record Office, Etton Inclosure notebook, minutes of proprietors meeting, 17 September 1817.

20 ibid., minutes of meeting held, 9 October 1817.

21 GLY 3162, East Sussex Record Office, copy of the Act for enclosing Ashdown Forest and Broyle Park.

22 Northamptonshire Inclosure Awards, Bound Volumes, Northamptonshire Record Office.

23 WD/HH/53, Cumbria (Kendal) Record Office, Dufton draft petition to enclose, c.1826.

24 Floor (Flower) enclosure, *Commons Journal*, p.600.

25 Mingay, G.E., *Parliamentary Enclosure in England* (Harlow, 1997), p.60.

26 D/St/E3/19/11(2), Durham Record Office, consents, c.1801.

27 D 4459/1/1/14, Derbyshire Record Office, consents, c.1802.

28 Cole, J., manuscript diary, *Northamptonshire Notes and Queries*, 2, 370, also reproduced in Jenkins, E., *Victorian Northamptonshire: the early years* (Rushden, 1993), p.188.

29 D/ELS M455, Hertfordshire Record Office, 'Orders for the Fields and Penalties', Maidford (1724).

30 Commander, J. (ed.), *Gilbert White's Year* (extracts from *The Garden Kalendar* and *The Naturalist's Journal*) (Oxford, 1982), p.10.

31 D/ELS M455, Hertfordshire Record Office, Presentment papers, Maidford.

32 *Notes and Queries*, 2nd ser. 10, p.285, reproduced in Morgan, *Harvesters*, pp.158–9; and Hutton, R., *The Stations of the Sun* (Oxford, 1997), p.335.

33 Humphries, J., 'Enclosures, Common Rights, and Women: The Proletarianisation of Families in the Late Eighteenth and Early Nineteenth Centuries', *JEH*, L (1990), pp.17–42.

34 Neeson, J.M., *Commoners: common right, enclosure and social change in England, 1700–1820* (Cambridge, 1993).

35 ibid., p.262.

36 ibid., p.262.

37 Turner, M.E., 'Economic Protest in Rural Society: Opposition to Parliamentary Enclosure in Buckinghamshire', *Southern History*, 10 (1988), p.100.

38 Neeson, *Commoners* ..., pp.269–70.

39 Turner, 'Economic Protest ...', p.105.

40 WDX 76, Cumbria (Kendal) Record Office, counter-petition, Ravenstonedale enclosure.

41 GLY 3172 and GLY 3173, East Sussex Record Office, counter-petitions.

42 GLY 3174, East Sussex Record Office, counter-petition, Broyle Park, 1767.

43 Anscomb, J.W., 'An Eighteenth Century Inclosure and Foot Ball Play at West Haddon', *Northamptonshire Past and Present*, 4 (Northampton, 1969), pp.177–8.

44 Mingay, G.E., *A Social History of the English Countryside* (1990), p.160.

45 Parliamentary Papers, *Report from the Select Committee on Agriculture with Minutes of Evidence*, 2 August 1837, p.449.

46 ibid., 4 March 1836, the evidence of John Houghton of Hannington and elsewhere, p.51.

Chapter 3: Processes of Parliamentary Enclosure: Stage II, pp.52–71

1 Mingay, G.E., *Parliamentary Inclosure in England* (Harlow, 1997), pp.59–60, based on Longleat MSS 845, Wiltshire Record Office.

2 Tate, W.E., *A Domesday of English Enclosure Acts and Awards* (ed. Turner, M.E.) (Reading, 1978), p.133.

3 ibid., p.280.

4 For this debate, see Turner, M.E., *English Parliamentary Inclosure: Its historical geography and economic history* (1980); Wordie, J.R., 'The Chronology of English Enclosure, 1500–1914', *Ec.HR*, 2nd ser. 36 (1983), pp.483-505; Chapman, J., 'The Nature and Extent of Parliamentary Enclosure', *Ag.HR*, 31 (1987), p.25; Walton, J.R., 'On Estimating the Extent of Parliamentary Enclosure', *Ag.HR*, 38 (1990), pp.79–82.

5 Bound Inclosure volumes, Northamptonshire Record Office, Wootton, 1778.

6 ibid., Hannington, 1803.

7 WQ/R/I Cumbria (Kendal) Record Office letter, George White to Messrs Caton & Beetson, 16 March 1803.

8 X7485, Uncatalogued B. S. & L. MSS, Northamptonshire Record Office.

9 Minutes of the House of Lords Committee, 14 March 1776, House of Lords Record Office.

10 Tate, *Domesday ...*, p.163.

11 L 1258/M/SS/L/13, Devon (Exeter) Record Office

12 Box 3/5, uncatalogued Honeybunn Sykes MSS, Northamptonshire Record Office; Shelton (Bedfordshire) Enclosure Act and Award.

13 Inclosure Act, Maidford, Northamptonshire (1778), House of Lords Record Office.

14 Chapman, J., *A Guide to Parliamentary Enclosures in Wales* (Cardiff, 1992), p.130.

15 ibid., p.54.

16 Northamptonshire Inclosure Awards, bound volumes, Northamptonshire Record Office

17 KY 16/23, Dorset Record Office, miscellaneous enclosure papers, *c.*1843–53.

18 KY 16/7, 16/38, Dorset Record Office, miscellaneous papers, *c.*1850.

19 Chapman, *A Guide ...*, p.60.

20 ibid., p.84.

21 ibid., p.109.

22 L 1258 M/SS/L/13, Devon (Exeter) Record Office Act for Inclosing Lands in the parishes of Tavistock, Milton Abbot, Brentor and Lamerton in the County of Devon ..., 3 July 1835.

23 D/St/E3/19/1, Durham Record Office, Draft Bill, Mickleton Moor, *c.*1801.

24 WPR 8/Acc. 630, Cumbria (Kendal) Record Office, Act for Inclosing Lands within the Townships or Divisions of Strickland Roger ..., 1838.

25 For example, the Moulton (Northamptonshire) enclosure, 1772.

26 For example, the Mickleton Moor enclosure, D/St/E3/19/1, Durham Record Office, Draft Bill, *c.*1801.

27 Private Act for enclosing Maidford, 1778, p.17.

28 Bound enclosure volume, DA/310, East Riding Record Office Etton enclosure, 1818.

29 Bound volumes, Northamptonshire Record Office, 1809.

30 ibid., 1819.

31 ibid., 1809.

32 Tate, *Domesday ...*, p.167.

33 ibid., p.149.

34 WPR 8/Acc. 630, Cumbria (Kendal) Record Office, Act for Inclosing lands within the Townships or Divisions of Strickland Roger ..., 1838.

35 Hammond, J.L. and B., *The Village Labourer, 1760–1832* (1911, 1978), pp.49–56.

36 During the first peak of enclosure activity in the late 1770s, many army officers and soldiers were fighting in the American War of Independence.

37 WPR 8/Acc. 630, Cumbria (Kendal) Record Office, Act for Inclosing lands within the Townships or Divisions of Strickland Roger …, 1838.

Chapter 4: Stage III: The Commissioners Take Over, pp.72–89

1 Homer, Rev. H., *An Essay on the Nature and Method of Ascertaining the Specifick Shares of the Proprietors, upon the Inclosure of Common Fields. With Observations upon the Inconveniences of Open Fields, and upon the Objections to their Inclosure particularly as far as they relate to the Publick and the Poor* (Oxford, 1766).

2 ibid., p.61.

3 Beresford, M.W., 'Commissioners of Enclosure', *Ec.HR*, 2nd ser. 16 (1946), p.131.

4 Turner, M.E., 'Enclosure Commissioners and Buckinghamshire Parliamentary Enclosure', *Ag.HR*, 25 (1977), pp.127–8. See also Turner, M.E., 'John Davis of Bloxham, Enclosure Commissioner', *Cake and Cockhorse* (1971), pp.175–7.

5 Hollowell, S.R., PhD Thesis, Nottingham University, 1998.

6 Mingay, G.E., *Parliamentary Enclosure in England* (Harlow, 1997), p.71.

7 Tate, W.E., *A Domesday of English Enclosure Acts and Awards* (ed. Turner, M.E.) (Reading, 1978), p.280.

8 ibid., p.228.

9 ibid., p.145.

10 ibid., p.62.

11 ibid.

12 ibid.

13 ibid., p.63.

14 Chapman, J., *A Guide to Parliamentary Enclosures in Wales* (Cardiff, 1992), pp.30–1.

15 Tate, W.E., *A Domesday of English Enclosure Acts and Awards* (ed. Turner, M.E.) (Reading, 1978), p.117.

16 ibid., p.119.

17 ibid., p.137.

18 X 7484-5, Burnham, Son and Lewin MSS, Northamptonshire Record Office.

19 ibid.

20 Honeybunn Sykes, Box 3/1, Northamptonshire Record Office.

21 Chapman, *A Guide* …, p.121.

22 D/LE/691, Flintshire Record Office, notice of perambulation of bounds, Kerry enclosure, 1 August 1797.

23 QSD/DS/2/11, Denbighshire Record Office, newspaper notices, c.1852, Ruthin enclosure.

24 WD/HH/137, Cumbria (Kendal) Record Office, miscellaneous working papers, Shap Rough Intake enclosure, c.1839.

25 D 4459/1/2, Derbyshire Record Office, Kirk Ireton claims, 1803.

26 D/St/E3/19/19(7), Durham Record Office, Mickleton enclosure, John Smith of Sunderland – Claims.

27 D/St/E3/19/22(1), Durham Record Office, Mickleton enclosure, Earl of Strathmore's claim, 20 April 1803.

28 Russell, E. and R., *Parliamentary Enclosure & New Landscapes in Lincolnshire* (Lincoln, 1987), p.15.

29 D/DM/101/1(e), Flintshire Record Office, Case of the Petitioners for the Shapwick Inclosure Bill (Somerset).

30 Mingay, G.E., *Parliamentary Enclosure in England* (Harlow, 1997), p.75.

31 Thompson, E.P., *Customs in Common* (1991), pp.97–8.

32 Broadbent, J.F., 'Dewsbury Inclosure 1796–1806', *Yorkshire Archaeological Journal*, 69 (1997), p.216.

33 ibid.

34 D4459/1/3/4, Derbyshire Record Office, Evidence of Henry Ford Sen., Kirk Ireton and Callow enclosure, c.1804.

35 D/St/E3/19/24, Durham Record Office, claims and objections, Mickleton, 1803.

36 D/LE/685, Flintshire Record Office, Mold enclosure, 1 November 1793.

37 D/LE/688, Flintshire Record Office, Hope enclosure, 13 November 1794. For more details on the Hope enclosure see Evans, D.G., 'The Hope Enclosure Act of 1791', *Flintshire Historical Society Journal*, 31 (1983–4), pp.161–86.
38 SAS/ACC/1100/1/1, East Sussex Record Office, Schedule of claims and objections, Washington enclosure, *c.*1849.
39 ibid.
40 D/St/E3/19/1, Durham Record Office, Mickleton Moor, Draft Enclosure Bill.
41 Tate, *Domesday …*, p.253.
42 SAS/ACC/1100/1/9, East Sussex Record Office, Assessment for the relief of the poor, Southease, 7 January 1845.

Chapter 5: Surveyors, Surveying and Awards, pp.90–108

1 Turner, M.E., 'Enclosure Commissioners and Buckinghamshire Parliamentary Enclosure', *Ag.HR*, 25 (1977).
2 ibid., p.126.
3 Crowther, J., *Enclosure Commissioners and Surveyors of the East Riding* (Beverley, 1986), p.18.
4 Homer, Rev. H., *An Essay on the Nature and Method of Ascertaining the Specifick Shares …*, p.52.
5 For example, the Maidford Inclosure Act, 1778.
6 ZB 71/9 (in X 678) Journal of Thomas Cowper, 1765–6; also, typescript by Joan Wake – ZB 71/11, both at Northamptonshire Record Office.
7 Stephen, L. and Lee, S., *Dictionary of National Biography* (1890), pp.350–1.
8 49 Long Buckby Quality Book: Northamptonshire Central Library Local Studies Collection, 1765–1766.
9 V3128, Quality Book, Badby (1779), Northamptonshire Record Office.
10 DDcc (2) 8/10, East Riding Record Office, Quality Book, Burton Pidsea (1761).
11 Inc. 29, Award, Northamptonshire Record Office, Farthingstone (1751).
12 Hall, D., *NP and P*, 9 (3) (1996–7), pp.203–4.
13 SAS/ACC/1100/1/1, East Sussex Record Office, enclosure summary sheet 27 September 1849, Washington and Ashington enclosure.
14 SAS/ACC 1100/1/9, East Sussex Record Office, Notice of roads, 24 April 1844, Southease enclosure.
15 QSD/DS/1/2, Denbighshire Record Office, Road Certificate for Llanarmon and Llandegla, 18 November 1819.

Chapter 6: Enclosure: The Issues, pp.109–135

1 Turner, M.E., *English Parliamentary Enclosure: its Historical Geography and Economic History* (Folkestone, 1980), pp.179–81.
2 Chapman, J., 'The Nature and Extent of Parliamentary Enclosure', *Ag.HR*, 31 (1987), p.25.
3 Wordie, J.R., 'The Chronology of English Enclosure, 1500–1914', *Ec.HR*, 2nd ser. 36 (1983).
4 Butlin, R.A., 'The Enclosure of Open Fields and Extinction of Common Rights in England *c.*1600–1750: A Review', in Fox, H.S.A. and Butlin, R.A. (eds.), *Change in the Countryside: essays in rural England, 1500–1900*, Institute of British Geographers, Special Publications 10 (1979), pp.65–82.
5 Beckett, J.V., *Agricultural Revolution* (Oxford, 1990), p.35.
6 Chapman, J., 'The Chronology of English Enclosure', *Ec.HR*, 2nd ser. 37 (1984), pp.557–9.
7 Wordie, J.R., 'The Chronology of Enclosure: A Reply', *Ec.HR*, 2nd ser. 37 (1984), pp.560–2.
8 Tate, W.E., *A Domesday of English Enclosure Acts and Awards* (ed. Turner, M.E.) (Reading, 1978).
9 Chapman, J., *A Guide to Parliamentary Enclosure in Wales* (Cardiff, 1992).
10 Chapman, 'The Nature and Extent …', p.25.
11 Walton, J.R., 'On Estimating the Extent of Parliamentary Enclosure', *Ag.HR*, 38 (1990), pp.79–83.
12 Chapman, J. 'The Bootstrap and Dr Walton's Red Herrings', *Ag.HR*, 39 (1991), pp.167–8.
13 Turner, *English Parliamentary Enclosure …*, p.131.
14 Searle, C.E., 'Customary Tenants and the Enclosure of the Cumbrian Commons', *Northern History*, 29 (Leeds, 1993), pp.126–53.

15 Martin, J.M., 'The Cost of Parliamentary Enclosure in Warwickshire', *University of Birmingham, Historical Journal*, 9 (1964), pp.144–62.

16 Tate, W.E., 'The Cost of Parliamentary Enclosure in England (with special reference to the County of Oxfordshire)', *Ec.HR*, 2nd ser. 5 (1952), pp.258–65.

17 Swales, T.H., 'The Parliamentary Enclosures of Lindsey', *Reports and Papers of the Architectural and Archaeological Societies of Lincolnshire and Northamptonshire*, 42 (1937), pp.233–75 and 2 (1938), pp.85–120.

18 Turner, M.E., 'The Cost of Parliamentary Enclosure in Buckinghamshire', *Ag.HR*, 21 (1973), pp.35–46.

19 Northamptonshire Inclosures, bound volumes, Northamptonshire Record Office, Upper and Lower Boddington Inclosure, 1758.

20 D4459/1/5/19, Derbyshire Record Office, 'Account of Expenses in Passing the Kirk Ireton Inclosure Act', 1803.

21 3704 M/SS/I/5, North Devon (Barnstaple) Record Office, Braunton Marsh Inclosure, Poster, 'To Be Sold', 1813.

22 DDX 309, East Riding Record Office, Etton Inclosure Tax (1818).

23 WD/HH/53, Cumbria (Kendal) Record Office, Dufton Inclosure Assessments, *c*.1828

24 D/KK/457/6, Flintshire Record Office, receipt for Ralph Richardson for Caerwys Enclosure, 8 October 1812.

25 Marx, K., *Das Kapital*, 1 (reprinted in English, 1954), p.676.

26 Gray, H.L., 'Yeoman Farming in Oxfordshire from the Sixteenth Century to the Nineteenth', *Quarterly Journal of Economics*, 24 (1910).

27 Tawney, R.H., *The Agrarian Problem in the Sixteenth Century* (London, 1912).

28 Ernle, Lord, *English Farming: Past and Present* (1912).

29 Hammond, J.L. and B., *The Village Labourer 1760–1832* (1911).

30 Hammond, J.L. and B., *The Town Labourer 1760–1832* (1917).

31 Hammond, J.L. and B., *The Skilled Labourer 1760–1832* (1920).

32 Tate, W.E., 'Members of Parliament and the Proceedings upon Enclosure Bills', *Ec.HR*, 1st ser. 12 (1942).

33 Lavrovsky, V.M., 'Parliamentary Enclosure of the Common Fields in England at the end of the Eighteenth Century and the Beginning of the Nineteenth Century' (review by C. Hill), *Ec.HR*, 1st ser. 12 (1942).

34 Chambers, J.D., 'Enclosure and the Small Landowner', *Ec.HR*, 1st ser. 10 (1940).

35 Hunt, H.G., 'Land Ownership and Enclosure, 1750–1830', *Ec.HR*, 2nd ser. 11 (1958–9), p.501.

36 Chambers, J.D. and Mingay, G.E., *The Agricultural Revolution* (1966) and also Mingay, G.E., *Enclosure and the Small Farmer in the Age of the Industrial Revolution* (1968).

37 ibid., p.14.

38 Turner, *Enclosures in Britain 1750-1830* (1984), pp.74–5.

39 Martin, J.M., 'The Small Landowner and Parliamentary Enclosure in Warwickshire', *Ec.HR*, 2nd ser. 32 (1979), p.335.

40 Beckett, J.V., 'The Pattern of Land Ownership in England and Wales, 1660–1880', *Ec.HR*, 2nd ser. 37 (1985), pp.1–22.

41 Beckett, J.V., 'The Decline of the Small Landowner in England and Wales, 1690–1900', in Thompson, F.M.L. (ed.), *Landowners, Capitalists and Entrepreneurs – Essays for Sir John Habakkuk* (Oxford, 1994), pp.89–112.

42 Ginter, D.E., *A Measure of Wealth* (1992), pp.3–4.

43 Hollowell, S.R., *Irthlingborough 1770–1820: The Implementation of Parliamentary Inclosure* (Northampton, 1993) at Northamptonshire Libraries Local Studies Collection, Table 6, p.101.

44 Turner, M.E., 'Parliamentary Enclosure and Landownership Change in Buckinghamshire', *Ec.HR*, 2nd ser. 28 (1975), p.565.

45 Alcock, N.W., *Old Title Deeds: A Guide for Local and Family Historians* (Chichester, 1986).

46 X5143, Northamptonshire Record Office, Conditional Surrender, Irthlingborough Manor (1770).

47 Mingay, G.E., *English Landed Society in the Eighteenth Century* (1963).

48 McCloskey, D.N., 'The Persistence of English Common Fields' in Parker, W.N. and Jones, E.L. (eds.), *European Peasants and Their Markets: Essays in Agrarian History* (1975), p.5.

49 Kerridge, E., *The Agricultural Revolution* (1967), pp.94-5.

50 Beckett, J.V., *The Agricultural Revolution* (Oxford, 1990), p.39.

51 Turner, *Enclosures in Britain ...*, p.37.
52 Turner, M.E., 'English Open Fields and Enclosures: Retardation or Productivity Improvements?', *JEH*, 46 (1986), p.669.
53 Homer, Rev. H., *An Essay on the Nature and Method of Ascertaining the Specifick Shares of Proprietors, upon the Inclosure of Common Fields* (Oxford, 1766), p.64.
54 Hillyard, C., *Practical Farming and Grazing* (Northampton, 1840), p.60.
55 Stratton, J.M., *Agricultural Records AD 220–1968* (1969), pp.89–93.
56 HO 67, Parish Acreage Returns (1801), Public Record Office.
57 List and Index Society, Turner, M.E. (ed.), *Home Office Acreage Returns (HO67) 1801* (1982).
58 Collyweston, Farthingstone and Hemington, all also in Northamptonshire.
59 Vamplew, W., 'Tithes and Agriculture: Some Comments on Commutation', *Ec.HR*, 2nd ser. 34 (1981).
60 IR 18, *c*.1837, Public Record Office.
61 Kain, R., *An Atlas and Index of the Tithe Files of Mid-Nineteenth Century England* (1986).
62 Clay, C., 'The Price of Freehold Land in the Later Seventeenth and Eighteenth Centuries', *Ec.HR*, 2nd ser. 27 (1974), pp.173–89.
63 As a typical example, see Hammond, J.L. and B., *The Village Labourer 1760–1832* (1911).
64 Neeson, J.M., *Commoners: common right, enclosure and social change in England, 1700–1820* (Cambridge, 1993), p.281.
65 Thompson, E.P., *Customs in Common* (1991), p.121.
66 Mingay, G.E., *A Social History of the English Countryside* (1990), p.59.
67 Jones, E.L., *Seasons and Prices* (1964).
68 ibid.
69 *Northampton Mercury*, 24 July 1830, p.3.
70 ibid., 9 October 1830, p.4.
71 ibid., 30 October 1830, p.4.
72 Mingay, *A Social History ...*, p.163.
73 *Northampton Mercury*, 30 October 1830, p.4.
74 ibid.
75 ibid.
76 ibid., 27 November 1830, p.1.
77 ibid., p.3.
78 ibid., p.2.
79 ibid., p.3.
80 ibid., 18 December 1830, p.3.
81 Report from the Select Committee on Agriculture with Minutes of Evidence, Minutes of First Report, 4 March 1836.
82 ibid., minutes of 25 June 1837.

Epilogue: Enclosure and the Law Today, pp.136–142

 1 For example, Inclosure Act for Alderton, Northamptonshire (1819), Northamptonshire Central Library Local Studies Collection, bound Acts and Bills.
 2 Box 3/5, uncatalogued Honeybunn and Sykes MSS, Northamptonshire Record Office; Denford (Northamptonshire) Inclosure Act and Award.
 3 Northamptonshire Inclosures, bound Awards, Moulton (1772), Northamptonshire Record Office.
 4 Box 3/5, uncatalogued Honeybunn and Sykes MSS, Northamptonshire Record Office; Shelton (Bedfordshire) Enclosure Act and Award.
 5 For example, Aynho (Northamptonshire) Inclosure Act (1792), Northamptonshire Central Library Local Studies Collection, bound Acts and Bills.
 6 Lawrence, J. in Vowles v. Miller (1810), 3 Taunt. 137, 138.
 7 Access to Neighbouring Land Act, 1992.
 8 Neeson, J.M., *Commoners: common right, enclosure and social change in England, 1700–1820* (Cambridge, 1993), p.2.
 9 Clare, J., 'The Mores', in Robinson E. and Summerfield G. (eds.), *Selected Poems and Prose of John Clare* (Oxford, 1988), p.170.
10 ibid.

Bibliography

ABBREVIATIONS

Ag.HR   *Agricultural History Review*
Ec.HR   *Economic History Review*
EEH   *Explorations in Economic History*
H.L.   House of Lords
JEH   *Journal of Economic History*
NCLLS   Northamptonshire Central Library Local Studies Collection
NP and P   *Northamptonshire Past and Present*
NRO   Northamptonshire Record Office
PRO   Public Record Office
QJE   *Quarterly Journal of Economics*
RCAM   Royal Commission on Ancient Monuments (now English Heritage)

PRINTED PRIMARY SOURCES

Anscomb, J.W., *Northamptonshire Inclosure Acts and Awards* (Northampton, undated, at NRO)

Board of Agriculture, *General Report on Enclosures* (1808)

Board of Agriculture, *The Agricultural State of the Kingdom, 1816* (1816)

Bridges, J., *The History and Antiquities of Northamptonshire* (Oxford, 1791)

Cole, J., *The History and Antiquities of Wellingborough* (Wellingborough, 1837)

Dictionary of National Biography, Stephen, L. (ed.), 15 (1888) and Lee, S. (ed.), 45 (1896)

Cowper, W. in *The Poetical Works of William Cowper* (London and Edinburgh, *c*.1853)

Donaldson, J., *General View of the Agriculture of the County of Northampton with Observations on Its Means of Improvement* (Board of Agriculture Report, Edinburgh, 1794)

Eyre, T., *Map of the County of Northampton* (revised by T. Jeffery, 1779)

Fream, W., *Elements of Agriculture*, 8th edition (ed. Ainsworth-Davis, J.R., 1911)

Hillyard, C., *Practical Farming and Grazing* (Northampton, 1840)

Home Office Acreage Returns, HO 67 (PRO) (1801), List and Index Society, 190

Homer, Rev. H., *An Essay on the Nature and Method of Ascertaining the Specifick Shares of Proprietors upon the Inclosure of Common Fields with Observations upon the Inconveniences of Open Fields, and upon the Objections to their Inclosure particularly as far as they relate to the Publick and the Poor* (Oxford, 1766)

Macaulay, T.B., *The State of England in 1685*, Clement Notcutt, H. (ed.) (*c*.1852)

McConnell, P., *Notebook of Agricultural Facts and Figures for Farmers and Farm Students* (1883)

Marshall, W., *Review and Abstracts of the County Reports to the Board of Agriculture—Midland Department* (York, 1818)

More, Sir T., *Utopia* (1516–17)

Pitt, W., *General View of the Agriculture of the County of Northampton* (drawn up for the Board of Agriculture, Report 1809)

RCAM, RAF aerial photographs (1945–50)

Rous, J., *Historia Regum Angliae* (*c*.1459, 2nd edn., Oxford, 1745)

Stone, T., *Suggestions for Rendering the Inclosure of Common Fields and Waste Lands a Source of Population and Riches* (1787)

Stow, J., *Annals* (1615), p. 889, quoted in Tate, W.E., 'Inclosure Movements in Northamptonshire', *NP and P*, 1, no. 2 (1949)

Young, A., *The Farmer's Tour through the East of England* (1771)

Young, A., *Observations on the Present State of the Waste Lands of Great Britain* (1773)

Young, A., *General Report on Enclosures* (Board of Agriculture Report, 1808)

Young, A., *General View of the Agriculture of Oxfordshire* (Board of Agriculture Report, 1813)

Secondary Sources: Books

(Place of publication London unless stated)

Adams, I.H., *Agrarian Landscape Terms: A Glossary for Historical Geography*, special publication no. 9, the Institute of British Geographers (1976)

Alcock, N.W., *Old Title Deeds: A Guide for Local and Family Historians* (Chichester, 1986)

Allen, R.C., *Enclosure and the Yeoman* (Oxford, 1992)

Baker, A.R.H. and Butlin, R.A. (eds.), *Studies of Field Systems in the British Isles* (Cambridge, 1973)

Beckett, J.V., *A History of Laxton: England's last open-field village* (1989)

Beckett, J.V., *The Agricultural Revolution* (Oxford, 1990)

Beckett, J.V., 'The Disappearance of the Cottager and the Squatter from the English Countryside: The Hammonds Revisited', in Holderness, B.A. and Turner, M.E. (eds.), *Land, Labour and Agriculture: Essays Presented to Gordon Mingay* (1991)

Beckett, J.V., 'The Decline of the Small Landowner in England and Wales, 1660–1900', in Thompson, F.M.L. (ed.), *Landowners, Capitalists and Entrepreneurs—Essays for Sir John Habakkuk* (Oxford, 1994)

Beresford, M.W., 'Habitation versus Improvement: The Debate on Inclosure by Agreement', in Fisher, F.J. (ed.), *Essays on the Economic and Social History of Tudor and Stuart England* (1961)

Beresford, M. and Hurst, G. (eds.), *Deserted Medieval Villages: Studies* (1971)

Bird, R., *Osborn's Concise Law Dictionary* (1983)

Bowden, P.J., 'Agricultural Prices, Wages, Farm Profits and Rents', in Thirsk, J. (ed.), *Agrarian History of England and Wales*, 5, 2 (Cambridge, 1985)

Butlin, R.A., 'The Enclosure of Open Fields in England *c*.1600–1750: a Review', in Fox, H.S.A. and Butlin, R.A. (eds.), *Change in the Countryside: essays in rural England, 1500–1900* (1979)

Chambers, J.D., *Nottinghamshire in the Eighteenth Century* (1932)

Chambers, J.D. and Mingay, G.E., *The Agricultural Revolution* (1966)

Chapman, J., *A Guide to Parliamentary Enclosures in Wales* (Cardiff, 1992)

Clare, J., 'The Mores', in Robinson, E. and Summerfield, G. (eds.), *Selected Poems and Prose of John Clare* (Oxford, 1967)

Crowther, J., *Enclosure Commissioners and Surveyors of the East Riding* (Beverley, 1986)

Dahlman, C., *The Open Field System and Beyond: A Property Rights Analysis of an Economic Institution* (1980)

Darby, H.C., *Historical Geography of England before 1800* (1936)

Darby, H.C., 'The Age of the Improver: 1600–1800', in Darby, H.C. (ed.), *A New Historical Geography of England* (1973)

Deane, P. and Cole, W.A., *British Economic Growth, 1688–1959* (Cambridge, 1969)

Ernle (Lord), *English Farming: Past and Present* (1912)

Ernle (Lord), 'Obstacles to Progress', in Jones, E.L. (ed.), *Agriculture and Economic Growth in England 1650–1815* (1967)

Fryde, E.B. and Fryde, N., 'Peasant Rebellion and Peasant Discontents', in Miller, E. (ed.), *The Agrarian History of England and Wales*, 3 (Cambridge, 1991)

Gilbert, K., *Life in a Hampshire Village: The History of Ashley* (Winchester, 1992)

Ginter, D.E., 'Measuring the Decline of the Small Landowner', in Holderness, B.A. and Turner, M.E. (eds.), *Land, Labour and Agriculture: Essays Presented to Gordon Mingay* (1991)

Ginter, D.E., *A Measure of Wealth* (1992)

Gonner, E.C.K., *Common Land and Inclosure* (1912)

Gray, H.L., *English Open Fields* (1955)

Hall, D.N., *The Open Fields of Northamptonshire* (Northampton, 1995)

Hammond, J.L. and B., *The Village Labourer 1760–1832* (1911)

Hammond, J.L. and B., *The Town Labourer 1760–1832* (1917)

Hammond, J.L. and B., *The Skilled Labourer 1760–1832* (1920)

Harvey, N., *The Industrial Archaeology of Farming in England and Wales* (1980)

Hatley, V.A., *Northamptonshire Militia Lists 1777* (Northampton, 1973)

Holderness, B.A., 'Capital Formation in Agriculture 1750–1850', in Higgins, J.P.P. and Pollard, S. (eds.), *Aspects of Capital Investment in Great Britain 1750–1850* (1971)

Holderness, B.A., 'Prices, Productivity and Output', in Mingay, G.E. (ed.), *The Agrarian History of England and Wales*, 6 (Cambridge, 1984)

Holderness, B.A. and Turner, M.E. (eds.), *Land, Labour and Agriculture: Essays Presented to Gordon Mingay* (1991)

Hoskins, W.G., *The Making of the English Landscape* (1955)

Hoskins, W.G., *The Midland Peasant* (1957)

Hoskins, W.G. and Stamp, L.D., *The Common Lands of England and Wales* (1963)

Hutton, R., *The Stations of the Sun* (Oxford, 1997)

Jenkins, E., *Victorian Northamptonshire: the early years* (Rushden, 1993)

John, A.H., 'Farming in Wartime: 1793–1815', in Jones, E.L. and Mingay, G.E. (eds.), *Land, Labour and Population during the Industrial Revolution* (1967)

John, A.H. (ed.), *Enclosure and Population* (1973)

Johnson, A.H., *The Disappearance of the Small Landowner* (Oxford, 1909)

Jones, E.L., *Seasons and Prices* (1964)

Jones, E.L. (ed.), *Agriculture and Economic Growth in England 1650–1815* (1967)

Kain, R., *An Atlas and Index of the Tithe Files of Mid-Nineteenth Century England* (1986)

Kerridge, E., *The Agricultural Revolution* (1967)

Kerridge, E., *Agrarian Problems in the Sixteenth Century and After* (1969)

Kussmaul, A.S., *A General View of the Rural Economy of England, 1538–1840* (Cambridge, 1990)

Laslett, P., *The World We Have Lost—Further Explored* (Cambridge, 1983)

Lavrovsky, V.M., *Parliamentary Enclosure of the Common Fields in England at the End of the Eighteenth Century and Beginning of the Nineteenth* (Moscow, Leningrad, 1940)

Leadham, I.S., *The Domesday of Inclosures* (1897)

McCloskey, D.N., 'The Persistence of English Common Fields', in Parker, W.N. and Jones, E.L. (eds.), *European Peasants and Their Markets: Essays in Agrarian History* (Princeton, 1975)

Mantoux, P., *The Industrial Revolution in the Eighteenth Century* (1961)

Martin, J.M., 'The Cost of Parliamentary Enclosure in Warwickshire', in Jones, E.L. (ed.), *Agriculture and Economic Growth in England 1650–1815* (1967)

Marx, K., *Das Kapital* (reprinted in English, 1954)

Mingay, G.E., *English Landed Society in the Eighteenth Century* (1963)

Mingay, G.E., *Enclosure and the Small Farmer in the Age of the Industrial Revolution* (1968)

Mingay, G.E., 'The East Midlands', in Thirsk, J. (ed.), *Agrarian History of England and Wales*, 5, 1 (Cambridge, 1984)

Mingay, G.E., *The Unquiet Countryside* (1989)

Mingay, G.E., *A Social History of the English Countryside* (1990)

Mingay, G.E., *Parliamentary Enclosure in England* (1997)

Mitchell, B.R., *Abstract of British Historical Statistics* (Cambridge, 1992)

Neeson, J.M., *Commoners: common right, enclosure and social change in England, 1700–1820* (Cambridge, 1993)

Orwin, C.S. and Orwin, C.S., *The Open Fields* (Oxford, 1938)

Overton, M., 'Agricultural Revolution? Development of the Agrarian Economy in Early Modern England', in Baker, A.R.H. and Gregory, D.J. (eds.), *Explorations in Historical Geography* (Cambridge, 1984)

Overton, M., 'The Determinants of Crop Yields in Early Modern England', in Campbell, B.M.S. and Overton, M. (eds.), *Land, Labour and Livestock: Historical Studies in European Agricultural Productivity* (Manchester, 1991)

Parker, W.N. and Jones, E.L. (eds.), *European Peasants and Their Markets: Essays in Agrarian History* (Princeton, 1975)

Passmore, J.B., *The English Plough* (1930)

Reed, M., 'Class and Conflict in Rural England: Some Reflections on a Debate', in Reed, M. and Wells, R. (eds.), *Class, Conflict and Protest in the English Countryside 1700–1880* (1990)

Russell, R.C., *The Logic of Open Field Systems: Fifteen Maps of Groups of Common Fields on the Eve of Enclosure* (Standing Conference for Local History, 1974)

Russell, E. and R., *Parliamentary Enclosure & New Landscapes in Lincolnshire* (Lincoln, 1987)

Seebohm, F., *The English Village Community* (1915)

Slater, G., *The English Peasantry and the Enclosure of Common Fields* (1907)

Snell, K.D.M., *Annals of the Labouring Poor: Social Change and Agrarian England 1660–1900* (Cambridge, 1985)

Spufford, M., *A Cambridgeshire Community: Chippenham from Settlement to Enclosure* (Leicester, 1965)

Stamp, L.D. and Hoskins, W.G., *The Common Lands of England and Wales* (1963)

Stratton, J.M. and Brown, J.H., *Agricultural Records, AD 220–1977* (1978)

Stuart, D., *Manorial Records* (Chichester, 1992)

Tate, W.E., *A Handlist of Buckinghamshire Enclosure Acts and Awards* (Aylesbury, 1946)

Tate, W.E., *The Parish Chest* (Cambridge, 1946)

Tate, W.E., *The English Village Community and the Enclosure Movements* (1967)

Tate, W.E., *A Domesday of English Enclosure Acts and Awards*, Turner, M.E. (ed.) (Reading, 1978)

Tawney, R.H., *The Agrarian Problem in the Sixteenth Century* (1912)

Thirsk, J., 'Agrarian History, 1540–1950', *Victoria County History, Leicestershire*, 2 (Oxford, 1954)

Thirsk, J., *Tudor Enclosures* (Historical Association, general ser. 41, 1959)

Thirsk, J., 'Industries in the Countryside', in Fisher, F.J. (ed.), *Essays in the Economic and Social History of Tudor and Stuart England* (1961)

Thirsk, J., 'Enclosing and Engrossing', in Finberg, H.P.R. (ed.), *The Agrarian History of England and Wales*, 4 (Cambridge, 1967)

Thirsk, J. (ed.), *The Agrarian History of England and Wales*, 4 (Cambridge, 1967), 5, Parts I and II (Cambridge, 1984, 1985)

Thirsk, J., 'Field Systems of the East Midlands', in Baker, A.R.H. and Butlin, R.A. (eds.), *Studies of Field Systems in the British Isles* (Cambridge, 1973)

Thirsk, J., *Alternative Agriculture* (Oxford, 1997)

Thompson, E.P., *The Making of the English Working Class* (1963)

Thompson, E.P., *Customs in Common* (1991)

Thompson, F.M.L., 'The Land Market in the Nineteenth Century', in Minchinton, W.E. (ed.), *Essays in Agrarian History*, 2 (Newton Abbot, 1968)

Thoyts, E.E., *How to Read Old Documents* (Chichester, 1980)

Trow-Smith, R., *A History of British Livestock Husbandry 1700–1900* (1959)

Turner, M.E., *English Parliamentary Enclosure, its Historical Geography and Economic History* (Folkestone, 1980)

Turner, M.E., *Enclosures in Britain 1750–1830* (1984)

Turner, M.E., 'The Landscape of Parliamentary Enclosure' in Reed, M. (ed.), *Discovering Past Landscapes* (1984)

Turner, M.E. and Mills, D. (eds.), *Land and Property: The English Land Tax, 1692–1832* (Gloucester, 1986)

Walton, J., 'The Residential Mobility of Farmers and its Relationship to the Parliamentary

Enclosure Movement in Oxfordshire', in Phillips, A.D.M. and Turton, B.J. (eds.), *Environment, Man and Economic Change* (1975)

White, G., *Gilbert White's Year, Passages from the Garden Kalendar & The Naturalist's Journal*, Commander, J. and Mabey, R. (eds.) (1982)

Wrigley, E.A., 'Men on the Land and Men in the Countryside: employment in agriculture in early nineteenth-century England', in Bonfield, L., Smith, R. and Wrightson, K. (eds.), *The World We Have Gained* (Cambridge, 1986)

Yelling, J.A., *Common Field and Enclosure in England 1450–1850* (1977)

SECONDARY SOURCES: ARTICLES

Allen, R.C., 'The Efficiency and Distributional Consequences of 18th Century Enclosures', *Economic Journal*, 92 (1982)

Allen, R.C., 'The Price of Freehold Land and the Interest Rate in the 17th and 18th Centuries', *Ec.HR*, 2nd ser. 41 (1988)

Allen, R.C., 'Inferring Yields from Probate Inventories', *JEH*, 48 (1988)

Anscomb, J.W., 'An 18th Century Inclosure and Foot Ball Play at West Haddon', *NP and P*, 4 (Northampton, 1969)

Anscomb, J.W., 'Parliamentary Enclosure in Northamptonshire: Process and Procedures', *NP and P*, 7 (Northampton, 1988)

Baack, B.D. and Thomas, R.P., 'The Enclosure Movement and the Supply of Labour during the Industrial Revolution', *Journal of European Economic History*, 3 (1974)

Ballard, A., 'The Management of Open Fields', *Report* (Oxfordshire Archaeological Society, 1913)

Beckett, J.V., 'Regional Variation and the Agricultural Depression', *Ec.HR*, 2nd ser. 35 (1982)

Beckett, J.V., 'The Pattern of Land Ownership in England and Wales, 1660–1880', *Ec.HR*, 2nd ser. 37 (1984)

Beckett, J.V., 'English Rural Society, 1750–1914', *Historian*, 38 (1993)

Beckwith, I.S., 'The Present State of Enclosure Studies in Lincolnshire', *Bulletin of Local History, East Midlands Region*, 6 (1971)

Beresford, M.W., 'The Commissioners of Enclosure', *Ec.HR*, 1st ser. 16 (1946)

Beresford, M.W., 'Glebe Terriers and open field Yorkshire', *Yorkshire Archaeological Journal*, 37 (1950)

Beresford, M.W., 'The Decree Rolls of Chancery as a Source of Economic History, 1547–c.1700', *Ec.HR*, 2nd ser. 32 (1979)

Billson, C.J., 'Open Fields of Leicester', *Transactions of the Leicester Archaeological Society*, 14 (1925–6)

Blum, J., 'Review Article. English Parliamentary Enclosure', *Journal of Modern History*, 103 (1981)

Broadbent, J.F., 'Dewsbury Inclosure 1796–1806', *Yorkshire Archaeological Journal*, 69 (1997)

Buchanan, B.J., 'The Financing of Parliamentary Waste Land Enclosure: Some Evidence from North Somerset, 1770–1830', *Ag.HR*, 30 (1982)

Butlin, R.A., 'Some Terms used in Agrarian History: A Glossary', *Ag.HR*, 9 (1961)

Campbell, B.M.S., 'The Extent and Layout of Common Fields in Eastern Norfolk', *Norfolk Archaeology*, 38 (1981)

Campbell, B.M.S., 'The Regional Uniqueness of English Field Systems? Some Evidence from East Norfolk', *Ag.HR*, 29 (1987)

Chambers, J.D., 'Enclosure and the Small Landowner', *Ec.HR*, 1st ser. 10 (1940)

Chambers, J.D., 'Enclosure and the Small Landowner in Lindsey', *The Lincolnshire Historian*, 1 (1947)

Chambers, J.D., 'Enclosure and Labour Supply in the Industrial Revolution', *Ec.HR*, 2nd ser. 5 (1953)

Chapman, J., 'Some Problems in the Interpretation of Enclosure Awards', *Ag.HR*, 26 (1978)

Chapman, J. and Harris, T.M., 'The Accuracy of Enclosure Estimates: Some Evidence from Northern England', *Journal of Historical Geography*, 8 (1982)

Chapman, J., 'The Nature and Extent of Parliamentary Enclosure', *Ag.HR*, 35 (1987)

Chapman, J., 'The Bootstrap and Dr. Walton's Red Herrings', *Ag.HR*, 39 (1991)

Chapman, J. and Seeliger, S., 'Enclosure by Non-Parliamentary Means: Some Comments on the Records', *Archives*, 22, no. 95 (1996)

Chartres, J.A., 'Market Integration and Agricultural Output in Seventeenth, Eighteenth and Early Nineteenth Centuries', *Ag.HR*, 43 (1995)

Chorley, G.P.H., 'The Agricultural Revolution in Northern Europe, 1750–1880: Nitrogen, Legumes and Crop Productivity', *Ec.HR*, 2nd ser. 34 (1981)

Clark, G., 'Productivity Growth without Technical Change in European Agriculture before 1850', *JEH*, 47 (1987)

Clark, G., 'Yields per Acre in English Agriculture, 1250–1860', *Ec.HR*, 2nd ser. 44 (1991)

Clay, C., 'The Price of Freehold Land in the Later 17th and 18th Centuries', *Ec.HR*, 2nd ser. 27 (1974)

Collins, E.J.T., 'Historical Farm Records', *Archives*, 7 (1966)

Collins, K., 'Marx on the English Agricultural Revolution: Theory and Evidence', *History and Theory: Studies in the Philosophy of History*, 6 (1967)

Cooke, J.R., 'Timber-Stealing Riots in Whittlebury and Salcey Forests in 1727–8', *Northamptonshire Notes and Queries*, 1 (1886)

Crafts, N.F.R., 'Enclosure and Labour Supply Revisited', *EEH*, 14 (1977)

Davies, E., 'The Small Landowner, 1780–1832, in the Light of the Land Tax Assessments', *Ec.HR*, 1st ser. 1 (1927)

Fussell, G.E., 'Population and Wheat Production in the 18th Century', *The History Teachers' Miscellany*, 7 (1929)

Fussell, G.E. and Compton, M., 'Agricultural Adjustments after the Napoleonic Wars', *Economic History*, 3 (1939)

Gay, E.F., 'Inclosures in England in the 16th Century', *Quarterly Journal of Economics*, 17 (1902–3)

Gay, E.F., 'The Midland Revolt and the Inquisition of Depopulation', *Trans. RHS*, new ser. 18 (1904)

Gray, H.L., 'Yeoman Farming in Oxfordshire from the 16th Century to the 19th', *QJE*, 24 (1910)

Grigg, D.B., 'The Land Tax Returns', *Ag.HR*, 11 (1963)

Grigg, D.B., 'A Source on Land Ownership: The Land Tax Returns', *Amateur Historian*, 6 (1964)

Habakkuk, H.J., 'English Landownership 1680–1740', *Ec.HR*, 1st ser. 10 (1940)

Havinden, M., 'Agricultural Progress in Open Field Oxfordshire', *Ag.HR*, 9 (1961)

Holderness, B.A., '"Open" and "Closed" Parishes in England in the 18th and 19th Centuries', *Ag.HR*, 20 (1972)

Hoskins, W.G., 'The Leicestershire Farmer in the 17th Century', *Ag.HR*, 25 (1951)

Hueckel, G., 'War and the British Economy, 1793–1815: A General Equilibrium Analysis', *EEH*, 10 (1973)

Hueckel, G., 'Relative Prices and Supply Response in English Agriculture during the Napoleonic Wars', *Ec.HR*, 29 (1976)

Humphries, J., 'Enclosures, Common Rights, and Women: The Proletarianisation of Families in the Late Eighteenth and Early Nineteenth Centuries', *JEH*, 1 (1990)

Hunt, H.G., 'The Chronology of Parliamentary Enclosure in Leicestershire', *Ec.HR*, 2nd ser. 10 (1957)

Hunt, H.G., 'Land Ownership and Enclosure, 1750–1830', *Ec.HR*, 2nd ser. 11 (1958–9)

Jones, E.L. and Collins, E.J.T., 'The Collection and Analysis of Farm Record Books', *Journal of the Society of Archivists*, 3 (1965)

Kerridge, E., 'The Returns of the Inquisitions of Depopulation', *English Historical Review*, 70 (1955)

Lavrovsky, V.M., 'Parliamentary Enclosure of the Common Fields in England at the End of the Eighteenth Century and the Beginning of the Nineteenth Century', review by C. Hill, *Ec.HR*, 1st ser. 12 (1942)

Lavrovsky, V.M., 'The Expropriation of the English Peasantry in the Eighteenth Century', *Ec.HR*, 2nd ser. 9 (1956–7)

McCloskey, D.N., 'The Enclosure of Open Fields: Preface to a Study of its Impact on the Efficiency of English Agriculture in the Eighteenth Century', *JEH*, 32 (1972)

McCloskey, D.N., 'English Open Fields as Behaviour Towards Risk', *Research in Economic History*, 1 (1976)

Martin, J., 'Enclosure and the Inquisitions of 1607: An Examination of Dr. Kerridge's Article, "The Returns of the Inquisitions of Depopulation"', *Ag.HR*, 7 (1959)

Martin, J., 'Sheep and Enclosure in Sixteenth-Century Northamptonshire', *Ag.HR*, 36 (1988)

Martin, J.M., 'The Cost of Parliamentary Enclosure in Warwickshire', *University of Birmingham, Historical Journal*, 9 (1964)

Martin, J.M., 'Land Ownership and the Land Tax Returns', *Ag.HR*, 14 (1966)

Martin, J.M., 'The Parliamentary Enclosure Movement and Rural Society in Warwickshire', *Ag.HR*, 15 (1967)

Martin, J.M., 'Members of Parliament and Enclosure: A Reconsideration', *Ag.HR*, 27 (1979)

Martin, J.M., 'The Small Landowner and Parliamentary Enclosure in Warwickshire', *Ec.HR*, 2nd ser. 32 (1979)

Minchinton, W.E., 'Agricultural Returns and the Government during the Napoleonic Wars', *Ag.HR*, 1 (1953)

Mingay, G.E., 'The Agricultural Depression, 1730–50', *Ag.HR*, 8 (1956)

Mingay, G.E., 'The Size of Farms in the Eighteenth Century', *Ec.HR*, 2nd ser. 14 (1962)

Mingay, G.E., 'The Land Tax Assessments and the Small Landowner', *Ec.HR*, 2nd ser. 7 (1964–5)

Morris, J. and Draper, J., 'The "Enclosure" of Fordington Fields and the Development of Dorchester, 1874–1903', *Dorset Natural History and Archaeological Society Proceedings*, 117 (1995)

Neeson, J.M., 'The Opponents of Enclosure in Eighteenth Century Northamptonshire', *Past & Present*, 5 (1984)

Neeson, J.M., 'Parliamentary Enclosure and the Disappearance of the English Peasantry, Revisited', *Research in Economic History* (1989)

Overton, M., 'Agricultural Productivity in Eighteenth Century England: Some Further Speculations', *Ec.HR*, 2nd ser. 37 (1984)

Overton, M., 'Re-estimating Crop Yields from Probate Inventories', *JEH*, 50 (1990)

Parton, A.G., 'Parliamentary Enclosure in Nineteenth-Century Surrey—Some Perspectives on the Evaluation of Land Potential', *Ag.HR*, 33 (1985)

Philpot, G., 'Enclosure and Population Growth in Eighteenth Century England', *EEH*, 12 (1975)

Philpot, G., 'Parliamentary Enclosure and Population Change in England, 1750–1830: Reply' (to M.E. Turner), *EEH*, 13 (1976)

Purdum, J.L., 'Profitability and Timing of Parliamentary Land Enclosures', *EEH*, 15 (1978)

Rae, J., 'Why have the Yeomanry Perished?', *Contemporary Review*, 44 (1883)

Ranson, S., 'Finedon Inclosure 1804–08', *NP and P*, 3 (Northampton, 1966)

Reed, M., 'The Peasantry of Nineteenth-Century England: A Neglected Class?', *History Workshop Journal*, 18 (1984)

Rogers, G., 'Custom and Common Right: Waste Land Enclosure and Social Change in West Lancashire', *Ag.HR*, 41 (1993)

Searle, C.E., 'Customary Tenants and the Enclosure of the Cumbrian Commons', *Northern History*, 29 (Leeds, 1993)

Snell, K.D.M., 'Agrarian Histories and Our Rural Past', *Journal of Historical Geography*, 17 (1991)

Swales, T.H., 'The Parliamentary Enclosures of Lindsey', *Reports and Papers of the Architectural and Archaeological Societies of Lincolnshire and Northamptonshire*, old ser. 42 (1937) and new ser. 2 (1938)

Tate, W.E., 'Members of Parliament and the Proceedings upon Enclosure Bills', *Ec.HR*, 1st ser. 12 (1942)

Tate, W.E., 'Some Unexplored Records of the Enclosure Movement', *English Historical Review*, 57 (1942)

Tate, W.E., 'Parliamentary Counter-Petitions During the Enclosures of the Eighteenth and Nineteenth Centuries', *English Historical Review*, 59 (1944)

Tate, W.E., 'The *Commons Journals* as Sources of Information Concerning the Eighteenth-Century Enclosure Movement', *Economic Journal*, 54 (1944)

Tate, W.E., 'Opposition to Parliamentary Enclosure in Eighteenth Century England', *Agricultural History*, 19 (1945)

Tate, W.E., 'Members of Parliament and Their Personal Relations to Enclosure', *Agricultural History*, 23 (1949)

Tate, W.E., 'Inclosure Movements in Northamptonshire', *NP and P*, 1 (Northampton, 1951)

Tate, W.E., 'The Cost of Parliamentary Enclosure in England (with special reference to the

County of Oxfordshire)', *Ec.HR*, 2nd ser. 5 (1952)

Thirsk, J., 'The Common Fields', *Past & Present*, 29 (1964)

Turner, M.E., 'John Davis of Bloxham, Enclosure Commissioner', *Cake and Cockhorse* (1971)

Turner, M.E., 'The Cost of Parliamentary Enclosure in Buckinghamshire', *Ag.HR*, 21 (1973)

Turner, M.E., 'Parliamentary Enclosure and Landownership Change in Buckinghamshire', *Ec.HR*, 2nd ser. 28 (1975)

Turner, M.E., 'Parliamentary Enclosure and Population Change in England, 1750–1830', *EEH*, 13 (1976)

Turner, M.E., 'Recent Progress in the Study of Parliamentary Enclosure', *The Local Historian*, 12 (February 1976)

Turner, M.E., 'Enclosure Commissioners and Buckinghamshire Parliamentary Enclosure', *Ag.HR*, 25 (1977)

Turner, M.E., 'Cost, Finance and Parliamentary Enclosure', *Ec.HR*, 2nd ser. 34 (1981)

Turner, M.E., 'Arable in England and Wales: Estimates from the 1801 Crop Returns', *Journal of Historical Geography*, 7 (1981)

Turner, M.E., 'Agricultural Productivity in England in the Eighteenth Century', *Ec.HR*, 2nd ser. 35 (1982)

Turner, M.E., 'English Open Fields and Enclosures: Retardation or Productivity Improvements?', *JEH*, 46 (1986)

Turner, M.E., 'Economic Protest in a Rural Society: Opposition to Parliamentary Enclosure in Buckinghamshire', *Southern History*, 10 (1988)

Turner, M.E., 'Benefits but at a Cost: The Debates about Parliamentary Enclosure', *Research in Economic History*, Supp. 5 (1989)

Turner, M.E., Beckett, J.V. and Afton, B., 'Taking Stock: Farmers, Farm Records and Agricultural Output in England, 1700–1850', *Ag.HR*, 44 (1996)

Turner, M.E. and Wray, T., 'A Survey of Sources for Parliamentary Enclosure: The House of Commons Journal and Commissioners' Working Papers', *Archives*, 19 (April 1991)

Tyley, J., (Halton, D. translation.) 'Inclosure of Open Fields in Northamptonshire', *NP and P*, 1 (Northampton, 1951)

Tyson, B., 'Murton Great Field, near Appleby', *Trans. of the Cumberland & Westmorland Antiquarian & Archaeological Society*, 92 (1992)

Vamplew, W., 'Tithes and Agriculture: Some comments on commutation', *Ec.HR*, 2nd ser. 34 (1981)

Walton, J.R., 'On Estimating the Extent of Parliamentary Enclosure', *Ag.HR*, 38 (1990)

Watts, K., 'Wiltshire Deer Parks: An Introductory Survey', *The Wiltshire Archaeological and Natural History Magazine*, 89 (1996)

Watts, K., 'Some Wiltshire Deer Parks', *The Wiltshire Archaeological and Natural History Magazine*, 91 (1998)

Watts, S., 'Glebe Terriers and Local History: Shifnal 1612–1853', *Shropshire History and Archaeology*, 71 (1996)

Wells, R.A.E., 'The Development of the English Rural Proletariat and Social Protest, 1700–1850', *Journal of Peasant Studies*, 7 (1979)

Williams, M., 'The Enclosure and Reclamation of Wasteland in England and Wales in the

18th and 19th Centuries', *Transactions and Papers of the Institute of British Geographers*, 51 (1970)

Williams, M., 'The Enclosure and Reclamation of the Mendip Hills', *Ag.HR*, 19 (1971)

Williams, M., 'The Enclosure of Waste Land in Somerset', *Transactions of the Institute of British Geographers*, 57 (1972)

Wordie, J.R., 'The Chronology of English Enclosure, 1500–1914', *Ec.HR*, 2nd ser. 36 (November 1983)

Yelling, J.A., 'Common Land and Enclosure in East Worcestershire, 1540–1870', *Transactions and Papers of the Institute of British Geographers* (1968)

Yelling, J.A., 'Changes in Crop Production in East Worcestershire, 1540–1867', *Ag.HR*, 21 (1973)

Yelling, J.A., 'Rationality in the Common Fields', *Ec.HR*, 2nd ser. 35 (1982)

THESES

Bond, D., 'Pre-Enclosure Field Patterns in the Peterborough Locality', M.A. thesis (University of Nottingham, 1985)

Havinden, M.A., 'The Rural Economy of Oxfordshire, 1580–1730', B. Litt. thesis (University of Oxford, 1961)

Hollowell, S.R., 'Maidford 1718–88', M.A. thesis (University of Nottingham, 1989)

Hollowell, S.R., 'Aspects of Northamptonshire Inclosure', Ph.D. thesis (University of Nottingham, 1998)

Martin, J.M., 'Economic and Social Trends in the Rural West Midlands 1770–1825', M.Com. thesis (University of Birmingham, 1960)

Neeson, J.M., 'Common Right and Enclosure in 18th Century Northamptonshire', Ph.D. thesis (University of Warwick, 1978)

Turner, M.E., 'Some Social and Economic Considerations of Parliamentary Enclosure in Buckinghamshire, 1738–1865', Ph.D. thesis (University of Sheffield, 1973)

Glossary of useful terms

The following is a list of some of the more common terms found in the study of enclosure and agricultural history. There are wide regional variations in all such terms and this list is far from exhaustive. For less commonly recurring words, readers may wish to consult two other useful sources, both of which appear in the bibliography. R.A. Butlin's article, 'Some Terms used in Agrarian History' appeared in Volume 9 (1961) of *Agricultural History Review* and I.H. Adams produced 'Agrarian Landscape Terms: A Glossary for Historical Geography' as a special publication (number 9, 1976) for the *Institute of British Geographers*.

ABUTTAL	Owners or occupiers of land adjoining or adjacent to the land under consideration.
ACRE	Largest unit of area in pre-metric common usage, approximately equivalent to 0.4 hectares. Originally, it was conceived as the amount of land that a single team could plough in a day.
ACT	An Act of Parliament, being part of the Statute law.
ADMEASURE	The measurement of large areas such as of land.
AMERCEMENT	A small fine levied on a proprietor by the manor court—usually for a transgression in the open fields.
ASSIGNEE	Usually in a property transaction, the person to whom rights have been transferred.
AWARD	The final document produced in an enclosure process, detailing all the decisions made by the commissioners or arbitrators.
BAILIFF	A senior member of the manor court, second only to the steward. Often charged with carrying out the wishes of the court such as collecting amercements or fines.
BALK (BAULK)	A narrow strip of grass in a common arable field. Used for access, grazing, etc.
BEAST	Usually a bullock or steer.
BILL	A draft Act of Parliament—not yet agreed.
BOVATE	See Oxgang.
BUSHEL	An imperial measure of capacity equal to 8 gallons. Used for small quantities of grain, also fruit and some vegetables.
CANDLEMAS	2 February.
CARR	Wet, boggy land—pasture reclaimed from fen.
CARUCATE	The amount of land which could be tilled in a year using one plough and a team of eight oxen. Common in the north of England.
CHAIN	A unit of length: 22 yards, equal to 100 links or a tenth of a change. See Gunter's Chain.

CHANGE	A unit of length—220 yards or 10 chains or 1 furlong.
CLAIM	Usually a written declaration of amount of land held in open fields, commons and wastes at the time of enclosure.
CLERK OF THE GAITS	See Hayward.
CLOSES	Small enclosed fields not included in the open and common field system. Usually situated near to the village and the farmsteads.
CONSIDERATION	The sum payable in exchange for land or property.
COPY OF COURT ROLL	Copy of extract of court roll, recording the admission of a tenant to copyhold property. See Court Roll.
COPYHOLD	Tenure of land or property held by virtue of the evidence provided by a copy of the court roll. See Court Roll.
COURT ROLL	Minutes or proceedings of a manor court, traditionally written on a long roll of parchment. See Copy of Court Roll and Copyhold.
COTTAGE COW COMMON	The right of pasture for one cow when it was attached to a property, i.e. a cottage. See also Cow Gate.
COVENANT	An agreement.
COW GATE (COWGAIT)	Right of pasture for one cow.
CROFT	See Toft.
CUSTOMARY COURT	A name sometimes used for a manor court.
CUSTOMARY TENANT	A tenant of copyhold land or property. See Copyhold.
CURTILAGE	The land or yards immediately adjacent to a building.
DECINER	In some manors, deciners were appointed to represent the court between sittings, dealing especially with land transfers which were later confirmed by the court.
DEMESNE	The home farm, belonging to and farmed by the lord of the manor.
DOLE MEADOW	Common meadow divided into portions or doles.
ENCLOSURE	See Inclosure.
ENROLMENT (ENROLLMENT)	The entering of an agreement or transaction in to the records of a court.
EXECUTOR (-TRIX)	Person(s) appointed by a testator(-trix) to carry out the provisions of his/her will.
EXTENT	A survey and subsequent valuation of a manor.
FALLOW	An arable field being 'rested', i.e. not having a crop. There are different forms of fallow depending on the crops previous and following.
FIELD	(i) A collection of furlongs in the pre-enclosure period sometimes with many farmers. (ii) An enclosure allotment usually with only one proprietor.
FIELD BOOK	A written record of all the lands, furlongs, fields and commons in a manor.
FIELD REEVES	Officials of the manor court responsible for the open fields and ensuring their proper use.
FINE	Initial sum paid upon entry to a copyhold property.
FREEHOLD	Absolute tenure of a property, usually, by the 18th century, free of

	obligations to the lord of the manor.
FURLONG	(i) A unit of linear measure—220 yards or a change or one-eighth of a mile.
	(ii) A collection of lands or strips usually making a rectilinear area and part of an open field. Usually containing land belonging to several farmers.
FURROW	The trench formed down an arable field by a plough with a single share and board. See also Ridge and Furrow
GELDING	A castrated horse.
GLEBE	The farm belonging to the rector.
GUNTER'S CHAIN	Light-gauge steel chain used by surveyors for measuring linear distances. Invented by Edmund Gunter, English mathematician (16th/17th century).
HAYWARD	A manor court official who was responsible for the open field pasture. Similar to the Clerk of the Gates (gaits) in northern areas.
HEADLAND	The strip of land at the ends of the other strips in a furlong (making it a strip itself but at right angles to the others) wide enough for the farmers to turn their plough team at the end of each furrow.
HERIOT	According to local custom but usually took the form of the best animal or chattel (or a money equivalent) of a deceased tenant which was given to his lord.
HOGGERELS (EWE HOGGERELS)	Sheep.
INCLOSURE	(i) The physical dividing up by hedges, fences or walls of the former open fields or wastes.
	(ii) The legal process which authorised the division of the open fields and wastes and created farming in severalty.
INDENTURE	A deed or agreement with the top of the membrane indented (wavy-edged) so that two or more could be matched together.
INROLMENT (INROLLMENT)	See Enrolment.
INTAKE	Land enclosed from former wastes.
LADY DAY	25 March, one of the quarter or rent days.
LAMMAS	(i) Traditionally, 1 August and Harvest Festival.
	(ii) An early strain of wheat.
LAMMAS LAND	Common lands thrown open for loose grazing between Lammas Day and Lady Day.
LAND	(i) Collective term for the countryside.
	(ii) A narrow strip of land in a furlong, what today is known as ridge and furrow. They usually occur in what is known as a reverse S pattern.
LEASE	A grant of real property to a tenant for a specified number of years or lives of people (tenants).
LEASEHOLD	Tenure of land or property by lease.
LEY	Temporary pasture.

LINK	Unit of linear measurement approximately equal to 7.92 inches or one-hundredth of a chain.
MANOR COURT	There were many variations, called variously the Court Baron, the Customary Court and the Court Leet, each with its own terms of reference which in practice became increasingly confused. By the 18th and 19th centuries their business tended to change from the regulation of the open fields and pastures to the supervision of copyhold land transactions.
MAST	Fruit of forest trees such as beech. Used for feeding pigs.
MESNE LORD	A lord of the manor with a superior lord usually holding several manors.
MESSUAGE	Real property including a house, e.g. a farmstead.
MICHAELMAS	29 September, one of the quarter or rent days.
MOIETY	Originally a half but, later, any share.
MOUND	The spoil excavated from a ditch upon which hedges were often planted.
OPEN FIELD	Generally, the pre-enclosure arrangement of two, three or more common fields, divided into a number of furlongs and these in turn consisting of strips farmed by individual proprietors. In practice, there were usually at least some enclosed fields as well.
OXGANG	An imprecise unit of area of land being one-eighth of a carucate. It varied from 10 to 18 acres. Common in northern England. Sometimes called a bovate.
PARISH	(i) Until 1894, it was an ecclesiastical area only which was centred on a church. Historically, the incumbent could claim tithes. (ii) After the Local Government Act, 1894, civil parishes headed by parish councils were created to take over some of the responsibilities of the vestry.
PARISH CONSTABLE	A forerunner of the modern policeman but appointed by some manor courts.
PERCH	Usually, a unit of area equal to 30¼ square yards but, more importantly, one-fortieth of a rood.
PINFOLD	Small, usually walled, enclosure where stray animals were locked in until claimed by their owners who usually had to pay a small fine or amercement.
POLE	See Perch.
POUND	See Pinfold.
QUALITY BOOK	A book containing the results of a survey of quality and quantity carried out during the process of enclosure by Act of Parliament.
QUARTER	Imperial measure of capacity equal to eight bushels. Often used for grain.
QUARTER DAY	The traditional rent days: 25 March (Lady Day); 24 June (Midsummer Day); 29 September (Michaelmas); 25 December (Christmas Day).
QUICKSETS	Young hawthorn plants used for hedging.
QUIT RENT	A small annual payment made by copyholders to their lord.
QUITCLAIM	A deed which renounces any right to a property.

RACK RENT	A very high rent—virtually the full annual value of the land.
REVERSION	The granting of a property sometimes following the termination of a former lease.
RIDGE AND FURROW	The modern name given to the medieval lands, because they were constantly ploughed the same way—towards the middle—and the soil moved away from the edges creating an undulating corrugated effect.
RIGHTS	Certain privileges such as: Rights of estover—usually the right to collect wood for fuel or building materials; Rights of fishery (or piscary)—the right to fish, usually from the river bank; Rights of pannage—the right to allow pigs to feed on fallen beech mast and acorns in woods and forests; Rights of pasture—the right to graze sheep or cattle in the common pasture; Right of soil—mineral rights, usually retained by the lord of the manor; Right of turbary—the right to dig peat or turf from the wastes to use as fuel; Right of warren—the right to hunt rabbits, usually retained by the lord of the manor.
ROD	A symbolic or actual wooden rod used to represent copyhold land at a time of transfer of title. The original title-holder, for example, 'surrendered the land by the rod'.
ROOD	A unit of area equal to forty perch or one-quarter of an acre.
SCITE	The site of a former cottage or homestead, now derelict and perhaps grazed.
SELION	See Land (ii).
SEVERALTY	Alternative method of holding land to the open and common field system, whereby each farmer alone occupies his own land and is able to make farming decisions without reference to the manor court or the other farmers.
SHEEP GATE (SHEEPGAIT)	The right to graze a sheep on the common pasture.
SHEEPFOLD	Usually a temporary shelter erected in the fields to house the ewes at lambing time.
SHEEPWALK	An area of land kept clear for sheep grazing.
SHIPPES (SHEPE)	Sheep
STINT	The number of cattle, sheep or other stock allowed to graze on the common pasture. In times of shortage of grazing, stinting was a means of sharing it out fairly—sometimes in proportion to the amount of arable land held by each proprietor in the open fields.
SWANIMOTE	Forest court. Historically met three times per year to arrange pannage of forest. See Rights.
TEG	A sheep in its second year.
TENEMENT	Any type of real property but especially that which contains one or more dwellings.
TENURE	The nature of the title to land or property, e.g. knight service, leasehold, copyhold, freehold, etc.
TERRIER	A detailed list of all a farmer's lands in the open fields giving the size

of each, its position with respect to neighbours and the furlong and the field in which it lay.

THIRDBOROUGH	An ancient manorial office but, by the 18th century, thirdboroughs were usually assistants to the parish constable.
TITHE	A tenth of the crops of a village which were claimed by the titheholder as a tax. Most titheholders were usually ecclesiastical bodies. The local rector (if there was one) claimed the rectorial or great tithes of hay and corn. A vicar claimed the lesser tithes which varied according to local tradition. An impropriate rector was a lay rector who held land which had once been ecclesiastical property. Tithes were originally paid in kind but later came to be replaced by moduses or compositions (money in lieu). Later, during parliamentary enclosure, land was awarded as a final payment instead of tithes.
TOFT	A farmstead with at least some land.
TON	The largest imperial measure of weight.
TOWNSHIP	The village or manor with a self-contained farming system.
VIRGATE	See Yardland.
WATER MEADOW	Meadows situated in valley basins where controlled flooding introduced beneficial silts and nutrients to improve the quality of hay and fodder crops.
YARDLAND	An imprecise area of land ranging from as little as 18 acres to as much as 50 acres or more. Generally reckoned to constitute a farm in the open fields, being scattered in many small parcels across the furlongs.

Index

Numbers in **bold** type indicate the page numbers on which the document illustrations appear.